RACIAL CONFLICT
AND NEGOTIATIONS

RACIAL CONFLICT
AND NEGOTIATIONS
Perspectives and First Case Studies

Edited by
W. ELLISON CHALMERS
GERALD W. CORMICK

Contributing Authors

W. ELLISON CHALMERS
GERALD W. CORMICK

PRESTON WILCOX

F. RAY MARSHALL
ARVIL VAN ADAMS

JAMES E. BLACKWELL
MARIE R. HAUG

ANN ARBOR

INSTITUTE OF LABOR AND INDUSTRIAL RELATIONS
THE UNIVERSITY OF MICHIGAN—WAYNE STATE UNIVERSITY
AND THE
NATIONAL CENTER FOR DISPUTE SETTLEMENT
OF THE AMERICAN ARBITRATION ASSOCIATION

1971

This study was supported by a grant from the
Ford Foundation. The opinions expressed are
those of the authors and do not necessarily
reflect those of either the Ford Foundation
or the American Arbitration Association.

1-L

PREFACE

THIS volume is the first formal publication of materials from the Racial Negotiations Project. The Project was established in the Institute of Labor and Industrial Relations at The University of Michigan—Wayne State University in August, 1968. Funded by the Ford Foundation for a two-year period, its purpose is to study the negotiations process in racial confrontations.

The case study method has been used as the basic research approach for the Project. The specific conflicts to be studied were selected by the Project staff. Various scholars were then commissioned to execute the studies within a common framework. A total of 16 case studies have been undertaken, and future publications will include some of these individual case studies as well as comparative analyses and overall generalizations.

Part 1 of this volume is designed to put the material here presented into some larger perspective and to describe the dimensions of the study and the criteria for the selection of the cases. Part 2 presents the views of a black activist on the utilization of the negotiations process between groups of blacks and institutions dominated by whites.

The last two parts are the first of the full case studies carried on in the course of gathering the data for the total Project. The first of these deals with the 1968 strike of black garbage workers in Memphis, Tennessee, and the second with a wildcat strike of black water works employees in Cleveland, Ohio. As with other cases now being completed, these two studies were designed to be included in the exploration of patterns of negotiations in a variety of racial conflicts. Each is also, however, a unit complete in itself and can be read as a discrete and insightful analysis of a specific situation.

The basic data for both the Memphis and Cleveland cases were collected by a series of interviews with participants from both sides as well as local observers. This was, of course, supplemented by documentary material as well. In appendix E of this volume will be found a series of excerpts from some of the interviews conducted for the Memphis study. Within some of these interviews, omissions are made because of space limitations and because the authors did not consider the sections omitted to be essential to the analysis. In addition, the participants in the interviews may have wished to have some of their responses treated in confidence. Interviews with numerous other participants and local observers have been omitted for one or more of the same reasons. It is unfortunate that we are unable to reproduce here any of the interview material obtained from the participants on the "establishment side."

The Cleveland material was obtained by Blackwell and Haug in the same manner. In this case, however, the participants did not wish to have their interviews reproduced for publication—a wish which we have, of course, honored.

The I.S. 201 material has been reported from the intimate view of a participant observer.

Louis A. Ferman, director of the Research Division of the Institute of Labor and Industrial Relations of The University of Michigan-Wayne State University when the Project began was deeply involved both in the early formulation of the Project and in the continuing development of conceptual material. Thelma Fox Chalmers has been the technical editor of this volume as she is for the entire Project. Joe A. Miller, acting director of the Research Division, was the assistant director of this project for the first year.

Also involved in many of the discussions were personnel from the National Center for Dispute Settlement of the American Arbitration Association. These include: Samuel C. Jackson, the first director, now assistant secretary for metropolitan development at the Department of Housing and Urban Development; Willoughby Abner, director of the National Center for Dispute Settlement; Donald B. Straus, president, American Arbitration Association.

General support has been provided by the co-directors of the Institute of Labor and Industrial Relations, Charles M. Rehmus and Ronald W. Haughton. The latter was particularly involved in this Project's development.

W. ELLISON CHALMERS
GERALD W. CORMICK

July 1970

CONTENTS

RACIAL CONFLICT
AND NEGOTIATIONS

PART 1

Some Perspectives on Racial Negotiations

W. ELLISON CHALMERS
GERALD W. CORMICK

Editors' Introduction

THIS part is designed to serve two purposes: first, to describe the broad outlines of the two-year research project from which this volume is derived, and, second, to provide some general perspectives on the potentials for the negotiating process in racial conflict, the subject matter of that project.

The nation has experienced serious conflicts between black protest groups and white-dominated institutions that are likely to continue and even intensify. This overall project seeks to explore whether or not a negotiating process provides a mechanism that can be used by both the black protesters and the institutions to work out their differences in such a way that a satisfactory rate of change is achieved without tearing the nation apart.

In this part we have summarized our reasons for using a series of case studies as the major source of information about the utility of negotiations in such confrontations. This part also includes our criteria for case selection and the general framework of our overall study.

Two of these case studies appear in this volume. This part attempts to suggest not only the range of other studies that are still in process but also the relation of these two studies to the larger research design. To provide some perspective for the reader, we have also presented some highly tentative ways in which the two cases may be interpreted toward the development of more general answers.

Finally, this part develops our reasons for seeking and some of our reactions to a black point of view to this "negotiating" approach to racial conflicts. From this is developed some first "hunches" as to the factors involved in the decision of black groups to enter into negotiations.

Some Perspectives on Racial Negotiations

THE PROBLEM EXPLORED BY THE RACIAL NEGOTIATIONS PROJECT

MANY black leaders express the widely held and deeply felt conviction that the discriminatory characteristics of what they view as a white racist society can be changed rapidly and profoundly enough to be meaningful *only* when black Americans possess sufficient coercive power to force change upon that society. This is countered by the equally widely held and deeply felt conviction of many whites that adequate methods for change already exist, that progress toward equality is being made through these accepted methods, and that no group has the "right" to force changes, but only to operate in accordance with established rules and through established channels.

When black demands for change are rejected by an establishment,* and when black leaders are willing and able to make use of the coercive powers at their disposal either by direct action or by threats of such action, a confrontation develops.

The question we are investigating is "What happens next?" Are the protagonists likely to use a negotiating process in an attempt to work out their differences and to find a formula acceptable to both for adjusting their conflicting positions? In many other social situations today, negotiations appear as an acceptable method of accomodating conflicting interests, particularly when each side has some coercive potential in relation to the other. Does this approach

---

* In this section, the term "establishment" is used to refer to a single formal organization with sets of rules and both internal and external relationships already defined and a recognized set of functions and outputs. We shall use the term "institution" to refer to a category of establishments which are grouped together because they have common functions, structures, and outputs in American society, e.g., public schools, universities, and city governments. We are not here using the term "The Establishment" or "The White Power Structure," but think of the concepts those terms connote as wider and more general than either "establishment" or "institution."

also make sense in racial conflicts? More specifically, we are investigating: (1) whether, how, and why negotiations develop when black leaders challenge the functioning of specific establishments dominated by decision-makers who are white; and (2) whether, how, and why such negotiations are carried to what kind of a mutually acceptable conclusion—with or without the assistance of third parties.

Behind these questions, of course, lies the uncertainty of whether the protagonists *want* to use the negotiating process. We shall use a labor-management analogy to explore their reaction to the same criteria that are used in judgments about collective bargaining. Is "peace" desirable and what is the possibility of achieving it instead of open conflict? What is the possibility of achieving a satisfactory reallocation of resources? What is the possibility of an agreement on a satisfactory involvement by protesters in establishment decisions? However, we cannot extend that analogy too far. In the labor area, unions, management, and the public, i.e., "government," reach sufficiently affirmative answers to these questions to use and support the negotiations process. In racial confrontations, on the other hand, the questions are just beginning to be asked. And the answers of both participants and potential participants are by no means clear.

The two full case studies included in this volume and the others now being concluded focus on an immediate situation. In this sense they cannot yet be analyzed within a perspective of their longer term results because the cases are too recent. Thus we cannot yet supply the data for a crucial test of the negotiating process in racial conflicts, i.e., whether it provides a viable route for the resolution of racial disputes. Nor do we yet have the data with which to appraise whether or not, over time, this process is a step toward a *basic* change in the status of blacks within American society.

It needs to be noted that numerous black scholars and activists with whom we have explored these issues in conferences and in the development of these case studies have expressed a profound skepticism as to the utility of achieving more than minor change through negotiations. Such skepticism is frequently documented by reference to experiences in attempting, as they say, to "change the system." Some of these difficulties may be inherent in the nature of institutions, and some data on the difficulties of making such changes are illustrated in the cases reported here and the other cases being de-

veloped within our total project. But, in addition, some of the difficulties must be attributed to the inherent racism of our society.

Perhaps one of the most penetrating comments made by any of the
authors included in this volume is that judgment of Wilcox that
"there is no major effort in this country to end racism." He argues
that the symptoms are being addressed but that racism remains, only
to emerge in different places and in different forms.

In addition Wilcox throws out a challenge to this whole research
project which we have also heard from other black scholars and activists: Is the exploration of the negotiations potential only a device
for the further co-optation of black dissidents? In part this goes to
the question of "values" which we have discussed at some length in
an article.[1] However, our response is in two parts: (1) the *purpose*
of this study is not co-optation, but rather the exploration of the usefulness of the negotiating process as a means of achieving significant
changes in resources and in power, and (2) as in all research, the
uses that are made of the results are beyond the control of the researcher.

THE RESEARCH DESIGN

How can one develop answers or even hunches of possible answers
for the analytical problems that we have set for ourselves? There are
no already developed theories on which we can build. It is not infrequently asserted that racial negotiations are probably sufficiently
like labor negotiations that we could build a research design by ex-
ploring common and perhaps also variant characteristics of union-
management collective bargaining. Elsewhere, however, we have identified some of the numerous contrasts between the labor relations patterns and those that might be found in racial conflicts and there concluded that we could not simply borrow, modify, and refine theory
from that area, but needed to build our own.[2]

This conclusion led us to develop a research design to explore a
new social phenomenon, and we chose the device of a set of case
studies with an emphasis on the exploratory character of each, but
with a common framework. We are, of course, seeking not so much

1. W. Ellison Chalmers and Gerald W. Cormick, "Collective Bargaining in Racial
Disputes?," *Issues in Industrial Society,* I (1970) .
  2. *Ibid.*

the description and understanding of any specific racial conflict, but rather what each incident might suggest about patterns of racial confrontations that may be expected to recur.

The total project includes some 16 different case studies that have this common research design: each study is done by a team, usually a black and a white scholar; each team has conducted a set of interviews of the principal participants in a recent specific confrontation in which there was the experimental use of negotiations; each report seeks not only to describe the relevant events, but also to set it into a larger context and to search for the explanations of the major moves made by each of the participants.

Since the study of race relations not only includes the several judgments and complexities referred to above but is widely interdisciplinary in nature, we have engaged scholars from a variety of the pertinent disciplines.

Selection of the cases was guided by such considerations as: that it was desirable to include a variety of social institutions; that for comparative purposes it would be useful to consider each of these institutions in more than one situation; that both "northern" and "southern" confrontations should be included; and that qualified scholars, familiar with the general environment within which a particular situation occurs, be both interested and available. Two of these case studies are reported in this volume (parts 3 and 4).

The cases thus selected[3] and now in varying stages of completion fall into eight broad institutional categories: public employers, private employers, universities, school systems, welfare agencies, nonprofit organizations, building trades unions, and federal aid.

From the analyses of these individual cases as well as the insights provided by our contacts with other interested practitioners and scholars, the Ann Arbor staff will attempt to analyze the more general significance of these findings.

THE FRAMEWORK OF INQUIRY

In order to ensure that the separate studies and separate analyses add up to some general answers to our questions, a research frame-

3. Certain additional cases are being developed on a more limited basis in order to provide further comparative insights. Some of them have been researched in some depth elsewhere, while for others the data are less complete.

work was developed, and each team of scholars was instructed to organize the investigation and collection of data and to construct the study around that general model.

As it began, the general framework included (1) the characteristics of the black protesting group, including the nature of the protest, the leadership-constituency relationships, and the identifications with larger community groupings; (2) characteristics of the institution being challenged, including its structure, its decision-making processes, its outputs, and its environmental constraints; (3) the degrees of relative coercive power* available to each side distinguished by issues and over time; (4) the alternative and conflicting objectives of those involved in the racial confrontation and the judgments of each side as it considers whether or not to engage in negotiations; (5) the negotiations process, with particular reference to the communications patterns and the degree to which each side seeks a settlement on the basis of power and/or by the development of shared objectives or programs; and (6) the terms of possible settlements, distinguishing between changes in outputs and changes in procedures of the establishment.

However, as the project has developed, it has become increasingly apparent that the racial characteristics of the conflicts being studied require that certain elements of the framework be elaborated. Thus although establishment leaders may consider that it and they are racially neutral, from the point of view of the black protesters, the institution which they are challenging is perceived as a "white racist" institution because: (1) it is controlled by whites; (2) it was developed by and functions to the advantage of whites and the disadvantage of blacks; and (3) these whites have prejudices which affect the ways in which they perceive blacks and black demands, evaluate social change, guide establishment choices, and relate to the larger society.

---

* The concept of "relative coercive power" is complex. The use of physical violence by either side against the other is only one extreme form. It also includes a wide range of other actions that can be taken by one side against the other, e.g., disruption, damage to standing and reputation, loss of support from constituents, etc. Additionally, it refers to both the actual performance and the credible threat of these actions and to both the "reality" and the perceptions of the prospects of damage. Finally, the word "relative" includes the notion that each party must judge the degree to which such coercive actions will damage not only his opponent but also himself.

We also needed to extend our analysis of the nature of the black challenge. For that purpose, we classified alternate black programs for change as: (1) the refusal to participate within a society which they reject as "racist"; or (2) the development of separate black identity and an insistence on the independent role of black leaders in shaping the pattern of black participation within the larger society; or (3) the joint participation of blacks with whites in common programs for political, social, and economic change.

Our research is directed to the second of these alternative black perspectives.

PATTERNS OF ANALYSIS

In working toward general conclusions out of the enormous amount and variation of data and analysis in the 16 case studies, we are formulating generalizations at three levels; *idiosyncratic, patterns of conflict,* and *general tendencies.*

The Idiosyncratic

Each case has a peculiar combination of circumstances that can never be reproduced nor spontaneously recur elsewhere. The two major cases in this volume and each of the 16 cases in the total project have their own special meaning for the participants *and* the observers. As the cases in this volume are examined, the reader will be aware of striking differences in the facts of one case as compared to the other. Obviously, then, it would be a mistake to assume that the development of one case can be exactly repeated in another. Indeed, as each of the two case analyses indicates, even the same scene changes so drastically from one year to the next that neither the later conflicts nor the later results duplicate the earlier experience.

There is a second set of contrasts among cases that derives from the ways in which they are reported and analyzed. The Memphis case study was prepared by two labor economists, both white, while the Cleveland study was prepared by two sociologists, one black and one white. Thus even the commonalities of the two cases may be blurred or hidden by the different perspectives of the scholars deriving from their disciplines and/or their color.

Therefore, in attempting any cross-analysis of the cases which make up the total project, it will be necessary to search for generalizations which go beyond those idiosyncrasies which result from the research design and those which are actually a part of the individual situations.

Patterns of Conflict

We consider that an identification of general conflict patterns is desirable not only to improve our understanding of the group of cases under study, but also to provide a basis for extending such understanding to other similar situations. Thus, for example, there are obviously ways in which the cases reported in parts 3 and 4 are similar. Some material on another of our cases suggests similar characteristics.

Examination of data from a variety of sources in this area suggests at least four alternative classifications of patterns of conflict: time, geography, type of black organization, and type of institutional setting. While it is the fourth of these which formed a basis for the selection of our cases and is, therefore, primary to our analysis, note is made here of the others in the hope that they will stimulate other scholars.

1. *Time.* In some ways, the fundamental characteristics of race relationships in America change very slowly. But in other ways the interactions are changing rapidly. Both of the cases we report here and, indeed, all of our 16 cases fall within a quite narrow time period—1968-1970. It could be that there are important similarities among all of our cases that contrast with different characteristics of cases that arose in an earlier period or that will be developing within the next few years.

2. *Geography.* Memphis and Cleveland may be thought of as in two quite different sections of the country. Our 16 cases could be divided among, for instance, "South," "West," and "North." We speculate that these labels may group and distinguish important sets of variables, but we have not tried this arrangement of our cases.

3. *Type of Black Organization.* The two cases reported in parts 3 and 4 of this volume involve a rather unusual type of "separate" black organization—a black-employee grouping within a larger union organization. In most of the other cases under study, quite different

types of black organizations appear. Since the phenomenon that we are studying begins with an organization of black protest, there might be important commonalities and/or differences to be discovered by identifying and comparing black leader-constituency relationships. Some of the key variables may be: characteristics of the leaders, the fluid quality of negotiating teams, the characteristics of the relevant black community including its size and the degree of its ghetto concentrations, the number and kinds of issues that draw the group together and whether the group is ad hoc or continuous.

Of course, the characteristics of black organizations are influenced by the kind of white institution that is being challenged. Thus, the grouping by institutions, developed below, in substantial degree overlaps with the grouping by black organizations.

4. *Type of Institutional Setting.* It is our assumption that the nature of the institutional setting to a large degree shapes the patterns of conflict which arise within it. The structure of the institution, the relationships of the protagonists to that institution, and the degree of dependence of the institution on society as a whole are some of the factors which shape both the conflict and the way in which that conflict develops and is resolved.

Different types of institutions within which racial confrontations occur will require different kinds of generalizations about the prospects for negotiations. Not only is there variation in the degree of importance of the racial factor in the negotiations, but also in the institutional response. This is not surprising, for we are dealing with institutions that have different structures, different decision-making processes, different outputs, and different environments. Accordingly, it appears likely that there will be significant differences among the categories of institutions in which we have chosen and grouped our cases. Thus race and the type of institution combine to create interrelated elements within the racial negotiations context.

We can illustrate the sharp contrasts between one institutional category and another by comparing the Memphis and Cleveland cases reported here with the school cases commented on in Part 2.

The case reports in parts 3 and 4 may be grouped together as a conflict pattern between a city administration and its black employees. Some of the important common characteristics of these two cases are:

1. Both the development and the outcomes of the black challenge

are shaped by political factors which affect the policies and procedures of the city administration.

2. City government has available to it the courts and the police force as its agents, and these limit the opportunity of the protesters to coerce the establishment. This became a critcal factor in Memphis but was a more peripheral concern in Cleveland.

3. The major output of the city is services; the consumers of these services are all the citizens. While this relationship does not indicate or define the interest conflict within either case, it nevertheless defines the degree of coercive power which is available to the black protesters.

4. The conflict in both cases is a black protest about treatment on the job by the city as employer.

5. The black workers organized their protest through membership in a local union affiliated with a national union of government employees. Through this relationship, there existed the potential of greater strength as well as negotiation and organizational expertise.

6. The formal rules of conflict resolution, in both cases, are the product of a set of union-management relationships whose *general* applicability was recognized, if not accepted by the protagonists.

However, even though conflicts reported in both parts 3 and 4 are importantly defined and largely contained within the usual rules and expectations of union-management collective bargaining, the recognition issue had a quite different significance to each side as compared to its usual meaning in labor relations. In both cases, the black demand was for a recognition by white administrators of the black identity of those workers, summarized in the Memphis case by the slogan: "I *AM* A MAN." This is a basic characteristic which, as we note below, reappears in different forms in all of our other cases as well and so becomes one of the categories that needs to be understood in all of the racial negotiations cases—no matter within what institutional setting.

In both cases the institutional setting provided not only the stimulus but also the mechanics for the expression of much more general black dissatisfaction with the white-controlled institution (s) since a city government has a relationship with all whites and all blacks residing within its boundaries.

Even more tentatively, we can begin to identify what appear to be more complex interrelationships that characterize this city-black employees conflict pattern:

1. Black workers draw significant and needed support from the black community.

2. A black local union group develops a wider power base by its affiliations within the labor movement although it encounters significant reluctance and even hostility from some white-dominated sections of the labor movement.

3. The pressures of white political constituencies significantly restrict the options available to a city administration.

4. Expressions and acts of prejudice by white administrators sharpen the conflict posture of black workers and their leaders.

Thus, these two cases have a specialized combination defined by the city government's relation to its black employees on the one hand and the involvement of black workers in a union on the other. Both deal with the efforts of those black workers to establish satisfactory bargaining relationships through union-management rules. These cases embody, then, not only the developing problems of collective bargaining for public employees but also the uses and limitations of public-employee bargaining for the channeling of racial conflicts.

From a section of the Wilcox analysis in Part 2, there emerge data that suggest a second patterning of racial conflicts—that between school boards on the one hand and black pupils, parents, and the black local community on the other.

Explicitly or implicitly within this analysis of the I.S. 201 experience in New York a few years ago are what may be some common characteristics appearing in public school conflicts: sharp dissent by a black community from the school board's judgments about the educational outputs of the system for ghetto children, the control mechanisms within the school system that resist black challenges for changes in the institution, the judgments of at least some protesting black parents and members of the black community that black "community control" provides the only route for achievement of "relevant" education for black children and others.

Incidentally, as Wilcox implies, the logic of the black demand for community control over ghetto schools can be extended to some other institutions, although he would, presumably, not define the needs of black workers employed by a city administration in that way. Perhaps this black perspective on the need for "community control" carries our analysis beyond the school conflict pattern, but is still somewhat short of a generalization applicable to all racial conflicts.

General Tendencies

The third and most difficult level of analysis toward which we are working is that which cuts across individual cases in various institutional settings to develop overall generalizations. Since this kind of analysis draws from both the idiosyncratic and the institutional types mentioned earlier, it attempts to pull together widely different patterns of data. It is toward these wider generalizations, however, that our research and analysis are directed. To date, such propositions can be labeled only as "preliminary hunches."

TENTATIVE GENERALIZATIONS

What follows are some tentative first generalizations drawn from the materials included in this volume as well as from preliminary data from other cases. They are included here to provide some general view of the direction and thrust of the Project.

Black Perspectives

Within a society where discrimination and segregation are enforced and where inferior social status is endemic, there is a strong insistence on black identity and black independence, that is, on "equality." This demand for recognition and status is clearly stated in many of our cases and is expressed here both in the I.S. 201 case (Part 2) and in the Memphis case (Part 3) to a very strong degree and is present, though not as strongly, in the Cleveland case (Part 4). The evidence from other cases lends support to the strength of this factor in racial confrontations in general.

Another proposition common to the whole range of black-white confrontations and the potential for negotiations is embodied in the question: "Who decides who speaks for blacks?" Negotiations can be seen as a white trap unless the answer accepted by the establishment is: "The black community speaks for itself and determines its own spokesmen and leaders through its own mechanisms." If there is a diversity of views and of leaderships among blacks, the establishment ought not interfere with nor seek to manipulate the processes by which the black community handles such internal conflicts. Within this volume, this point is central to the Wilcox thesis and is illustrated in both the text and the interviews of the Marshall-Adams chapter on Memphis as well.

In addition, Wilcox considers that there is an increasing tendency for black leaders to consider themselves accountable *only* to the black community. A different, and perhaps more difficult, aspect of this point is his judgment that black administrators within the establishment ought to owe their first allegiance to the black community. This question of accountability seems to be appearing in many of our cases.

Black perspectives on co-optation are very complex. Among the cases being analyzed within our project, there is considerable diversity on this dimension. In this volume, Wilcox, in Part 2, develops this point extensively. From his point of view, any black group that participates in the negotiations and settlement of their demands is being co-opted unless its independence and its authority to be *the* spokesmen for relevant black interests has been established.

To avoid co-optation then, in this view, there must be independent black involvement within a larger institution. The adoption of the principle of black community control followed by negotiations on the implementation of such a principle within the larger context of the central school board is advocated by Wilcox to this end. In this meaning of the term, co-optation occurs wherever a black group accepts an involvement in the activities of the major institution in a subservient role rather than as a spokesman for black interests.

Characteristics of White-Controlled Establishments

Each institution has an elaborate structure, including both internal and external decision-making processes and relationships in which the black protesters' involvement is either nonexistent or inadequate. Although some internal elements may coalesce with the black protesters in pressing for change in these institutional arrangements, the general thrust of the establishment is toward the continuation of the status quo and, therefore, resistance to the inclusion of independent black groups within the structure of the establishment.

Even before all of our data are in, it appears that it requires considerable coercive capacity on the part of black protesters to produce any change in the direction they desire. For instance, even with the formal rules for dissent and protest built into union-management relationships, the material in Part 3 suggests that the white Memphis mayor accepted recognition and collective bargaining with the black garbage workers only under considerable coercive pressures. In Part 4 Blackwell and Haug indicate that the black mayor of Cleveland and his white administrators moderated the punishment for a black shop steward only when convinced that the costs of not doing so were too high. The I.S. 201 incident in Part 2 illustrates the failure to achieve change because the black group was unable to mobilize sufficient coercive power. It is dramatically evident in other cases within this Project that established institutions are quite inflexible about including the black protesters in the decision-making processes unless *forced* to do so.

Another generalization about white-controlled institutions is that the establishments do, in fact, discriminate against blacks both in the way in which decisions are made and in the outputs that they provide.

The Judgments of Black Protesters on the Desirability of Negotiations

The issues of "recognition" and black organizational independence are generally considered to be nonnegotiable. Many of the cases which we are examining include reference to "nonnegotiable demands." In this volume, these appear in Memphis in the form of demands for recognition of black dignity and in Cleveland in the issue of the status and dignity of the black shop steward. This point is elaborated in Part 2 in which Wilcox differentiates between what is and what is not negotiable from the black point of view. From many of our cases, we, too, believe we see some kinds of situations in which there are black judgments that negotiations are desirable primarily in those areas that relate to the *specifics* of participation and to substantive demands.

The Judgments of White Institutional Decision-Makers on the Desirability of Negotiations

We have already speculated above that institutions tend to be resistant to change. Further, then, they will tend to reject or at least avoid, if possible, negotiating with black protesters. This resistance appears to be on both institutional and "racist" grounds, as is quite evident in Memphis but only more subtly apparent in Cleveland. Our other cases appear to bear out this reluctance. It is perhaps more manifest in cases involving universities and public schools than in others.

Further, we are finding in some of these cases what was especially apparent in Memphis: that when the establishment is forced to yield to a demand for inclusion of blacks within the decision-making structure, it will employ the device of privately accepting the actuality of black involvement in the bargaining while publicly denying it, at least symbolically. In Memphis, for example, the final agreement was in the form of a unilateral memorandum of the City Council. It is possible to speculate further that this is a form of denying the formal recognition that Wilcox refers to as the *sine qua non* of black participation in negotiations.

The Degree of Change in Establishment Procedures and Outputs

Our tentative conclusion on this point is that some modest changes in the patterns of black-white relationships in general and in the relationships between blacks and establishments are emerging from negotiations. In some of our cases, the negotiated results fell far short of the original demands of the blacks. In others such as Memphis and Cleveland, the black groups eventually achieved changes generally in line with their demands.

It appears that there may be two basic explanations of the minimal degree of these gains: (1) as in Memphis and Cleveland, blacks enter serious negotiations with "demands" already reduced from the ideal down to what may appear "practical" and/or "realistic" within the immediate situation; and (2) insofar as change depends on coercive power, the power equation is so heavily tipped to the side of the establishment and the status quo that no fundamental changes can be achieved, at least as far as the evidence of the studies included in this Project shows.

To some degree, the significance of the changes which have been achieved is dependent on one's value system. We hope to analyze this question more completely after all the case material has been analyzed and compared.

Third-Party Intervention

The evidence of our cases suggests that not infrequently the parties to a racial conflict need the assistance of a third party, provided he is mutually acceptable. In racial conflicts, however, "acceptability" is an urgent and not easily resolved problem because black leaders tend to insist that such an intervenor be committed to their thrust for both procedural and substantive change while the establishment may be unwilling to accept such deviation from their conception of "neutrality."

The third-party intervenor may be needed to provide help in understanding and using a negotiations process which may be unfamiliar to many black groups and perhaps even to some of the white-controlled institutions with little experience in bargaining. The I.S. 201 case, which did not utilize a third party, illustrates the difficulties of an inexperienced black group in the negotiating process. As is dramatically illustrated in the Cleveland case, the intervenor may be needed to work out misunderstandings which are particularly likely between black and white representatives. He may also be needed to act in the usual role of a mediator in any kind of a conflict, e.g., suggesting imaginative alternatives to deadlocked positions or taking public responsibility for terms with which neither side is happy.

In both the Memphis and the Cleveland cases reported here, a third party intervenor was instrumental in bringing the parties to an agreement. The I.S. 201 case, which failed of agreement, did not include the services of such an intervenor. There are many questions still to be examined as to the role of a third party. One deals with the color of the intervenor. In the Memphis case, the mediator was white, while in Cleveland he was black. In the latter case, that color identification appears to have been crucial. In general, does the color of the intervenor make a difference, and is it possible that a black-white mediating team would be likely to be more effective?

Additional questions which we are pursuing deal with the process through which the intervention is initiated; the kinds of roles possible and/or necessary in disputes in a racial framework; the assessment of "success" or "failure;" and the possible use of such intervention as a continuing device, particularly where the protesting organization has no status "inside" the establishment as is true, for example, in many of the school cases.

SUMMARY

We have attempted here to provide some general background and introduction to the three parts which follow. While the final format has not yet been determined, it is expected that more of our case studies will be published in a similar manner. It is hoped that these will be useful not only to the practitioner and the researcher but also as teaching materials.

The major emphasis of this project will, however, be on analyses across cases and an attempt to examine in depth the significance of negotiations in the resolution of racial conflict.

PART 2

To Negotiate or Not to Negotiate: Toward a Definition of a Black Position

PRESTON WILCOX

Editors' Introduction

THIS part performs a dual function. First, it describes an abortive attempt at negotiations between the black community involved with I.S. 201 in Harlem and the New York City Board of Education. Second, it develops a thoughtful analysis of the perspectives of a black activist about the potentials and limitations that need to be evaluated by blacks as they consider whether or not to participate in racial negotiations.

This challenge to the utility of the negotiations process in effecting basic, meaningful change in the status of blacks, so articulately expressed here by Mr. Wilcox, has been frequently encountered in the course of this Project. This view of the limited usefulness of negotiations and the skepticism with which black participants view them was so illuminating, particularly to the Project directors and to the white scholars involved in some of the Project conferences, that it was felt important to include it in this volume for the benefit of a wider audience.

Since Wilcox combined an academic background, an activist stance, and an intimate involvement in the drive for "community control," we considered him to be uniquely suited for the explication of a view of the negotiations process in racial conflicts from the black perspective. It is a viewpoint which needs to be recognized and understood by scholars and decision-makers alike. It is an added bonus that he has also brought to this volume a description of a racial negotiations which occurred in a school setting.

To Negotiate or Not to Negotiate:
Toward a Definition of a Black Position

INTRODUCTION

THIS statement deals with the question of the feasibility of the use of negotiation as a tool to resolve conflicts between Black dissidents and public organizations. It developed as a consequence of a Conference on Negotiations of Public Organizations with Black Dissidents sponsored by the Institute of Labor and Industrial Relations, The University of Michigan—Wayne State University in February 1969. The conference was convened and chaired by Dr. W. Ellison Chalmers, director of the Institute's Racial Negotiations Project.

The Racial Negotiations Project was an exploration of the function of negotiations in the adjustment of conflicts resulting from the demands of a dissident Black group for changes in the decision-making process, policies, practices, or outputs of public organizations dominated by whites, such as school boards, colleges, police departments, welfare agencies, housing authorities, and city planning agencies.[1] The conference was to consider such questions as:

1. contrasting the "usefulness" of negotiations with (a) a purely *advisory* role for Black representatives; (b) co-optation of individual Blacks within organizations; (c) adjustments of the perceptions and styles of existing leadership of the organization; or (d) other alternatives.

2. contrasting the characteristics of one public organization (sector) with another as these affect negotiating roles and prospects.

3. contrasting functions sought when Black dissidents are members within the white organization or are outsiders affected by the outputs of the white organization.[2]

1. "The Agenda for Conference on Negotiations of Public Organizations with Black Dissidents" (Ann Arbor: Institute of Labor and Industrial Relations, 1969), p. 1.
2. *Ibid.*

The conference in February 1969 was characterized by a continuing need to redefine terms, to clarify positions, and to reinterpret findings and observations. In itself it was a conflict of perceptions: the white liberal position versus the authentically Black position. This is important to understand, since the subject under discussion arises largely out of a need of white America to find a way to deal with its need to control Black people without actually giving up that control. The statement of purpose from which the above questions were taken poses negotiation as an alternative to "Black separation from the rest of America" or "violence, and perhaps eventually to a complete rebuilding of American society from the ground up."[3]

It can be inferred that the authors of this statement refuse to concede that Blacks and whites are already effectively separated and segregated from each other in terms of schools, housing, and employment. The failure to perceive Black separation as being synonymous with "Black control" or the loss of white control over Blacks is apparent and perhaps deliberate.[4]

To assert that Black separation is to be devalued while at the same time proposing that Blacks "build a power base and a degree of unity in order to participate in and change major social institutions"[5] is to blind one's readers through the use of the rhetoric of oppression. If Blacks have not built a power base, it is not solely because of their separation from the mainstream; it is because of the control of the *internal structure* of Black communities by whites. The combination of white racism and the subsequent dependence on governmental services for education and welfare have produced this situation.[6]

In an earlier draft of this statement an attempt was made through the use of a case history to demonstrate some of the difficulties of achieving a mutually satisfactory process for solving problems through negotiations because of the racist behavior of the repre-

3. W. Ellison Chalmers, *Racial Negotiations—A Project Statement* (Ann Arbor: Institute of Labor and Industrial Relations, 1968), p. 2.

4. Preston Wilcox, *Integration or Separatism in Education K-12* (New York: Afram Associates, Inc., 1969), p. 14 (mimeographed).

5. Chalmers, *Racial Negotiations,* p. 2.

6. Oscar Handlin, *The Newcomers: Negroes and Puerto Ricans in a Changing Society* (Garden City, N.Y.: Doubleday and Co., 1959), p. 121.

sentatives of the white institutions.[7] This paper will push that inquiry a little further by suggesting that the demand for community control over Harlem's Intermediate School 201 was less an attempt to influence the New York City Board of Education than it was an effort to assume control over the development of a local institution as it affects the life of the local community. It was an attempt to influence the internal Black agenda as distinguished from the external white agenda. In the process it was rediscovered that the two agendas were interlocked and were controlled by whites. The control over the Black community by whites has been firmly established. The Kerner Commission observed: "What white Americans have never fully understood—but what the Negro can never forget—is that white society is deeply implicated in the ghetto. *White institutions created it, white institutions maintain it and white society condones it.*"[8]

A corollary to this assertion is the recognized state of affairs which has conditioned white America to interpose prejudice and to nullify the laws set up to protect its victims.[9] Blacks have been the subject of a series of legislative and judicial actions to promote and protect their rights and victims of their own efforts to have their rights enforced. This is illustrated in the lives of Medgar Evers, Marcus Garvey, W. E. B. Dubois, Martin Luther King, Frederick Douglass, Booker T. Washington, Nat Turner, Denmark Vesey, Adam Clayton Powell, and Malcolm X. The point of it all is that, in most cases, Blacks have become victims largely because they believed that the rights and privileges presumptively bestowed upon them were legal entitlements guaranteed under the law—and not special privileges to be granted on the basis of the benevolent whims of white America.

Viewed from this perspective, the subject of negotiations takes on a different coloration. One has to discern the capability of white institutions of engaging in mutual transactions with Black dissidents, i.e., responding to Blacks as humans. A second concern relates to

7. Preston Wilcox, *To Negotiate or Not to Negotiate: Toward a Definition of a Black Position* (Ann Arbor: Institute of Labor and Industrial Relations, 1969) (1st draft).

8. *Report of the National Advisory Commission on Civil Disorders* (New York: E. P. Dutton and Co., Inc., 1969) , p. VII.

9. A. H. Yancey, *Interpositionullification* (New York: American Press, 1959) , p. 128.

whether or not Blacks should "negotiate" in order to control the communal institutions serving their private and ethnic interests. A more important strategy might be that of identifying those decisions which should be the exclusive function of Black communities.[10] Does negotiation have other functions apart from conflict resolution?

This statement is largely based on the interpretation and analysis of data drawn from interviews conducted with four Black dissidents and from the controversy at Harlem's I.S. 201. Findings and recommendations have been drawn from those two sources supplemented by a review of the literature.

Since the first draft was completed, I have been involved in attempting to effectuate a negotiating attitude between the Model Cities Planning Council and the Board of Education in Dayton, Ohio. The director of the Educational Component of the Model Cities Program had been fired by the Board of Education in violation of a written agreement prohibiting unilateral action by either one of the parties, the Model Cities Planning Council and the Dayton Board of Education. (See appendix C.) Efforts to have Arthur J. Goldberg mediate the conflict were also rejected.[11]

The director was Black; eight of nine members of the Board of Education were white. The Model Cities target area was predominantly Black. It is fair to surmise that, despite the signed agreement between the two bodies, an effective working relationship was never established, largely because of the inability of the Board to control the behavior of the Black director. Since there is little or no tradition for white men who direct programs in the Black community standing up against school systems, both the independence of the Black director and his ethnicity worked against him.[12]

White institutional resistance to effective Black leadership is legendary. In New York City alone, Herman Ferguson, John Hatchett, Albert Vann, Leslie Campbell, Leroy Watkins, Ralph Poynter,

10. Preston Wilcox, "Black Studies As An Academic Discipline: Toward A Definition" (New York: Afram Associates, Inc., 1969) (mimeographed) .

11. "Goldberg Mediation Denied Art Thomas," *Dayton Daily News*, November 9, 1969, p. 1.

12. Harlem's Elliot Shapiro is a major exception along with Evanston, Illinois's Gregory Coffin. Nat Hentoff has discussed Shapiro's work in *Our Children Are Dying* (New York: Viking Press, 1966) . Gregory Coffin is referred to elsewhere in this statement.

Rhody McCoy, Reverend Herbert Oliver, David X. Spencer, Charles Wilson, and Merle Stewart have all found themselves the targets of attack by white institutions. On the other hand, most enjoyed the respect of the Black communities they served.

I was also involved in a dispute in Honolulu where the Kalihi-Palama target area attempted to obtain the approval of the Hawaii Board of Education for the establishment of a Parent Advisory Committee. A confrontation occurred, and a negotiating meeting was effectuated and carried out. A meeting was then held in which at least four members of the Board became advocates for the citizen group, and on Thursday, October 23, 1969, the Parent Advisory Committee proposal was affirmed by the Board.[13, 14] I was the only Black involved—and then only as a consultant. There was a strong hint that the governor, who is up for reelection, wanted to make a favorable impression in the Kalihi-Palama area. If this is the case, it could have affected the response of the Hawaii Board of Education.

Having been a participant-observer-consultant in both of these actions, I noted that they differed largely on the basis of whether or not race was a factor. In Honolulu, it was a social class factor; several ethnic groups including whites were represented on both sides of the conflict. In Dayton, as in New York, it was largely a race issue; Black confrontations tended to stimulate militant white resistance.[15]

It might be instructive to include a reference to the events which prevented negotiations in Dayton and those which made them possible in Honolulu. The Dayton Model Cities Planning Council refused to negotiate with the Dayton Board of Education when the latter failed to honor the partnership agreement it had signed by refusing to rescind its unilateral decision to fire the director. The director later sued the Board of Education and was encouraged by the courts to pursue his libel suit against the Board of Education since the latter knew at the time the partnership agreement was signed that its participation in such an agreement was illegal.[16]

13. Monta Kinney, "Statement Presented Before the State Board of Education" (New York: Afram Associates, Inc., 1969) (mimeographed).

14. Harold Hostler, "School Board Backs Model Cities Plan," *Honolulu Advertiser*, October 24, 1969. p. 6.

15. Frances Fox Piven, "Militant Civil Servants in New York City," *Trans-Action*, VII (November, 1969), 24-28 and 55.

16. "Way Cleared for Thomas Hearing," *Dayton Daily News*, Nov. 8, 1969, p. 5.

The subsequent efforts to draw upon the mediating talents of Arthur Goldberg were designed to enable the Board to "save face" and to begin to effectuate the "working relationship" which must be developed in order to conduct a meaningful educational program. Even though the Model Cities Planning Council had developed a Community School Council for the 11 participating schools, the Board's staff moved into the community to set up a competing body: the Parent Advisory Council.[17] This move lent further support to the efforts of the Board of Education to control the educational programs within the Black community. It also began to divide the Black community.

The event which made negotiation possible in the Honolulu situation occurred when the Kalihi-Palama committee asked the Board itself to draw up an acceptable proposal. Earlier bickering over various aspects of the proposal—and the Board's efforts to avoid a conflict with the teachers' unions—stimulated the use of this strategy by the Kalihi-Palama committee. As it turned out, several of the Board members became advocates for the local community and gave evidence of having a genuine interest in the education of their children.

These additional experiences and my deepened comprehension of the issues at hand have shaped this statement. They have caused me to raise the following questions. Should negotiation be employed only as a tool to enable white institutions to give up the Black plantations without "losing face"? Should negotiations take place to plan to redistribute power and resources or to attempt to win them? The difference lies in whether one negotiates one's demands for control or refuses to negotiate until such demands have been granted and then uses negotiations to plan for the transfer of power, resources, and other rewards. How can one determine when negotiations are feasible and possible?

Considering the systematic denial of the rights of Black people by white America and the accompanying usurpation of the personal and ethnic rights of Black people by white America, a basic question should be raised as to whether the confrontations by Black dissidents are efforts to usurp power which justifiably belongs to whites

17. Discussion Guide for Citizens' School Seminars, Nov. 10-21, 1969, (Dayton: Dayton Public Schools, 1969).

or to return to Blacks those powers which justifiably belong to them. It seems to me that when Blacks talk about their non-negotiable rights, they are alluding to the legitimate right of Blacks to control the infrastructures of their own communities and the nature of the services delivered to them.

It is understandable that whites would wish to debate the division of the above-mentioned rights and that power must be taken rather than be granted. It still holds, however, that the rights and rewards which most Black dissident groups seek are long overdue and that the control over these rights and rewards by non-Blacks is a direct expression of white oppression—not white humanism.

My basic assumption, then, is that the very fact that Blacks have yet to gain through coercion and pressure the rights which most ethnic groups were granted solely because of the color of their skins is a reflection of the strength of white institutional racism. This introduces the question of whether Black-white transactions are characterized less by mutual interaction than by colonialistic tendencies and tactics.

It is the variable of racism and its impact on negotiations to which this paper is addressed. In the last analysis, negotiations between Black dissidents and white institutions must produce a joint peace and a redistribution of power and rewards. Within a racist context, Black-directed peace and humanism is "illegal" despite the avowed ideals of this nation. The trick becomes that of finding ways to use negotiations as a tool to remove racists from control over Black decisions. Stated in other terms, negotiations must become a tool to redefine Black-white relationships as they relate to the assignment of decision-making powers over particular spheres of interest.

The first part of this discussion describes a negotiating process in which I was involved at Harlem I.S. 201 in the fall of 1966 and is presented as a case history in order to provide a framework for further discussion, analysis, and interpretation.

The second part of this statement outlines a research effort designed to elicit the opinions and experiences of four Blacks who had been involved in negotiations with white institutions.

The statement ends with a set of conclusions and guidelines culled from the sources listed above. An effort is made to define a Black dissident model. Questions are raised for consideration as well as to suggest further study and investigation of the subject.

A CASE HISTORY: HARLEM'S I.S. 201

Participants and Issues

IN the fall of 1966 the Intermediate School 201 negotiating committee and Dr. Bernard Donovan, superintendent of the New York City school system, met for more than a week.

The negotiation process involved the following participants:

1. For I.S. 201: (a) Ten negotiators for the I.S. 201 negotiating committee plus two advisors, both professionals; (b) twenty-six observers from the I.S. 201 area.

2. For the Board of Education: Dr. Bernard A. Donovan, superintendent of schools, and two members of the human relations staff. From time to time selected members of the Board of Education joined Dr. Donovan in the negotiations.

The ten members of the I.S. 201 negotiating committee represented the prospective PTA of the host school and several locally based organizations. Most were local residents elected on the spot mainly from among those present at a meeting of the above groups. Official leadership positions and prior demonstrated leadership and involvement were the main criteria. *The question of negotiating skills was never considered.* The twenty-six observers from the I.S. 201 area were not allowed to negotiate but were empowered to pass notes to the negotiators. Their function was to "keep the negotiators honest" and to inform community individuals and groups of what was taking place. One of them was assigned as a runner to move back and forth from the negotiating room—a library on the second floor of the school—to the streets, where the press, onlookers, and the police remained. The negotiating site had political significance since it served to sustain local interest and support. The runner's job was to keep the community's onlookers informed—not the press and the police. Nightly meetings were also held to report to the community.

The issues under negotiation were the community's request for a Black principal selected by them and the establishment of a policy-determining community committee. The initial request for an *experiment* in community selection of principals had been made to

Dr. Donovan in March, 1966.[18] Discussions, letter writing, visits to the mayor, and even to Commissioner Harold Howe in Washington had failed earlier to get the Board of Education to transport white students for I.S. 201 in order to desegregate it. The move toward requests for decision-making had resulted.

The demand to be involved in the selection of their own principal was a strategy to increase the possibility that the principal would feel responsible to the host community. It was hoped that such a principal would become an advocate for the community. The community could then expend less energy blaming him for school failures than in helping him to do his job more effectively. The normal pattern of appointments makes the principal accountable to the Board of Education and not necessarily to the parent/community leaders of the student he serves.

The strategy behind the demand for decision-making powers began as an effort to arrive at a division of responsibility between the Board of Education and the local community. The selection of the principal was to become the first of such decisions. The hope at this time was that a mutual effort could be undertaken to redistribute powers so as to modify the role of the Board of Education to one of monitoring and standard-setting with related policies and actions being relegated to the local body.

The latent function of the negotiations was, then, to test out whether or not a workable relationship between the Board of Education and the I.S. 201 community was possible. To a degree, it was an experiment to determine whether a partnership arrangement could reap educational benefits for the students. Such an arrangement would bestow status on influential local citizens within a branch of the school system which tended to keep such persons as spectators. Importantly, the students could be afforded an opportunity to see their parent/community leaders function in leadership, status-bearing roles legitimated by the central system and by their own actions.[19, 20]

18. Preston Wilcox, "The Community-Centered School," *The School House in the City* (New York: Praeger and Company, 1969).

19. Some of the educational benefits deriving from the exercise of influence by local leaders have been discussed elsewhere by Wilcox (*Integration and Separatism in Education: K-12*, p. 5).

20. See also Mario D. Fantini, "Participation, Decentralization, Community

Negotiations and Agreement

While it is difficult to discern the actual event that produced the circumstances leading to negotiations, I can identify two such possible events.

First, a midnight visit to the home of one of the human relations staff who had been serving as an intermediary. (At least ten local resident/activists participated.) Although he was Negro, he has seldom revealed any comprehension of the demands of the Black community. Just before the picketing, he made a racial appeal to the group. By that time, it was too late. There is some evidence that when he reported the midnight visit to his home to the members of the Board, the Board decided to negotiate.

Second, the threats of violence as perceived by the white Board of Education based on the rhetoric of certain local residents.

The Board decided *not* to begin classes at I.S. 201 on the first day of school. It was a new school, to be opened for the first time. The Board also suggested the negotiations. (Or was it really a negotiation which was suggested?)

On the Sunday before school was to open, one of the local leaders had telephoned the Board which was meeting in special session. She spoke with Dr. Donovan and agreed to a negotiation. An agreement was also reached to send out a joint news release. I was asked by Dr. Donovan over the phone if the group was willing to negotiate. I said I thought they were. Since that time, I have always wondered if my word as a college professor was the *key* word. Or did my words merely confirm those of the leader to whom he had just spoken?

Within a half hour, at least 60 Harlemites were sitting in the Board Room at the Board of Education listening to the Board's president reading a news release in which the Board agreed not to open the school and to negotiate a settlement. After a few changes suggested by local leaders, the statement was released to the press. The suggested changes were made to *test* the willingness of the Board to cooperate. The changes did not alter the substantive content of the statement.

I was and still am convinced that Dr. Donovan negotiated in good

Control, and Quality Education," *Teachers College Record,* LXXI (September 1969), 106-107.

faith. His Irish background and the historic struggles associated with it seemed to heighten his recognition of the desire of the Black community to shape those institutions serving its own children. In fact, the negotiations resulted in an agreement:

1. to replace the white principal (he was actually transferred out of the school);
2. to name a Black assistant principal as an interim principal; and
3. to utilize the I.S. 201 negotiating committee as a planning committee during the transition in order to: (a) select a new principal, and (b) plan for a more meaningful role for the parent/community leaders in school affairs. A school-community committee was to be established.

The I.S. 201 negotiating committee had won everything it had sought; it thought!

Failure of Agreement

The agreements were later nullified. The United Federation of Teachers refused to honor the agreement since they were not involved in the negotiations and because they were ultimately against local control of schools by Blacks. The Board of Education also failed to support Dr. Donovan when he returned to the main headquarters. Before returning to his office, he had met with the teachers at I.S. 201 and had transferred the principal to the central office. The Negro and white liberal teachers at I.S. 201, many of whom were known to the protesting group, refused to support Dr. Donovan's actions. Les Campbell described the actions of the Negro teachers: "Seemingly they [the Black parents] had won a victory for improved education in the Black ghetto. Then the establishment turned to its secret weapon, the Negro professional. The Negro teachers at I.S. 201 helped transfer the victory into defeat."[21]

There is one other possible explanation for the reversal of the decision. The local group inadvertently leaked the agreement to the press before Dr. Donovan could meet with the union or the Board members. The local group had prepared mimeographed copies of the agreement and circulated them within the community. Newspaper reporters only had to stand in line to receive one. In retro-

21. Leslie Campbell, "The Difference," *Negro Teachers Forum,* I (December, 1966), 3.

spect, the inadvertent leak to the press may have occurred because of the community's deep distrust of the Board and its superintendent. There was a strong generalized basis for the distrust. The question is whether it was appropriate to display it in this manner.

The mass media slowly turned against the community interests as did the white principals of the other Harlem schools. It was the beginning of a mounting and organized effort to keep the Black schools in their places—controlled by white principals preoccupied with keeping their jobs. The New York Association of Black Supervisors and School Administrators remained silent throughout the early stages of the controversy.

When the white principal was returned to the school, the I.S. 201 negotiating committee found that its failure to organize its own community behind it was its major error. Its ability to keep students out of school, its most vaunted power, had fizzled.

Subsequent negotiations with the teachers' union were a complete waste of time. The union later agreed to a plan for three experimental districts. It then proceeded, along with the school system's middle management, to sabotage the effort.

At one point during the conflict, several Negro elder statesmen were called by the local activists in order to assist the local efforts. All agreed to support the local activist group *if* it took a position which the elder statesmen had in mind. They had obviously been in contact with the opposition before they arrived. They were acting as agents of the opposition and not as advocates of the local interests.

Racial Differentials

One can draw the following racial differentials from this sketchy case history:

1. Normally a request for an *experiment* is denied on some rational basis developed through, at least, partial agreements. To this observer, the request for an experiment was never seriously entertained or evaluated in the presence of the local group. There is a strong hint that a white community could have achieved an understanding through cooperative strategies. The requirement that conflict be employed to engage in an experiment appears to have stemmed from the racist attitudes of the Board.

2. The opposition by the Negro teachers to a demand by a pre-

dominantly Black community also appears to raise the issue of racism: racism by Blacks against Blacks. Stated otherwise, it was white racism in color. Richard Wright would describe their behavior as "negative loyalty."[22]

3. It is highly doubtful if the United Federation of Teachers would have opposed a white community which viewed a principal's ethnicity as a key variable and which also wanted a voice in the affairs of the school.

Hindsight: Analysis and Interpretation

FALSE NEGOTIATION

In retrospect, several factors become obvious. The superintendent of schools, who negotiated on behalf of the Board of Education, was, in fact, a negotiator without the authority to settle or the power to "sell" the agreement he made with the I.S. 201 negotiating committee to the Board of Education and the United Federation of Teachers, whose approval he was required to obtain. Even those Board members who participated in the process had to return to the entire Board to elicit a consensus.

It is worthy of note that the pattern of utilizing such impotent negotiators in Black-white confrontations was also found at Cornell, where the faculty originally refused to support the dean with whom the Black students had negotiated.[23] Similarly, when FIGHT negotiated a "settlement" with Kodak in Rochester, New York, only to find that Kodak's "negotiator" was reversed by his superiors, the same pattern was revealed. Kodak's "negotiator" had requested an opportunity to achieve "a better relationship with FIGHT," not to negotiate a settlement.[24]

A subsequent news story on the Rochester incident reveals that FIGHT had demanded 600 jobs for the hard-core unemployed over an 18-month period—with FIGHT picking the new workers. Kodak had instead proposed a *community-wide* quota of 1,500 jobs over the

22. Richard Wright, *White Man, Listen* (Garden City, N.Y.: Anchor Books, 1964), p. 16. Wright defines negative loyalty as a "kind of yearning under almost impossible conditions to identify with the values of the white world, since their own traditions have been shattered by that world." They are "not psychologically free enough to be traitors."

23. Othello Mahome, "Incident at Cornell," *Liberator*, IX (June, 1969), 4-7.

24. Robert Coulson, *How to Stay Out of Court* (New York: Crown Publishers, Inc., 1968), pp. 193-214.

same period—"with participation by all Rochester employers and agencies that deal with the poor." A new organization, Rochester Jobs Incorporated, was set up. In two years, more than 2,600 hard-core unemployed were hired.[25] It would be interesting to know how many of the jobs were actually provided by Kodak.

In the Rochester incident, the white institution utilized the negotiation process and the coercive forces of FIGHT to mute FIGHT's drive for unilateral power. By widening the employer group and by bringing in other employing agencies, Kodak was able to undercut FIGHT as a viable local organization and to encourage the development of one which was more responsive to control and/or manipulation by Kodak.

There is also a powerful basis for suspecting, and even possibly concluding, that original "agreements" are made by the white institution's negotiators in order to diminish the coercive thrust of the Black dissidents. A secondary establishment gain is to escalate white opposition to negotiating "under duress" applied by Blacks. (How else can negotiation be brought about?)

The use of such negotiators without authority or power approximates a human relations effort because it is not employed as a tool for *authentic* negotiations. Rather it appears to be a tool to assess the strength of the opposition and to determine what unilateral response of the establishment might be expected to anesthetize that opposition. Stated otherwise, it is "colonial relations" poorly concealed. Clearly, there is no intent to reach mutually-satisfying agreements in the designation of such a "negotiator." It would be interesting to determine whether this device is used more frequently in Black-white negotiations than in union-management negotiations. If this were so, we would have identified a *racist* differential.

There have, of course, been instances when union negotiators have been subsequently overruled by the rank and file. Evidence would suggest, however, that when this occurs, the union negotiators are, in fact, using the circumstance as a ploy to apply more pressure on the opposition.

The apparent openness of the school superintendent during the negotiations can now be understood. He was an intermediary who

25. "Answer to Riots—The Rochester Plan," *U.S. News and World Report*, August 4, 1969, pp. 58 and 59.

collected information, established rapport and reported back. But his decision-making powers were severely curtailed since he was required to seek confirmation from the Board of Education. I do not recall that the superintendent asked for the support and/or inputs of the I.S. 201 negotiating committee in seeking the Board's confirmation.

This evidence points up the failure of Black dissidents to identify the real sources of power. Recall that John F. Kennedy settled the Birmingham bus boycott by telephoning Pittsburgh, Birmingham steel's "Big Daddy." The I.S. 201 negotiators should have taken their case *directly* to the entire Board of Education and traded off with the United Federation of Teachers the right to participate in subsequent union negotiations with the Board. They also failed to establish the powers of the "negotiator" before proceeding to negotiate or to participate in the selection of a bona fide mediator.

In addition, they failed to identify the real role of the superintendent as given above, accepting him at times as a "negotiator" and at times as a "mediator," when, in fact, he was neither. In the first instance, he lacked the requisite power and influence; in the second, he was probably miscast. Theodore Kheel adds some perspective to this question in which the employer's interests compete with his ability to achieve a settlement: "We may also find a way to relieve our public officials of the job of trying to act in two conflicting roles simultaneously. During New York's transit strike, for example, Mayor Lindsay had to be both employer, resisting higher wages, and mediator seeking peace."[26]

The essence of Kheel's statement is that an authentic mediator cannot be a member of either system; i.e., he must be an external agent or third party. With this understanding, the model of an impotent negotiator engaged in diversionary tactics comes through as a tool of subordination. The masking of the fact-finder role as mediation and the utilization of a member of the white institution's system rather than a mutually selected third party compounds the trickery. A corollary to this analysis is the growing inability of white institutions to call upon their agents within the Black community to serve as intermediaries. In the Dayton conflict, mentioned above,

---

26. Theodore W. Kheel, "Can We Stand Strikes by Teachers, Police, Garbage Men, Etc.," *Reader's Digest*, August, 1969, p. 103.

when the only Negro member failed to be reelected to the Board, the Board expressed regret.[27] He had a record of voting against the interests of the Black community and consequently was needed by the establishment.

PLURALISM VS. ASSIMILATION

The I.S. 201 negotiating committee had sought to obtain the *exclusive power* to select their own principal and a *share* of the power to establish educational policy. To the degree that it obtained a redistribution of powers, it represented the creation of a *parallel* and a *shared* power system. The union-management model results in a shared power system to the degree that mutual survival depends on shared responsibility. Management has to earn profits in order to pay staff; unions have to provide skilled employees in order to aid in the production of profits.

As a public system accountable to the taxpayer, the school system's existence depends less on its management than it does on public approval. It could surrender the power to select principals to the public without tampering with its survival. It does not have to co-opt community groups in order to survive; management must co-opt the union in order to do so.

Successful union negotiations must inevitably involve some form of co-optation; formal or informal.[28] The institutionalized conflict between union and management has a built-in symbiosis: shop stewards get favors from management in turn for acting as "policemen" over their constituents—the workers. Management guarantees higher production by capitulating to union demands.

This discussion has been included because I recall my instinctive response at the moment the I.S. 201 negotiators thought they had reached an agreement. My first thought was that the I.S. 201 negotiating committee would have to go out and organize a counterco-optation force within the community in order to keep themselves "honest" to avoid complete co-optation themselves. I recalled how the observers to the negotiation process had kept the I.S. 201 negotiators responsive and accountable by feeding back their observations and by questioning the negotiating behavior of the local participants. On occasion,

27 See *Dayton Daily News,* **November 8, 1969.**
28. See discussion of co-optation in Philip Selznick, *TVA and the Grass Roots: A Study in the Sociology of Formal Organization* (New York: Harper and Row, 1966), pp. 13-15.

the observers would pass notes to the negotiators in order to suggest that certain questions be raised or that specific points be rammed home. The negotiators would use their own discretion in deciding whether to follow such leads from individual observers. However, if three or more observers made the same suggestion, their wishes would be carried out.

Not only was there fear of co-optation, there was the recognition that to become a part of the school system was to increase the committee's chances of emulating the system it was seeking to replace.[29]

DECIDING TO NEGOTIATE

What the I.S. 201 negotiators have learned—or should have learned —was that they should *not* have negotiated, since the Board was not prepared to accord them equal status at the negotiating table. Importantly, the Board agreed to feign negotiation as a tool to weaken the thrust. It never intended to share and/or redistribute power.

As one of the respondents puts it: "I would decide to negotiate or not to negotiate on the basis of my goals. If I want to integrate into the system—negotiate. If I want liberation for all Black people— don't negotiate."

The superintendent was subsequently quoted in the press as being against community control. The press reported: "Dr. Donovan said he believed effective decentralization of the city school system could contribute to bridging the gap between the people and the system by bringing parents into the schools to participate, but he said he felt that community control had no future and nothing to contribute."[30]

That Dr. Donovan and the Board of Education were attempting to turn back the clock is evident in the following assessment made by Urban America, Inc., and the Urban Coalition: "The major issue to emerge in the past year is that of decentralization or community control of schools. Its impact on the quality of slum-ghetto education cannot be fully evaluated."[31]

But there seem to be more important lessons to be learned based on a decision to *feign* negotiation as a means to purchase time:

29. Preston Wilcox, "Observations on the Transition From Centralization to Decentralization, *Foresight*, I (August, 1969) , 7-8.

30. M. S. Handler, "Donovan Expresses Optimism on Peace in Schools," *New York Times*, August 31, 1969, p. 32.

31. Urban America, Inc. and The Urban Coalition, *One Year Later* (New York: Frederick A. Praeger, 1969), p. 60.

1. to study the opposition and its system
2. to develop a counterco-optation force, i.e., a locally based constituency to which one is accountable
3. to mute opposing voices emanating from the local community either through internal community negotiations or public discrediting[32]
4. to force the opposition into fatal moves such as walking out of the negotiations, etc.
5. to put on public record the failures of the institution being confronted
6. to mount legislative and legal forms of protest
7. to keep public attention focused on the issue
8. to sharpen the understanding of the negotiation process and to develop negotiating skills
9. to develop "behind the scenes" contacts and informational sources
10. to *ascertain whether or not an authentic negotiation process is feasible*

A negotiation set (a workable relationship between the competing parties) can only be achieved after feigned negotiations are used to learn if *authentic* negotiation is possible and if trade-offs and settlements are desired by both groups. Attention must be given to the process as well as the goals of the negotiations. Since successful negotiation leads to a form of co-optation, the ability of the opposing groups to work together looms crucial.

As I now recall the negotiating process at I.S. 201, both the distrust of the local residents and their failure to adopt a negotiating stance may have prevented them from using the process for the purposes outlined above. They were seemingly more interested in having the school superintendent and Board grant their requests than in demonstrating throughout the process that a working relationship was possible. A change in their behavior might have had no impact on the outcome, but it would have increased their ability to mount a local constituency. Their own preassumption of a "victory" after the negotiations did not foster the sustaining of local pressure.

32. McCandlish Phillips, "Groups in Harlem Plan a Coalition," *New York Times,* July 14, 1969.

GAUGING THE OPPOSITION

The I.S. 201 activists obviously failed to calculate the strength of the opposition. Marilyn Gittell has ably documented the existence of the opposition. She describes the Council of Supervisory Associations—a professional organization made up of the various individual supervisory associations—as having a record of blocking change: "The council has openly opposed the Princeton Plan, school busing, the comprehensive high school plan, the dropping of the I.Q. examinations, and school pairing—*after* they were adopted as official policy by the Board and by the Superintendent."[33] Only one of the policies opposed by the Council of Supervisory Associations—the dropping of I.Q. examinations—was implemented.

Gittell identified the United Federation of Teachers as being one of the system's major policy-makers. Teacher salaries and benefits represented close to one half of the educational budget. On the other hand, there was little participation by the union in the development of curriculum and in other policy areas. She noted a conflict between educational and professional goals on one hand, and the narrow interests of the membership on the other.[34]

THE BLACK NEGOTIATING EXPERIENCE

The goal of this study is to collect data as a preliminary guide to the construction of models for effective resolution of racial conflicts involving white institutions and Black dissident organizations or groups.

Hypothesis

Based on a review of the resource materials listed in Appendix A, on the record of the consultation held in February, 1969, and on my experiences and knowledge, I decided to adopt the following hypothesis: Some confrontations by Black dissidents of white institutions can be resolved through the use of negotiations.

While stated in the affirmative here, during the study it was stated in the form of related questions. This was done to enable the respondents to arrive at their own conclusions. A corollary to this plan was to begin to identify a Black position, if one existed.

33. Marilyn Gittell, *Participants and Participation: A Study of School Policy in New York City* (New York: Frederick A. Praeger Publishers, 1967), p. 14.
34. *Ibid.*

Negro and Black Positions

The paucity of Black-controlled institutions and the lack of reasons, in most cases, for them to be confronted politically by Black dissidents suggests that there is no need to distinguish them in behavior and form from white-controlled institutions. One might add, however, that student confrontation of Negro institutions (for example, colleges and churches) have not usually resulted in negotiations, that is, the leadership of such institutions have refused to negotiate "under duress."[35, 36] What they seemed to be questioning is the necessity to negotiate with subordinates.

It seems appropriate at this point to distinguish between Negro-white negotiations and Black-white negotiations. One way to look at this issue is to recall the current discussions going on within the Black community and between it and the white community on the following issues:

1. Integration *vs.* separatism[37]
2. Black capitalism *vs.* cooperative economic development[38]
3. White philanthropy *vs.* restitution to Blacks[39]
4. School decentralization *vs.* Black community control[40]
5. White liberalism *vs.* white racism[41]

Joseph Pentecoste has defined integration as follows: "Integration as a theory is basically a willingness to give up one's own attributes and to lose one's self-identity by merging with the dominant group."[42] Pentecoste would probably assert that the Negro-white conflict reflects an encounter between those whites who want to *stop* the clock and those Negroes who want to be accepted by their masters. The Black-white conflict is based on a rejection by Blacks of whites as masters and a reluctance of whites to surrender the privilege of the white skin. In the first instance, there is a denial of the reality of

35. "Southern Campuses in Crisis," *New South,* XXIV (Spring, 1969), 2.
36. "State of the Southern States," *New South,* XXIV (Spring, 1969), 59.
37. Wilcox, *Integration or Separatism in Education: K-12.*
38. James Boggs, "The Myth and Irrationality of Black Capitalism" (New York: Interreligious Foundation for Community Organization, 1969) (mimeographed).
39. James Forman, "The Black Manifesto" (New York: Interreligious Foundation for Community Organization, 1969) (mimeographed).
40. Preston Wilcox, "The Crisis Over Who Shall Control the Schools: A Bibliography" (New York: Afram Associates, Inc., 1968).
41. Preston Wilcox, *Education for Black Humanism* (New York: Afram Associates, Inc., 1969).
42. Joseph Pentecoste, "Black Psychology," *Black Liberator,* V (June 1969), 4.

racism by whites and, at the same time, a concerted effort to conceal it. In the second instance, its existence is accorded by Blacks who are desirous of removing racists from control over their lives. The competition embedded in Negro-white conflict derives from the desire of Negroes to become psychological mirror images of non-Blacks, largely because they feel that they are "outcasts." These non-Blacks have based their economic and psychological existences on remaining non-Black. The Black-white competition is a struggle for the right to *define* the Black condition in cultural, political, and physical terms. The Blacks so engaged do not rely on white definitions of Blacks, nor do they want to replace their own values with those of whites.

Negro-white negotiations are possible and even desirable end goals. Recall the four basic nonviolent steps of the late Martin Luther King, Jr.: "In any nonviolent campaign there are four basic steps: (1) collection of the facts to determine whether injustices are alive, (2) negotiation, (3) self-purification, and (4) direct action."[43]

Direct action was seen as a technique to "create a situation so crisis packed that it will inevitably open the door to negotiation." Martin Luther King posed his challenge to the system as an alternative to the Muslims.[44] To this degree, it was divisive to the Black cause and a willingness to compromise on the terms of the opposition. The fact that his famous *Letter from a Birmingham Jail* was addressed to white antagonists rather than to Black protagonists supports this theme. It was an appeal to the white conscience, not an assertion of Black consciousness.

When Stokely Carmichael urged young white activists to return to the white community in order to confront Simon Legree's racist and oppressive behavior, he laid the seeds for a new kind of social order.[45, 46] Racist-free Blacks and whites were to work within their own communities in order to create a new order. The alternative was to urge Negroes to become "psychologically white" (*and* anti-

43. Martin Luther King, Jr. *Letter From a Birmingham Jail* (New York: Fellowship of Reconciliation, 1963), p. 4.

44. *Ibid.*, pp. 11-12.

45. Stokely Carmichael, "What We Want," *New York Review of Books,* III (September 22, 1966), 5-8

46. See also, "Excerpts From Paper on Which the 'Black Power' Philosophy is Based," *New York Times,* August 5, 1966, p. 10.

Black at the same time) in order to conceal the deficits within and to maintain the existing order.

The dichotomy might also be stated in the following fashion:

Civil Rights	*vs.*	*Black Power*
Search for new and kinder masters		No need for masters
Assimilation		Enculturation
White approval		Black approval
One-by-one improvements		En masse improvements
Reaction		Enactment
Confront the man		Confront themselves
Piece of white action		Redistribute white action
Individualism		Collectivism
Responsibility without power		Power and responsibility
"Whites on the mind"		"Blacks on the mind"
White curriculum		Multicultural curriculum
Equal to whites		Equal to occasion
Appeal to white conscience		Appeal to Black consciousness
Evacuate the ghetto		Elevate the ghetto
White integrated control		Parallel multicultural control
Aimed toward "talented tenth"		Aimed toward Black masses
Black capitalism		Economic socialism
Develops followers		Develops communal leadership
Advocates for system		Advocates for Blacks and Negroes
Deals with symptoms		Seeks out basic causes
Building white nationalism		Building Black nationalism

This paper will turn its attention to *a* Black position, not the Negro position. Negro groups are willing to participate in negotiations because of a latent need to be co-opted into the system. Not only are such negotiations not authentic, they are usually set up to avoid dealing with the basic issues. Their function is to encourage Negro "dissidents" to replace their own values with those of their oppressors: to become mainstream advocates against others like them.

A third way of looking at the question of the Negro-Black issue is to list the historical leadership counterparts:

Negro	Black
Booker T. Washington	W. E. B. Dubois
Father Divine	Marcus Garvey
Martin Luther King, Jr.	Malcolm X[47]

That this distinction is crucial is highlighted by the fact that during the March on Washington in 1963, there were ten leaders of national stature within the Black community participating not including Malcolm X.[48, 49] Yet, the Poor People's March of 1967 resulted from the singular leadership of the Reverend Ralph Abernathy, president of the Southern Christian Leadership Conference. He received very little support from other national Black leaders. Not only has there been a decline in the number of Black leaders who are accountable to the establishment, but there are a growing number of national organizations who deem themselves to be accountable *only* to the Black community. President Nixon's failure to attract established Negro leadership to his administration and the rejection of such offers by many of those who received them is another case in point.[50]

The articulation and identification of a Black position have gained importance. Recent rebellions in Youngstown and Columbus, Ohio, for example, suggest that the "cool out" efforts have not worked. The National Commission on Civil Disorders made a diagnosis, but its treatment plan had not gotten off the ground one year later.[51, 52] Uncle Toms are under attack, white liberals have been declared obsolete and the overt white racists are building up for oppression. The Black position is distinctive, then, largely because it fails to lend itself to easy co-optation and because its very exercise calls oppressive tactics into play.

Is not the real point of the Racial Negotiations Project to discern how to co-opt Black dissidents without introducing any basic changes?

47. See Louis E. Lomax, *To Kill a Black Man* (Los Angeles: Holloway House Publishing Co., 1968). Lomax discusses the parallels in the lives of Malcolm X and Martin Luther King, Jr.

48. Robert S. Bird, *Ten Negroes* (New York: *New York Herald Tribune*, 1963).

49. See also *The March on Washington: A Chronological History of Negro Contributions*, a recording narrated by Ralph Cooper.

50. Simeon Booker, "What Nixon Plans for Blacks: None Offered Cabinet Posts," *Jet*, December 26, 1968, pp. 14-19.

51. *Report of National Advisory Committee on Civil Disorders* (New York: E. P. Dutton and Co., Inc., 1968).

52. See also Urban Coalition, *One Year Later* (New York: Frederick A. Praeger, 1969).

White men who challenge the values of the dominant group of which they are members will understand this assessment. Gregory Coffin, recently fired as superintendent of schools, Evanston, Illinois, understands now to a minimal degree what it means to be Black in America. He was fired not because he desegregated Evanston's school but because he sought authentically to integrate them.[53]

Methodology

In seeking to test out the above hypothesis, several efforts were undertaken:

1. The I.S. 201—Board of Education negotiation of September 1966, was recalled, recorded, and analzyed; see above.
2. Selected literature was reviewed; see bibliography.
3. Four Black persons who had recently been involved in negotiations were interviewed by an assistant to the author.

INTERVIEWEES

The four interviewees were selected on the following bases:

1. They were Black.
2. With one exception, they had been involved recently in negotiation processes between white-controlled institutions and Black dissident groups.
3. They had some interest in the subject issue.
4. Three were effectively accountable to Black people as demonstrated by their past actions despite the sources of their incomes.
5. They had practical insights into "white tricknology" and the skills to "read" racist behavior.
6. They were able to think conceptually and abstractly.

The interviewees approximated the white middle class in terms of education, income, and place of residence. All were college graduates with credentials no less than masters' degrees. Two were lawyers. All were known to me as professional colleagues/ethnic Brothers. Most would tend to respond more readily to me and/or my representative than to a white social researcher. There was a distinct possibility that through free association and interaction additional insights would be revealed.

53. Valery Jo Bradley, "Integrationist Superintendent Fired Despite 'Opposition,'" *Jet,* July 10, 1969, pp. 50-51.

Two had been involved in the New York City school strike and the conflict over who should control the schools within the Black community. Although these two were paid by the New York City Board of Education, one had been arrested for defying oppressive orders from the Board. The other also publicly defied Board mandates. They would not submit to control by the white-controlled school system.

The third was a lawyer who had been hired by a Black and communally based federation of organizations to provide legal advice during a negotiation. The federated group had challenged the right of a white-controlled corporation, which had imposed itself on the community, to control the program of an operation for which it was committed to raising funds.

The last was employed by a diamond mining company. He was functioning as a negotiator for the company in transactions with African nations. His ethnicity was an integral part of his qualifications for the position. Having resided in and worked in Africa, he professed a great understanding of African values, mores, and customs. He was able to perceive when and how to negotiate and was more than "tolerated" by the Africans who tended to respond to whites in that fashion. He had earned a law degree.

The first two interviewees were involved in negotiations following crisis situations. The last two had agreed to negotiate; one to attempt to *avoid conflict,* the other to seal an economic contract. In the third instance, the anticipated conflict never came to fruition even though the Black communal group lost out in the negotiation.

The first three were seeking a redistribution of power; the last was interested in achieving the best economic arrangement possible. No tools were available to him other than that of negotiation.

INTERVIEWS

The interviews were structured so as to identify the components of the racial negotiations in which the interviewees had been involved. Particular attention was given to comparisons with the labor-management negotiation model.

Initially, each interviewee was to be asked to give a general statement about the negotiation process and to touch upon issues such as the establishment of the right of Blacks to negotiate with whites, techniques for unifying the Black side, Black/white differentials, attitude and/or approach of white institutions, issues of racism and colonialism, and "cool out" or co-optation efforts undertaken by white institutions. However, all of the interviewees were not asked all of the questions.

Findings

The following are excerpts from responses of the four interviewees to two questions. The first was a request for a general statement on Black-white Negotiations:

Respondent No. 1. Negotiation is a misnomer. When Blacks sit at the table with whites it is more an attempt to get justice. Negotiation implies an exchange of relative equality; both sides have something to offer.

Respondent No. 2. The key to negotiations as I see it is that they work directly or indirectly to keep Blacks divided and powerless (for example, militants *vs.* moderates), thereby obscuring the real issues. . . . The power order must compartmentalize and break down opposition into more manageable units. . . . Negotiation by Blacks with whites is based on the fraudulent assumption of some kind of *honor* between them. History says the answer is NO.

Respondent No. 3. Black people must acquire the power not to have to negotiate. . . . White people have the tendency to feel that "if you are Black, get back."

Respondent No. 4. It may be more relevant in Black/white negotiations to think of oneself (a Black) as a foreigner and to perceive whites as foreigners in order to become sensitive to limitations of role and behavior expectations and values.

The second question was a request for a statement on the right of Blacks to negotiate:

Respondent No. 1. The right of Blacks to negotiate with whites has never been established. There is no recognition on the part of whites of a need to negotiate with Blacks. What is involved is a *reaction to conflict* and confrontation which arise out of Blacks' need for survival.

Respondent No. 2. Negotiation assumes the power to make the other guy keep his bargain; at this point we cannot do this.

Respondent No. 3. The power (for Blacks) to negotiate with whites is not there.

Respondent No. 4. This respondent never questioned this issue.

Rather he proceeded to talk about the negotiation process, the requisite skills and techniques and behavioral differences between Africans and Europeans.

In response to the first question, all four respondents identified racial barriers to the use of the negotiation process. The fourth respondent took them into consideration and proceeded to view the opposition in the way in which he perceived he was viewed by it. He accommodated to the circumstances. In this instance, he was suggesting a model for negotiations rather than recalling an actual experience. He said later that "A key ability in negotiations is the ability to argue your own position using the other persons frame of reference."

Seemingly, since he was involved in a *compulsory negotiation process*, his energies were expended in acquiring the skills and insights to participate in it.

The first two respondents viewed encounters with white institutions as efforts to correct historical inequities. One talked of *social justice*. The second later discussed the basic *needs* of Blacks as being paramount while white institutional negotiators and even union negotiators go to the table "wanting things." Their point seemed to be that Blacks are seeking the attainment of inalienable rights which should be non-negotiable and, therefore, cannot be achieved through negotiations.

In response to the second question, again the first three interviewees agreed that the right to negotiate cannot be granted. It must be seized through the exercise of power. The function of a Black-initiated "negotiation," then, is *not* to merely achieve Black goals but to agree upon the *methods of implementation* and to build up monitoring and self-correcting checks and balances. The inference is that a Black-white "negotiation" can take place only *after* there has been recognition of the rights of Blacks to control of their own destinies. What follows is a working out of the details of the process whereby such control will be effected.

In the instance of FIGHT in Rochester, referred to earlier, FIGHT, perhaps, should not have "settled" until Kodak publicly announced and documented the 600 jobs which were offered by its representative. The distribution and assignment of jobs and the recruitment of Black employees should have been the subject of negotiation—not the granting of the jobs themselves.

Negotiation as a tool to resolve racial conflicts, then, is not a right but an obligation as a price for the order that the establishment seeks. The failure of white institutions to grant the Blacks the *right* to negotiate renders negotiation useless as a tool to resolve conflicts.

One respondent outlined the negotiation process as follows:

1. Conflict and confrontation by Blacks.
2. Agreement to negotiate *by whites*. (Recall that Blacks were not demanding *the right to negotiate;* they wanted a voice in the education of their children.)
3. Whites listen—then retire for deliberation.
4. In the interim, Black pressure diminishes because Black pressure is undermined.
5. Whites then decide what they will do and what they will not do.

This process turns out to be a *social study* by the Establishment of the demands of the natives. A unilateral decision is then made by whites alone as to what they will give up. Not only is this not a negotiation; it is not even an attempt to co-opt. On another level, it is a mere postponement of conflict and confrontation; it is not an effort to deal with basic needs and demands. What comes through is that step three above is a reporting of demands, a clarification of issues. Negotiation, if it is to take place, should begin after step five, accompanied by sustained disruptions and pressures.

Confirmation for this view is submitted by the first three respondents in their discussion of attempts to co-opt Black dissident groups:

> They deal in personalities—good white group *vs.* bad white group—perpetuating the myth that it is individuals rather than the institutions that need to be changed.

> The individual negotiator is much more vulnerable than the negotiating team. He can more easily be made the object of suspicion. He can be manipulated and isolated through creating distrust. Furthermore, no individual can adequately speak for the community.

One is told in confidential tones "we can talk to you" or "you are knowledgeable and you can make *them* understand."

Black negotiating groups are often restricted as to size, or only one person is spoken to—others are ignored.

Job offers are made indirectly, through an agent or crony or ally.

Attempts are made to provoke Blacks through familiarities, insults. etc. This tactic is designed to precipitate a catharsis.

Negotiation sites are usually in white territory.

In negotiation between Negro groups and white institutions, many of the board members of the Negro group (NAACP and Urban League) are on the boards of the white institutions. The interlocking boards operate to the detriment of Negro dissidents.

Another issue which was key to the respondents was how the negotiation process was used to dissipate the constituent support of the Black dissidents. Several techniques were noted:

1. Extending the negotiation over a period of time to conceal the overt expressions of the conflict.
2. The selection of leadership that is accountable to whites, not Blacks.
3. The absence of a self-policing apparatus within the Black community.[54]
4. The control over the sources of information by white institutions and the absence of indigenous Black research organizations.[55]
5. Authentic negotiation does not take place; the process is used to collect data, to react to conflict, and to maintain the status quo.

CONCLUSIONS AND GUIDELINES

Meaningful negotiations for Blacks can only occur when they are predicated on a policy which has been accepted by the white estab-

54. See Brian Vachon, "United Voice for Harlem Seen in Alliance of Black Groups," *New York Daily News*, July 10, 1969, p. M1.
55. An example of such an organization is the Black People's Topographical Research Center, 633 East 75th Street, Chicago, Ill.

lishment in advance: that Blacks are in control of their own destinies and that it is improper for whites to define Black interests or to control Blacks in support of white interests.

This general principle includes policy elements which need to be part of the acceptance of Black control over Black destiny:

(1) Blacks will work out for themselves who are to be their representatives in expressing Black interests and in dealing with the white establishment about them; (2) Those functions of the establishment that apply to the Black community should be under the control of Black representatives.

Once the white establishment has fully recognized the fact of an independent Black community and the necessity for localized control over the way institutions function within the Black community, negotiations can be used to work out the implementation of these general policies by determining what guidelines, if any, will be agreed upon between the white establishment and the Black sub-unit affecting the allocation and uses of resources, patterns of curricula, personnel policies, control of capital funds, etc.

The Decision to Negotiate

1. The first question Black dissidents should raise is, "Should we negotiate or not negotiate and, if so, for what purposes?":

a. to achieve a reconciliation?
b. to purchase time in order to study the opposition and to build a constituency, etc.?
c. to discern whether or not a working relationship is possible?
d. to develop advocates within the opposition's system?
e. to negotiate the implementation of a settlement previously agreed upon?

This position is based on the lack of prior evidence that negotiation is possible; that white institutions will respect the right of Black dissidents as equals at the bargaining table. Hence the "negotiation" must be utilized as a process to discern if an authentic negotiation is feasible and possible and for what purposes. The right to negotiate does not exist—nor can it be "granted."

If and when Black dissident groups develop the requisite power and achieve the appropriate recognition by the establishment to command an *authentic* negotiation, the following steps are suggested:

2. The decision to negotiate must be made by the Black dissidents and not the representatives of the white institution.

3. The decision to negotiate should be based on some *prior agreement* by the white institution to settle or to trade off certain benefits. It should stress the negotiation of the implementation procedures rather than the desired benefits. This process will require "behind-the-scenes negotiations," the continued application of pressure, the muting of local opposition, and the sustained mounting of community support.

Guidelines to the Negotiation Process

1. The negotiation of implementation procedures should involve only those representatives of the white institution who have been delegated the *power* to set and/or implement policy.

2. Prior decisions on the rules of the negotiation process should be established and compliance with them maintained.

3. Plans for monitoring of the implementation process should be viewed as being an integral part of the process. The power to negotiate is inseparable from one's ability to hold the opposition accountable for settlements achieved. Such "accountability" is much more difficult in cases where Blacks are operating from *outside* the system—unlike the unions, who can police the agreement from *within* the system.

4. Black dissidents should not utilize *single* negotiators; neither should the establishment decide upon the number of negotiators who will act on behalf of the Black dissidents.

5. Black intermediaries sent by the establishment to work out arrangements with the Black dissidents should be carefully screened and tested out. They should *not* be utilized as negotiators by the Black dissidents if they are in the employment of the establishment or cannot be held accountable to the Black community.

No mediator is completely neutral; his behavior is shaped by his frame of reference and his understanding of the issues. Preference should be given to those mediators who can and will *advocate* the Black position.

6. The goals of Black dissidents should involve a *redistribution of power and institutional change* leading to Black community autonomy.

7. The inability of Black dissident groups to control the behavior

of their constituents was viewed by one respondent as being an *asset*. Implicit violence can have an impact which explicit violence would lack because it would be suppressed by the police. Hollow threats should be avoided.

8. Successful negotiation produces co-optation as a corollary. Importantly, it co-opts the leadership and does not necessarily benefit the Black masses. It is a decision to *postpone* rebellions rather than to overcome the need for them. Related to this assessment is an evaluation of the outcomes along a spectrum of an apparent victory but little probability of long-term change, or an apparent defeat but laying the basis for the continuation and development of the struggle. The former would probably postpone rebellions; the latter might remove the need for them.

9. The street-oriented, picket line activists are *not* the persons who should participate in negotiations. Confrontations with police, the wear and tear of early morning rising and late meetings, and the accumulated tensions which develop limit the capacity and desire of such persons to compromise, to bluff, to finesse, and to agree to *legitimate* compromises. This occurs for two reasons:

a. Their roles as picket leaders make it difficult for them to "save face" with those they lead if they come up with anything less than "total success" during negotiations. In addition, their separation from their followers during the negotiation process heightens suspicions.

b. Such persons are reluctant to agree to any compromises, legitimate or illegitimate, unless they have the sanction of the groups to whom they are accountable. Usually such leaders do not have a "Plan B" which they are empowered to enact, nor do they have an easy way to canvass group opinion. Black caucuses are suggested for that purpose.

10. The need for behind-the-scenes "contact persons" in between and even during negotiating meetings is crucial.

11. The negotiators must stick to their roles; they must not vacillate between negotiator and mediator roles. Several times, some of the I.S. 201 negotiators became mediators between the opposing sides. This was particularly the case with an advisor to the I.S. 201 side.

12. It is necessary to establish a *negotiations set,* i.e., to establish pragmatically that a mutual *negotiation process* is possible and feasible. A major reason for this step is to ascertain the explicit powers which have been delegated to the negotiators for the opposition. The point is that prior experience has shown that the New York City Board of Education's staff was always prepared with an *alternative* plan without having discussed the original one proposed by the community. Either a committee was proposed, a delay in consideration was suggested, or an alternate Board proposal was submitted. This was often done in the name of negotiation, when, in fact, it was an effort to avoid that eventuality.

One was able to discern whether or not a negotiation set was possible by watching the Board's staff operate. If they "role played," communicated nonverbally (e.g., eye signals), passed the buck, gave lectures, behaved ingratiatingly, or waited to insert tricky questions, then it was stalling, not negotiation. A second pattern was that of trying to seduce the professional staff person into assuming leadership of the group, to serve in a liaison role between the school system and the community group, or to discredit his technical-consultative efforts.

13. Be sure that *none* of those on the negotiating team can be compromised by a job offer, praise, or subtle threats.

14. Public announcements of "victory" should be avoided. Rather, continuing efforts to ensure that agreements reached are sealed and implemented should be made. This is particularly the case when the negotiator for the white institution has to obtain the approval of his institution before confirming the agreement.

15. Organize and educate one's constituency as to the issues and how they can support you by educating others.

16. Develop a plan to mute and/or neutralize the expression of opposing sentiments by local spokesmen who do not speak for the local community or who are mainstream advocates. Hold private meetings with those residents or Blacks who sit on the white institution's board.

Other Uses of Negotiation

Negotiations can also be used:
1. as a tool to mediate conflicts between ethnic groups such as

Blacks and Puerto Ricans, [56, 57, 58] and

2. as a tool to build a community coalition. One of the respondents to the survey stated: "Negotiations might be useful for finding a *problem definition among Blacks.*" Such a process can be used to develop what Maulana Ron Karenga calls "operational unity": "Most people get ideal unity and operational unity mixed up; ideal unity is a false position, operational unity is what must be achieved."[59]

BLACK DISSIDENT MODEL: TOWARD A DEFINITION

The identification of a Black position, hopefully, lends greater clarity to this inquiry. The respondents have pushed the issue further. A deeper question relates to whether racism and its consequences can be muted through negotiation. To suggest that racism can be minimized through negotiation raises some fundamental questions. One could posit that white America is much more committed to concealing racism than it is to ending it. Conversely, one could posit that the Black Power ethos commits its constituents to the removing of racists from control over their lives more than it does toward ending racism itself. The fact of the matter is there is no major effort in this country to *end racism.*

The analogy to the union-management model helps to make this point clear. A "successful negotiation" between union and management can be thought of as a process of co-optation of the union by the management. Based on the union-management model, a "successful negotiation" in a racial case is a co-optation of the Black protest group by the establishment. Such an agreement leads to a shared commitment to conceal racism and leave racists in control over the lives of Blacks. It is an agreement to maintain the status quo. The Featherstone article listed in the bibliography attests to this. A spokesman for the female liberation movement makes this point sharply.

56. "Puerto Rican-Afro-American Squabble Growing in the Bronx," *New York Amsterdam News,* January 27, 1968, p. 1.

57. Gregory Simms, and Enrique Arnyo, "Report of the Conference Proceedings of the Borough Presidents of Manhattan and the Bronx Held on December 9, 1967" (Trenton, New Jersey: New Jersey Community Action Training Institute, 1968).

58. "Trio of Mediators Named in City Poverty Dispute," *New York Times,* November 30, 1969, p. 20.

59. Clyde Halisi, and James Mtume, *The Quotable Karenga* (Los Angeles: U.S. Organization, 1967), p. 17.

We conceptualize the significance of the marriage institution this way:

$$\frac{\text{Marriage}}{\text{Women}} = \frac{\text{Integration}}{\text{Blacks}}$$

Marriage, as we know it, is for women, as integration is for Blacks. It is the atomization of a sex so as to render it politically powerless.[60]

If the same paradigm is applied to the subject discussed here, it might look something like this:

$$\frac{\text{Labor negotiations}}{\text{Unions}} = \frac{\text{Racial negotiations}}{\text{Black dissidents}}$$

The *invisible* aspects of both paradigms—*men, whites, management,* and *white-controlled institutions*—are characterized by their superordinate roles. They also hold in common an ability to oppress, to resist change, to co-opt and to control as it relates to their subordinates. Importantly, those subordinates who replace their values with those of the superordinates become politically powerless in terms of their freedom to question their superordinates. The union movement in this country presents the classic evidence. The power of unions is characterized by their expression of the interests of the superordinates. They have not worked on behalf of subordinates in recent years, particularly Blacks. In fact, unions have become more powerful because they have kept Blacks out.

Beyond the co-optation element and the political difficulties of joining with one's oppressors is the reality of the differences in goals. Not only are unions capitalistic in behavior and operation, deep down they are not even reformers. Scratch a conservative and you locate a person who wants to turn the clock back. Scratch a reformer and you will find one who really believes in stylizing the status quo. The authentic goals of Blacks call for restructuring Black-white relationships to increase the possibility that whites will find their "need

60. Judith Brown, "Toward a Female Liberation Movement," Part II (Gainesville, Florida: SSOC/SDS Chapter, 1969) (mimeographed), p. 22.

to control Blacks" unfulfilled, and Blacks will find themselves giving up the need to be anointed by whites.

Negotiation as a tool for solving race conflicts can serve only to soften the impact of the oppression without changing the basic structure of relationships. Such a process does not assign to the Blacks a share of responsibility or authority which is the sole purview of the Black dissident group and the community it purports to represent. Rather, it maintains white control over the Black agenda. The "non-negotiable" rights of Blacks remain negotiable by whites. The Black dissident model must focus its attention, not on Black-white negotiations, but on building a unified communal force such that Black-white negotiations are based on a definition of how the power will be redistributed rather than on what whites can do for Blacks.

As a case in point, one might examine those instances wherein Black Studies Programs have been developed on white racist campuses. Such programs have often been established under Black leadership selected by Black students or with their consent. The programs have exposed the Black students to *Black-oriented content* without modifying the core curricula of the institutions themselves, whose racist-oriented curricula and practices have often remained undisturbed.[61]

Autonomy of Blacks

Of importance, in such instances, is the tacit autonomy which such programs assign to Blacks over *significantly Black decisions*: the recruitment, selection, orientation, financing, counseling, and guidance of Black students. A secondary gain is the institutionalization of a Black caucus: a structure which fosters group study, group decision-making, and group action toward the collective interests of Black students. This built-in Black advocacy system earns power to the degree that it is consulted regularly, is assigned a designated piece of the action, and forces the larger institution to take its concerns into consideration. Importantly, the informal system within such structures provides to their members the security through which they come to perceive that power can be attained. Self- and group-developmental autonomy are enhanced, if not the autonomy to act unilaterally within the framework of the larger institution.

61. See Wilcox, "Black Studies as an Academic Discipline."

Within a racist society whose key factor is the control over the Black experience by whites, the control over the Black experience by Blacks is, indeed, a new-found leverage for the development of power.

In a society that exercises controls over all of its members—Black and white—the sanctity of the development of the internal system of its special interest groups is its hallmark. When one considers the degree to which the infrastructure of the Black community has been controlled (Urban League, NAACP, churches, etc.) or destroyed (Universal Negro Improvement Association, etc.) by white America, autonomy over one's *internal affairs* looms very crucial.

This interpretation of autonomy may be the key for which I have been searching. Most observers think of autonomy in terms of control over one's external relationships. What America presumptively guarantees all groups except the poor and minorities is autonomy over their internal affairs. The genius of racism and capitalism has been their impact in "dividing and conquering" the poor and the minorities. When viewed from this perspective, racial negotiations have failed largely because whites are not only resisting sharing the rewards of affluency with Blacks; they are reluctant to permit Blacks to *control their own lives and experiences*. This is the fullest manifestation of white institutional racism.

That the lack of Black cohesion can be attributed to racism has been ably documented. The classic statement of this position was made by the National Advisory Commission on Civil Disorders, as noted earlier.

The table in Appendix C describing the reactions of whites and Blacks to caucus experience also supports this position.

When one considers the *non-negotiable items* that Blacks seek to negotiate and understands that most of what Blacks are struggling for is long overdue them as human beings, it may be that what they are demanding of white institutions is not a share of white power but the return to Blacks of their basic Black Power—the right to control their own destinies in concert with other groups. *They are struggling for self-autonomy for Blacks.* It is no irony in a racist society that a desire to secure *Black self-autonomy* is a threat to the status quo.

Black dissidents, when confronting white institutions, are seeking control over those informal and internal processes which affect the viability of the Black community: who works (males or females), who decides one's qualifications and prepares one for college (whites or Blacks), who selects Blacks for jobs, who determines which Blacks should be arrested (white cops or Black cops, etc.). Are not these the crucial issues for control and action?

The implications of this interpretation for racial negotiations is that such efforts should identify and assign to Blacks, those *significantly Black decisions*. The establishment usually hires a Negro for positions involving these decisions. His role is to prevent Blacks from advancing while using his position to give the illusion of progress. *Significantly Black decisions are those which can only be made for Blacks, with Blacks, and by Blacks.*

There is an implicit change in the structure of relationships between Black dissidents and white institutions when agreements that Blacks will make their own decisions are reached. The former can expend energy in their own development without having to brook white interference. The latter can reduce the energy they expend controlling Blacks and interest themselves in learning how to relate to Blacks on a humane level. This concept was stated in the constitution of the recently formed Texas Conference of Churches. It was formed by a merger of ten dioceses of Texas's Catholic Conference and the Texas Council of Churches, linking Protestants, Catholics, and Eastern Orthodox.

It states in part: "doing together all there is save those which we must in good conscience and obedience do separately, cultivating interchurch fellowships throughout the state, and fostering dialogue in the realm of faith and order."[62]

There is growing evidence of the thrust for internal organization within the Black community. The proliferation of Black Urban Coalitions provides one piece of evidence. On the weekend of November 16-18, 1969, the Committee for a United Newark held a convention to select candidates for public office. Harlem is planning to convene a two-day convention to determine who should speak for Harlem in reference to a planned construction of a state office building. When Harlem's United Federation of Black Community Organizations was formed on July 13, 1969, a Manifesto containing the following statement emerged as reported in the *New York Times:* "Since 'the public

62. "Coming Together, Texas-Style," *Time,* March 7, 1969, p. 67.

and private institutions and services' are 'owned, operated, and controlled by the outer society,' . . . the residents of black communities must 'end their victimized status through the utilization of their tremendous organizational potential."[63]

Procedures and Questions

The Black dissident model then must address itself to:

1. Developing a procedure and a process for determining *who speaks for the Black community* and the criteria for selecting legitimate spokesmen.[64]

2. Developing techniques and processes for developing *"operational unity"* among the various special-interest groups within the Black community: moderates to militants, middle class to lower class, public employees and elected officials and community workers and residents, business interests and the working class, etc.

3. Identifying those *decisions* that can be made *about* the Black community only *by* the legitimate spokesman of the Black community.

4. Studying and understanding the nature of decision-making (informal and formal) within white-controlled groups and the competing participants (teachers, supervisors, administrators, etc.) within such institutions and how they can be converted into advocates for the Black agenda in pursuit of their own special interests. Oppenheimer and Lakey have described the reactions of the white opposition to confrontations by Black dissidents in the following stages: (a) indifference, (b) active antagonism, (c) disunity, and (d) negotiation.[65]

Steps a and b are fairly well understood by Blacks. The skill to exploit disunity, Step c, is probably a key determinant. Item d, negotiation, provides a "face-saving" escape for the white institution since when white support is brought in, the change which occurs can be "accredited" to white forces rather than to the Black dissidents.[66]

63. Phillips, "Groups in Harlem," *New York Times,* July 14, 1969.
64. This requirement will force Blacks who speak for themselves as individuals or for special organizations only to qualify their statements accordingly.
65. Martin Oppenheimer and George Lakey. *A Manual for Direct Action: Strategy and Tactics for Civil Rights and All Other Non-Violent Protest Movements* (Chicago: Quadrangle Books, Inc., 1964-65) , p. 22.
66. *Ibid.,* p. 35.

5. Establishing a procedure for the *control over information and its flow.* Edwards, an I.S. 201 activist, has noted: "The pattern which sees information flow from black professionals to white professionals to the lay white community to the lay black (usually via the mass media) is directly contributing to the colonization of our community. In its stead must be substituted a pattern of information flow from Black professionals to the lay Black community back to Black professionals for implementation of the ideas."[67]

The emphasis on the articulation of a Black dissident model as a prerequisite to negotiating with white-controlled institutions received its firmest support during the efforts to resolve Black urban rebellions. In only two cities was there a positive change in governmental grievance channels or procedures although negotiations took place in all of the disorders surveyed by the National Advisory Commission on Civil Disorders.[68]

The issue for Black dissidents becomes one of how to prepare themselves and their constituents to come to the negotiating table. They should be prepared even before asking themselves whether to negotiate or not. The following are questions Black dissidents should ask themselves before making that decision.

1. Who initiates the request for a negotiation?

2. Is the negotiator who represents the white institution empowered to settle?

3. What are the criteria for determining whether or not to negotiate? Lack of other alternatives available to either side? Establishment of legal rights to certain benefits? The development of the requisite power to enforce one's will on the establishment?

4. Should Black dissident groups ever agree to settle during the negotiation process itself?

5. How can Black dissidents ensure that benefits pledged by the white institutions are subsequently delivered? Signed statements? Continuing pressure? Disruptive tactics?

6. How does one ensure the selection of negotiators based on an assessment of their negotiation skills rather than through popular vote?

67. E. Babette Edwards, "The Black Professional—Judas in the Living Room?" *Kweli,* June, 1969, p. 2.
68. *Report of National Advisory Commission on Civil Disorders,* pp. 7 and 156.

7. After a negotiation has been agreed upon, what are the techniques for testing out whether or not an authentic mutual process is possible and capable of persisting?

8. How do Black dissident groups bring pressure on the apex of the power structure being challenged? What techniques are available for discerning the views of such persons through communication with their intermediaries?

9. What are the keys for determining when one shifts from a conflict model to a cooperative model?

10. What are the tasks involved in enabling a representative to have settlements confirmed subsequently by his superiors?

11. What are the alternatives to "refusing to negotiate?"

12. How can the negotiation process be structured so as to enhance the sustained involvement and operational unity of one's constituents?

13. How can one report back to his constituency without at the same time making important information available to the press?

14. What tools are available for educating one's constituency as to how to respond to reports in the mass media defensively? How can reports in the mass media be appropriately *reinterpreted* to one's constituents during conflicts?

15. How does one regain constituent interest after having lost a negotiation?

16. How can negotiation be used as a probe (a tactic) rather than as a strategy to resolve tensions and conflicts?

17. How can heightened conflict be used as a tool to help the Black community bring to public visibility usually overlooked evidence and insights?

18. Can negotiation be employed as a tool to bring about Black operational unity?

19. What kinds of training opportunities and/or materials, resources, and techniques are available for mass education of the Black community?

SUMMARY

This statement does not lead to any single conclusion. It is an attempt to define why *authentic* negotiations between white institutions and Black dissident groups within a racist society are only possible *after* the white establishment has fully recognized the inherent right of Blacks to control their own destinies through control of those institutions and parts of institutions which affect them. Once this is achieved, negotiations should be utilized as a tool to work out the details and monitor the implementation of a set of demands stemming from those rights. A second area relates to efforts to factor out a Black negotiation position, should negotiation be appropriate. Thirdly, an attempt is made to articulate a Black dissident model as it relates to philosophy, goals, non-negotiable issues, and the process of developing "operational unity" within the Black Community.

An analysis of the negotiating process in which the I.S. 201 activists were involved reveals that they failed to discern whether or not an authentic negotiation process was possible before they actually engaged themselves in it. On the other side of the table, the representatives of the Board of Education were not really engaged in a negotiating process. They used negotiations as a mask for a study process: an attempt to discern how little they could get away with giving up. An alternative goal of the Board of Education was to co-opt (and control) the I.S. 201 activists.

The four interviewees—three of whom questioned the feasibility of negotiations between white institutions and Black dissidents—agreed that racial barriers existed; only the fourth was able to make appropriate adjustments. He did so by perceiving himself as a "foreigner" and by arguing his position by using the frame of reference of the opposition. Seemingly, he focused his attention on the process of the negotiation as a first order of business and the goals as a second order of business. The failure of the I.S. 201 negotiating committee to direct their attention to the process has already been noted.

Several themes become apparent when this paper is viewed from this perspective.

1. Every confrontation has a potential negotiation built into its potential termination.

2. Every negotiation leads to co-optation—informal or formal.

3. Non-negotiable issues should remain that: non-negotiable. Non-negotiable issues become negotiable the moment they are negotiated.

4. "Mutuality" cannot be negotiated; it has to be actualized by a display of the requisite power and community support.

5. Black dissidence is a healthy and appropriate position for Blacks; it is not an anomaly within a racist society.

6. The goal of all negotiations in which Blacks are engaged should be that of monitoring the implementation of the demands; not the achievement of a settlement. The *redistribution of power* cannot be achieved through negotiating. Negotiation functions to redistribute services, resources, and opportunities as a consequence of the exercise of power.

7. White institutions do not seek to negotiate with Black dissidents; they are more interested in discerning how to prevent giving up anything to them.

What I feel that I have detected is the consequence of the self-fulfilling prophecy and its counterpart, the self-fulfilling delusion. Whites have deceived far too many Blacks about the presumed superiority of whites while concealing the reality of racism. On the other hand, Blacks are aware of the reality of racism but fail to make adjustments for it when they go to the bargaining table. They hold a belief deep down within themselves that oppressors have a conscience. They may have, but it becomes visible and apparent only when they have no alternative because of the power of their opponents. What whites perceive as the way things are supposed to be, Blacks perceive as an injustice. White justice equals Black oppression: that's the real formula.

Black dissident groups will have to develop the degree of "operational unity" needed to prevent the exercise by whites of divide-and-conquer tactics. They must also begin to exercise control over their own internal affairs as a means to demonstrate to themselves and white institutions that their communities cannot be controlled from the outside. They must be able to close their schools indefinitely, to boycott white-owned businesses, to exercise effective control over the institutions which serve them, and to apply legal harassment against those causing social injustices. The import of these activities is their function in educating the Pan-African community to understand and resist white oppression. A second function is to attract white allies who will begin to *confront* the white system themselves instead of engineering Black confrontations of the system. The Kent State murders served a dual function: they revealed the depth of the system's tendencies toward violence and that white students who sought to act out their dissent also became niggers.

The issue is not negotiation. Rather, the question remains how Blacks learn how *not* to participate in their own oppression. Negotiating for settlements is a sophisticated way of doing so. Negotiating only the implementation of demands switches the balance of power.

This analysis raises three basic questions:

1. *What are the requisites for making the negotiating of the implementation of demands a possibility?* This question was partially dealt with under the discussion of the Black dissident model. It requires the development of effective "operational unity" within the dissident community.

2. *What do we mean by non-negotiability?* The suggestion, here, is that the definition of this concept is multidimensional. It involves control over the internal structure and relationships of the dissident community. It involves those demands the exercise of which is the sole purview of the dissident community: the selection of principals, and the content of the curriculum as it relates to culture, politics, values, the concept and philosophy of education, and the like. It involves a decision to entertain a set of inseparable demands or *none* at all. It involves a refusal to comply with any procedures or policies that demean the status or interests of the dissident groups. Non-negotiable demands are presented: not discussed and debated. They are implemented by the dissident community with or without the support and encouragement of white institutions.

3. *What do we mean by victory?* The I.S. 201 activists sensed that they had "won" because the superintendent of schools agreed with their demands initially. They actually lost on *one* score because they were unable to implement their demands. But they also won because their supporting community began to understand the relationship between power and justice. Justice is not bestowed upon Black people; they must make continued injustice uncomfortable for the oppressors. As Martin Luther King, Jr., put it: "First, the line of progress is never straight. . . . A final victory is the accumulation of many short-term encounters. To lightly dismiss a success because it does not usher in a complete order of justice is to fail to comprehend the process of achieving full victory. It underestimates the

value of confrontation and dissolves the confidence born of a partial victory by which new efforts are powered."[69]

In discussing the same concept, Montgomery writes: "It is clear that victory is related to power. This means that victory can only be attained to the ability of an individual or group to exercise his power through force or persuasion. . . . It is well to understand that victory is relative. To experience a success, we must accept and exploit the relative value of victory."[70]

The I.S. 201 activists perceived themselves as having won because the school superintendent said they had. Had they viewed victory as a factor of their own power, they might not have announced the "victory," and they might have followed up differently. Both King and Montgomery seem to be implying that confrontation is a tool *to build supportive power* within the dissident community rather than a tool to overcome resistance by persuasion.

One point needs to be made in relation to negotiation skills. No assumption should be made here about the preeminence of the skills of negotiation possessed by white institutions. It's the imbalance of power that makes the difference. What Pan-African communities must build and not expect white institutions to impart to them is the requisite power to render the skills of negotiation irrelevant or, at the most, ancillary or supplemental.

69. Martin Luther King, Jr., *Where Do We Go From Here: Chaos or Community?* (New York: Bantam Books, 1968), p. 14.

70. M. Lee Montgomery, "The Concept of Victory" (Philadelphia: Center for Urban Affairs, Temple University, 1970) (mimeographed), pp. 1-2.

PART 3

The Memphis Public Employees Strike

F. RAY MARSHALL
ARVIL VAN ADAMS

Editors' Introduction

THIS is the first of our in-depth case studies. It deals with the patterns of conflict and the eventual achievement of an agreement in the now-famous strike of black garbage workers in Memphis, Tennessee, in the course of which Martin Luther King, Jr., was assassinated.

This case (and the Cleveland case that follows) is in the area of employment and thus is most directly analogous to the labor-management model of dispute settlement. Further, the workers involved were organized into a union and thus had a stable organizational base from which to challenge the establishment. Since the case lies in the area of public employment, however, there are additional and/or different factors involved than are found in the usual labor-management dispute in the private sector.

However, in addition to the traditional public-employee dispute factors, Memphis was selected because it contained a strong strain of racial conflict. The union in the Memphis case was predominantly black, and the dispute grew to include a large segment of the black community as well as segments of organized labor. Some observers described this strike as the first successful attempt to weld labor and civil rights groups in pursuance of black demands. This pattern has since been repeated in such locales as Charleston, South Carolina, and Baltimore, Maryland. Since there is reason to believe that public-employee unions will include increasingly large segments of blacks and that disputes between them and governmental bodies will continue to include racial factors, if not coalitions, this case was considered an important one for inclusion in this project. Memphis also offered an opportunity to study a continuing relationship between black and white. The 1968 strike and settlement was followed by new negotiations in 1969, which are also briefly reported. Further rounds of negotiations will provide a continuing relationship between black and white for other studies.

F. Ray Marshall is widely known as a labor economist and for his research and involvement in the area of relations between unions and black efforts to achieve economic equality. Thus he brought to this study of Memphis many valuable insights and perspectives. The co-author, Arvil Van Adams, not only contributed a major part of the research effort, but, having lived in Memphis, he was also able to provide an understanding of the environment within which the dispute occurred.

The Memphis Public Works Employees Strike*

THE American social fabric is being rent in many directions by the discontent and frustrations of black Americans. The source of their discontent is the unsatisfactory response of white-dominated institutions to black demands, which Negroes seek to achieve through a variety of philosophies and strategies. Some blacks would destroy the existing structures hoping to build from the rubble a new system free from the inequities built into the old system by prejudice. Others advocate complete separatism with the development of parallel black-dominated institutions. Still others would build a black power base with which existing institutions could be challenged for participation with a subsequent alteration in the process and product of these institutions. For all black strategies except the elimination of whites and the institutions they control, the negotiation process offers the best chance for peaceful settlement of differences.

This paper explores this method and provides an example of how negotiations can be used to resolve racial conflict.[1] The confrontation that took place in Memphis, Tennessee, during a strike of Public Works employees in 1968, will be described. The background of the dispute is outlined, and the parties involved are identified. This is followed by an analysis of the issues, the negotiation process, and the interaction of forces that led to the settlement.

The objective is to identify the major contributing factors that led to this dispute and its resolution. A better understanding of these factors might provide a guide to the usefulness of negotiations in resolving racial conflicts.

* Data gathered for this case study came from a series of interviews conducted with observers and participants in the dispute. Additional information came from the files of the AFL-CIO Labor Council in Memphis and other documentary materials gathered by the authors.

1. Some of the interview material gathered for this case study appears in Appendix E. Unfortunately we were unable to get permission to print any of the interviews with city officials and members of the Memphis business community.

BACKGROUND

Race Relations

The Memphis strike of Public Works employees began and ended as a labor dispute between Local 1733 of the American Federation of State, County, and Municipal Employees and the City of Memphis. The membership of Local 1733 was predominantly Negro and numbered over 1300. The majority of its members were sanitation workers. Surrounding the economic issues in the dispute was the underlying issue of race. Although Memphis,[2] unlike other southern cities of its size in the sixties, basked in relative racial tranquility, the surface changes in its public institutions obscured the perpetuation of economic and educational inequities. The support given Local 1733 by the Negro community during the dispute was a sign of racial dissatisfaction, the roots of which were far deeper than the basic economic issues of the strike itself. By drawing the Negro community together and providing articulate spokesmen, the strike revealed the nature of the black workers' problems to upper-class Negroes as well as whites. A 1964 report to the Southern Regional Council[3] concluded:

> In view of its heavy Negro population and its Deep South location, the progress of Memphis toward the elimination of race discrimination is remarkable. . . . Memphis has made conspicuous, though still [token] strides toward desegregation and equality of treatment in school and employment. In the desegregation of public, cultural, and recreational facilities, of places of amusement and of public accommodation, Memphis desegregation has gone well beyond the token stage.

Hearings conducted in Memphis in 1966 by the Tennessee State Advisory Committee to the United States Commission on Civil Rights presented the record of Negro employment in private in-

2. A special census conducted in Memphis in 1967 by the Bureau of the Census showed its population to be 536,585. Of the total, 323,548 are listed as white and 213,037 nonwhite. The nonwhite group comprises 39.7 percent of the total population. Negroes represent over 99 percent of the nonwhite population.

3. Benjamin Muse, *Memphis* (Atlanta: Southern Regional Council, 1964), pp. 1-2.

dustry and government agencies.[4] These hearings concluded: "In the area of employment, the need for training opportunities for Negro youth and adults is paramount. . . . old patterns of discrimination and exclusion on the part of employers have not disappeared totally. The problem seems most acute in the area of upgrading and promotion, and in the use of Negroes in supervisory positions."

The record for employment of Negroes was somewhat better at the county and federal government levels than at the city level. In the 1966 hearings, the city personnel director testified that there was no municipal regulation covering discrimination by hiring departments. He admitted that such discrimination could take place.

The desegregation of the Memphis city schools began in October 1961. In 1968, 53 percent of the 125,000 children in the school system were Negro, over 80 percent of whom were still attending predominantly Negro schools.[5]

Dissatisfactions of Negroes also extended to housing and police treatment. The Negro community was particularly incensed at such injustices by the Memphis police force as were reported by the 1966 Civil Rights Commission hearings:[6] "Relations between the police and the Negro community are in a sad state of disrepair. Only prompt, bold, and decisive leadership on the part of the highest officials of the city and county can avert the disaster which may coincide with the next incident."

Thus there existed prior to the strike a general dissatisfaction within the Negro community with the white power structure. Progress in resolving this dissatisfaction had come too slowly and frequently was nonexistent. The strike and its issues, therefore, served as a rallying point for airing the deeper dissatisfactions of the Negro community. The black community in Memphis could readily identify with the sanitation workers because the City's refusal to recognize their

4. According to the 1964 report for the 50 Plans for Progress firms in Memphis, 42 of these firms had Negro employees. These firms had 17,808 employees of which 3,363 or 18.8 percent were Negro. Of the Negro employees, 2.2 percent held white collar jobs, whereas 41.5 percent of the white labor force held white collar jobs. Research currently underway by the authors shows little perceptible change in these patterns. U.S. Commission on Civil Rights, Hearings held in Memphis, Tennessee (Washington: U.S. Government Printing Office, 1966), p. 6.

5. Data were obtained from the Memphis Board of Education.

6. U.S. Civil Rights Commission, *Hearings in Memphis*, p. 44.

union was similar to the white power structure's unwillingness to recognize Negroes as equals and as persons with the right to decide their own destinies. (See interview with Dr. Ralph Jackson in Appendix E.)

Community Organization

"Prior to the strike there never had been a more divided community than the Memphis Negro community," said Baxton Bryant, the white executive director of the Tennessee Council of Human Relations.[7] There was a natural rivalry provided by the churches, which competed fiercely for members and sometimes forgot ethics. Each minister dominated his own fiefdom, and agreement and coordination between ministers was infrequent.

There was also a spirited political rivalry within the Negro community. Dan Powell, the white southeastern regional director of the AFL-CIO Committee on Political Education (COPE), noted that the Negro vote[8] had been split in the 1966 gubernatorial election and again in the 1967 election of the mayor and councilmen. In the 1967 mayoral race with six candidates, the Negro vote was split between A. W. Willis, a Negro attorney and representative to the Tennessee House, and William Ingram, the white incumbent mayor. No candidate received a majority of the votes, and a runoff election was held between the two top candidates, Ingram and Henry Loeb. With the strength of the white vote, Loeb won the runoff election. According to an NAACP estimate, Henry Loeb received less than two percent of the Negro vote. The Council races also pitted Negro candidates against each other in two districts in the runoff election.

The strike had a unifying influence on the Negro community, and the union served as a common denominator for various factions which had been split by religious and political differences. Although its members belonged to the various churches and supported the separate Negro candidates, the union's determination to seek econom-

7. Unless otherwise indicated, all quotes, direct and indirect, are taken from personal interviews with the individuals quoted. Excerpts from some of these interviews are included in Appendix E.

8. According to the Shelby County Election Commission, Negroes constituted 34.3 percent of the 260,730 registered voters in Memphis as of March 31, 1969. They represented 30.5 percent of the registered voters in Shelby County, Tennessee on the same date.

ic justice for its members caused the Negro community to close ranks in support of the black strikers.

Union Organization

The problems facing the Negro community and the union did not appear overnight. From the receipt of its charter to the beginning of the strike, a period of three and a half years, the union had sought unsuccessfully to gain recognition from the City as sole bargaining agent. Local 1733 of AFSCME was chartered by the international union on October 13, 1964, but operated informally because the City refused to recognize any union as sole bargaining agent for a group of employees. Commissioner T. E. Sisson, a white, elected commissioner of public works in 1963, allegedly promised the union recognition in exchange for its political support. Sisson later denied this, contending that the City was prevented by law[9] from negotiating with a union.

Local 1733 attempted to strike for recognition in 1965, but that effort was poorly organized. Word leaked to the city administration about the union's plans and, before the walkout could start, an injunction against the strike was obtained by city attorneys in Chancery Court. The judge based his ruling on the earlier Tennessee Supreme Court decision noted above, but he carried his decision beyond that of the Supreme Court by ruling that it was also illegal to picket.

Added to the lack of organization of the strike was the presence of a political leader whose popularity made it difficult to gather support for the strike from members of Local 1733 and the Negro community. Because of his relatively fair treatment of Negroes when he was city judge, William Ingram, elected mayor in 1963, won the support and respect of the Negro community. It was suggested, however, by Ingram's adversaries that he really didn't like Negroes; he just hated the police more. Nevertheless, Ingram's popularity in the Negro community helped him win election as mayor. This popularity, W. T. Ross, white executive secretary of the Memphis AFL-CIO

9. The "law" being cited was actually a decision handed down by the Tennessee Supreme Court in two separate cases which held that strikes against the public were illegal. Neither the legal right to form a public employees' union, nor the right of a public body to recognize and negotiate with such a union was ruled upon.

Labor Council, pointed out, "definitely had an impact in blunting support [in the Negro community] for the strike in 1965." Many members of the Negro community and the local were hesitant to cross the political path of the man judged to be their friend. Because of this attitude, the injunction, and the lack of organization, the strike never got off the ground.

The commission form of government also had been a nemesis to the union because, as Ross noted, the commissioners hid behind one another in refusing to establish a policy of recognition for public-employee unions. This picture changed in 1968, however, when a new form of government took the place of the commission form. The mayor-council system enabled the mayor alone to establish the policy of recognition. No longer would there by any vacillation on the issue. "This was fine," noted Dan Powell, "except the wrong man was elected mayor."

Mayor Henry Loeb, unlike his predecessor, did not enjoy the support of the Negro community. He was considered anticivil rights and antiunion because of earlier actions while in city government. Once he took a position against the union, it took little effort to rally the Negro community against him and the City.

The mayor did not stand alone on the issue of recognition of public-employee unions. As Baxton Bryant pointed out, "Public-employee unions and strikes against the government are bad words to the American public." Before and during the strike, the mayor enjoyed the widespread support of the white community in Memphis.[10] The issue of race need not have been in the picture to have attracted the white community's support for the mayor, but it undoubtedly made white support stronger than it otherwise would have been.

Thus the intensification of dissatisfaction with the responsiveness of the white power structure to the needs of the Negro community, the fragmentation of the Negro community with the presence of the union as a unifying force, effective Negro leadership, and an untried political structure, coupled with an unacceptable political personality, provided the setting for the confrontation. The negotiation process that was to follow was heavily influenced by this combination of factors.

10. J. Edwin Stanfield, *In Memphis: Mirror to America* (Atlanta: Southern Regional Council, 1968), p. 23.

THE STRIKE AND NEGOTIATIONS

The strike started on February 12, 1968, and, before it was settled about two months later, resulted in riots and disorder, a Negro boycott of downtown white businesses, and the tragic assassination of Dr. Martin Luther King, Jr.[11] Although working conditions were the immediate cause of the dispute, these cannot be separated from the larger racial issues which were raised by this strike and the events leading up to it. Indeed, the walkout itself was not carefully planned, but was almost a spontaneous reaction by Negro workers to what they considered to be unfair treatment by the Department of Public Works.

The incident which sparked the strike occurred on January 31, 1968, when 22 Negro employees of the Sewer and Drain Maintenance Division of the Department of Public Works (DPW)[12] were sent home because of rain while white employees in identical work classifications were allowed to work and receive a full day's pay. The black workers complained to the DPW on pay day when they discovered the discriminatory wage payment. The City responded to the Negro workers' complaints by unilaterally paying them two hours' call-up pay, but this was not satisfactory to the workers. A meeting was therefore called of Local 1733, which sought to represent all DPW workers but which had no white members when the strike started, and on February 12, after considerable discussion, the union's president, T. O. Jones, led his men out on a strike. The local's all-black membership had many grievances, but they were particularly concerned about racial discrimination, and there was little opposition to the decision to strike. According to Jesse Epps, special assistant to the president of AFSCME, the International was reluctant to support the strike at first, primarily because proper preparation had not been made for a strike, and the timing was not good because garbage strikes are more effective in the summer than in the winter. However, the determination of Local 1733's membership caused the international to give the strikers full support.

There was no precedent in Memphis for dealing with a striking

11. See Appendix D for chronology of the strike.
12. The Department of Public Works was divided into three divisions: Sewer and Drain Maintenance (with 170 Negro and 52 white employees), Street Maintenance, and Sanitation. An NAACP survey six months before the strike revealed 2175 employees in the department, 1,597 of whom were black.

public-employees' union. The mayor, the City Council, and the mayor-council form of government were new.[13] Thus, what was to develop as a negotiation procedure long known to students of collective bargaining came about through a series of haphazard events.

There were both formal and informal negotiations aided by "neutral" third parties during the strike. The formal negotiations joined the mayor's representatives and the union's representatives with a mediator who had been appointed by a City Council resolution. The informal negotiations consisted of interested third parties who sought to bring the union and the City together by creating a dialogue on the issues.

The mayor, Henry Loeb, was the dominant figure representing the city through both formal and informal negotiations. The City Council interpreted the settlement of the dispute to be an executive function, and therefore would not intervene directly.

The mayor was described by friends and foes alike as a hard-driving, ambitious, shirt sleeves type of politician. Born in Memphis of an old-line Jewish family, he was educated in the East at Phillips Academy in Andover, Massachusetts, and Brown University. During World War II, he commanded a PT boat in the Mediterranean. He was elected public works commissioner for Memphis in 1956 and mayor in 1960. He resigned from office at the death of his father to take over the family laundry business, which he helped operate until 1966, when he sold his interest to his brother, William. Loeb was succeeded as mayor by William Ingram, who was elected in 1963 and took office January 1, 1964.

Initial Positions

Initially, Mayor Loeb considered the strike to be illegal. He refused to recognize the AFSCME as sole bargaining agent for the Public Works employees and remained adamant on this and the dues checkoff issue throughout the strike. In a mass meeting with union members on February 13, he said, "This is not New York. [Reference to the on-going New York sanitation strike] Nobody can break the

13. A new mayor-council system had been approved in a 1966 referendum in Memphis. It replaced a commission form of government, in which there also had been a mayor. The mayor and the City Council had been elected in a November 1967 run-off election and had come into office with the new form of government on January 1, 1968. This was 43 days prior to the strike.

law. You are putting my back against the wall, and I am not going to budge."[14]

Mayor Loeb was described by Baxton Bryant as a man who wanted to be fair, but whose definition of fairness came out of a white middle-class society. The mayor's position apparently was taken not so much on the race issue as against the union. He was quoted by one source as saying that he would not be the first mayor in the South to recognize a public-employee union.

Thus early in the strike the central figure for the City became committed to a stand that was difficult to back away from. He sought compromise on all issues except recognition and dues checkoff. He continued to talk informally throughout the strike, but his listeners from the union and the Negro community became fewer and fewer in number. Jesse Epps said that at one point in the strike Baxton Bryant was the sole contact the union had with the mayor.

The union had unwittingly chosen to make its stand on organizing public employees in the South here in Memphis. "We didn't think it [the strike] would escalate as it did," said Jesse Epps. "In the second week, we saw the City's position harden. We saw the strike growing and becoming important in our plans for southern organization." Memphis became very crucial to the AFSCME and, as a result, the international became deeply committed to the local dispute.

The action taken February 12, 1968, was not a wildcat reaction to an unresolved grievance. Local 1733 had been chartered nearly three and a half years when the strike began. Ross remarked that it was uncommon to find an informal organization of employees that had stood together with such resolve as long as had Local 1733. Its president T.O. Jones (black), had been fired by William Farris, public works commissioner, in the organizing effort of 1963.

These elements influenced the attitude that the union took into the strike and to the bargaining table. It sought economic equality for its members and to establish a foothold in the door of southern organization. This was, as the *New York Times*[15] reported May 6, 1968, the coalition of labor and the civil rights movement so eagerly encouraged by Dr. Martin Luther King, Jr., in 1961.

There were many third parties involved in informal negotiations

14. *New York Times,* February 14, 1968, p. 31.
15. Editorial, *New York Times,* May 6, 1968, p. 46C.

throughout the strike. A local business leader, Frank Miles, former mediator with the Federal Mediation and Conciliation Service, who served as mediator in the formal negotiations, reported that the most substantive effort to bring the parties together for dialogue was made by a few members of the Ministerial Alliance. This effort was made early in the strike, on February 18. The mayor, representing the City, and Jerry Wurf, international president of AFSCME, representing the union, were brought together with the ministers serving as moderators. The parties met over a period of five days in these sessions. Their confrontation was described by observers as a three-way dialogue with each side directing its comments to the other side via the moderator. From the time these sessions ended, there were no direct negotiations between the parties until formal negotiations were begun by Frank Miles on March 23.

The ministers conducting these sessions were white. However, Ed Stanfield[16] reports that "the white churches and churchmen of Memphis were not notably involved" throughout the strike, and our information confirms this conclusion. Indeed, the all-white Second Baptist Church in East Memphis split over its minister's participation in the strike on behalf of the union.

There were many individuals such as Frank Miles in the community who were deeply concerned at the outset. "It seemed," said Miles, "as though every Saturday somebody had a new idea they wanted to try out to resolve this thing. All these attempts were sincere, but I'd have to say they were not realistic in attempting to deal with collective bargaining problems." The background of Frank Miles as a mediator and as director of industrial relations with Plough, Inc., and E. L. Bruce & Co., both Memphis firms, generated his professional interest in the strike, and at the request of other interested third parties he became involved in an effort to resolve the dispute. Frank Miles said of himself, "[My] concern at the beginning of this dispute, which was purely and simply a labor dispute, was that if it was not controlled to the point that it could be settled as a labor dispute, then it was liable to spill over into racial conflict." A former mayor, Edmund Orgill, also was actively interested in this strike. As a member of the Memphis Committee on Human Rela-

---

16. J. Edwin Stanfield, *In Memphis: More than a Garbage Strike*, (Atlanta: Southern Regional Council, 1968), p. 41.

tions, he had long been involved with efforts in Memphis to provide interracial harmony. He therefore worked with others to seek a peaceful resolution of the dispute. Baxton Bryant, in his capacity as director of the Tennessee Council of Human Relations, became an important intermediary throughout the conflict.

An ad hoc group of Negro ministers, the Committee on the Move for Equality (C.O.M.E.), was formed to support the strike. Indeed, the Negro community became organized as never before under the leadership of such men as Dr. Ralph Jackson, Reverend S. B. Kyles, and Reverend James Lawson. They communicated effectively the spirit and fiber of the Negro community's solidarity for the strikers and were able to mount nonviolent coercive pressures on the City and the white business community to support the strikers' demands. They also broke a local news freeze on the strike, got national support for the strikers, and embarrassed the local power structure by involving well-known national civil rights leaders in the strike on behalf of the union. The best expression of their ability to control is represented by the limited amount of violence that took place in the explosive environment surrounding the marches and Dr. King's assassination and the sizes of the crowds they were able to rally in support of the strikers. Although we have no objective measures of its impact, the ministers also mounted what observers and participants generally agree was a very effective black boycott of downtown Memphis merchants.

The Issues

The issues of the dispute, as seen by the union, were outlined on February 8 in a letter[17] from P. J. Ciampa, field director for the International, to Charles Blackburn, director of the Department of Public Works. This followed an earlier meeting between Blackburn and Ciampa. The City's failure to take action to resolve the dispute at this point resulted in the walkout.

The substantive economic issues of the strike reflected the Negro community's desire to change the process and product of the white-dominated power structure. This was a demand for a change in the institutional structure as well as a demand for a change in the output of the institutions. The racial issues were symbolized by the demand

17. Files of the Memphis AFL-CIO Labor Council. See Appendix G.

for recognition of the Negroes' right to participate in economic and political decisions affecting their lives. These issues led to the dispute, surrounded the bargaining process, and played a large role in determining the content and form of the negotiation process.

The major collective bargaining issues of the strike were recognition and dues checkoff. The City had already recognized several unions informally, and was willing to deal informally with the AFSCME as well, which suggests that the City's position was not necessarily against unions per se. However, it had never recognized as sole bargaining agent, signed a collective bargaining agreement with, or granted a dues checkoff to any union. These AFSCME demands were, therefore, the major hurdles that had to be overcome at the bargaining table.

Recognition, the main issue between the City and the union since Local 1733's inception in 1964, was the single most important issue of the strike. The remaining issues (dues checkoff, a grievance procedure, merit promotion, and wages) could have been resolved only after recognition of the Public Works Department employees' right to chose their own bargaining representative. The recognition issue was important not only because the Local could not compromise it, but also because the City took the position that it would be illegal for it to recognize any union as sole bargaining agent. The city continued to base its resistance to the union on the decision regarding public-employee unions handed down by the Tennessee Supreme Court.

The dominance of the recognition issue highlighted the initial confrontation and resulting negotiations. In this instance, the change in process overshadowed the change in output of the existing institutions. There was tremendous resistance by the white-dominated power structure to the union's inclusion in the decision-making process, especially when that union was predominately black and had black leadership. The mayor's strong antiunion position was supported by many elements in the white community, at least at the outset of the strike, though there apparently were some shifts in white attitudes as the strike went on.

The attitude of many Negroes toward the recognition issue was symbolized by a picket sign that appeared in the daily marches on City Hall which read "I *AM* A MAN." Its implication, which was discussed at length in the black community, was that no longer were Negroes in Memphis willing to let one white man, or a group of white men, control their destiny. The issue to these men was one of black identity. The recognition of themselves as men with certain rights was the first step in the process of change that was to follow. The second step was the exercise of these rights by gaining a role for the union in decision-making.

AFSCME sought recognition of the right of the employee to determine freely who would represent him in any bilateral policy-making process. Thus, the issue of black identity caused the recognition question to become a race issue. Collective bargaining meant replacing the unilateralism of Old South politics with the bilateralism of the New South.

The Role of the Mayor

Since he considered the strike to be illegal, Mayor Loeb initially took the position that the workers would have to return to work before their grievances could be discussed. Although legality undoubtedly concerned the mayor, he obviously also thought collective bargaining was unnecessary in view of his "open door" policy, a position which caused Stanfield[18] to label him a "plantation politician."

Loeb undoubtedly understood that recognition of the AFSCME would have changed the City's decision-making process. As generally defined, recognition would have represented an obligation for the City and the union to meet and discuss wages, hours, and conditions of employment. In this instance recognition would have meant the entrance of the union and the Negro into the white decision-making process. It was this change that the mayor seemed to resist so vehemently.

The union, however, was only the vehicle of change. The real force of change came from the Negro community itself through the concept of black identity, the strength of which apparently was underestimated by white leaders. In his effort to defeat the union, it is questionable whether the mayor understood the significance of this force.

The mayor also refused to compromise on the dues checkoff system,

18. Stanfield, *In Memphis: More Than A Garbage Strike*, p. 24.

which was a crucial security issue for the AFSCME because Tennessee is a "right to work" state. Therefore, no provisions for membership maintenance were available to the union except through a checkoff of dues. Thus, the checkoff was a key issue in any hope the mayor had for diluting the union's strength.

In a typical paternalistic delusion, Mayor Loeb took the position that the union leaders and the ministers really did not represent the employees. He therefore refused to deal with representatives of the strikers and made a unilateral offer directly to the strikers through an open letter, published in a local newspaper on February 29. In this letter, he offered the strikers a wage increase of eight cents an hour, a grievance procedure, and certain insurance and overtime benefits. The wage increase was to be written into the City's budget to begin with the new fiscal year, July 1. The mayor remained adamant, however, in refusing to recognize the union or grant the checkoff.

On February 12, shortly after the walkout, the mayor challenged the extent to which the union actually spoke for the employees; the union answered his challenge with a march on City Hall by over a thousand union members. The mayor met with these men in Ellis Auditorium, next to City Hall, on February 13 and received a rude reception after outlining his stand against the strike and the union. Indeed, his reception was so rude that he ultimately walked out on the meeting.

The remaining portion of the first five weeks of the dispute was marked by one more meeting between the mayor and union representatives and a series of informal negotiations. These informal sessions included efforts by individual citizens and the ministers from the Ministerial Alliance, all of whom sought unsuccessfully to establish a dialogue between the parties.

Representatives of the union and the City searched for a means to settle the dispute. The Mayor stated his willingness to compromise all issues except recognition and dues checkoff, and AFSCME reportedly was willing to accept an informal exchange of letters between the mayor and the union in lieu of formal recognition.[19] The informal exchange of letters would have provided the mayor a face-saving device for his adamant stand against recognition. The union also was willing to work out a checkoff of dues with the inde-

19. *Ibid.*, p. 26.

pendent employees' credit union rather than directly from the City's payroll. However, the negative position taken by the mayor on these issues thwarted any hope of compromise.

Attempting to soften the mayor's stand, Baxton Bryant, in many informal conferences with the mayor, tried to explain the growth of black identity as an issue and what it meant to Negro union members. "At the close of each of these meetings," Bryant said, "the mayor would seem to understand this concept as a reason for the strength of the Negro commitment to the strike, but, by the next meeting, conservative elements seemed to get hold of him and he would remain unrelenting."

"The mayor continued to refer to his term as public works commissioner and how he understood 'his' men. He never could accept the idea that the men wanted the union," said Bryant. "He seemed to feel that the union organizers were 'outsiders' who weren't speaking for the men. He ignored the large numbers of workers appearing at the union meetings and instead pointed to the smaller numbers appearing for the daily marches as a sign of diminishing support for the strike."

The Use of Coercion

During the strike, coercive pressures were applied by both sides. The union, with the support of the Negro community, reinforced its demands by daily marches, picketing of City Hall, and boycotts of downtown stores, the two daily newspapers, and firms doing business under the name of "Loeb." In addition, a growing militant mood among younger Negroes, though more a figment of journalistic sensationalism and white fears than a real force in the black community, placed further pressure on the City.

The City responded with legal tactics designed to halt the strike: the hiring of strikebreakers, continued garbage collection on a limited scale, and a show of large numbers of policemen at Council meetings and marches downtown. The deployment of police in excessive numbers had been a practice of the City throughout its early civil rights history, noted Benjamin Muse in his special report in 1964 to the Southern Regional Council. The show of police force was especially significant in view of the deterioration of Negro-police relations that had happened earlier.

The Use of a Mediator

By resolution of the City Council, Frank Miles was asked to serve as mediator between the union and the mayor in the dispute. This was the first direct effort by the Council to resolve the conflict, and it came after Mayor Loeb's opposition to third-party intervention was overcome. The mayor confused the neutral assistance of the mediator with the binding decision of an arbitrator and agreed to mediation only after this distinction was explained to him. Up to this point, the City Council had maintained that the settlement of this matter was an executive and not a legislative function. In explaining their belated intervention, Councilman Lewis R. Donelson said, "It [the strike] had gotten past an administrative decision and had become a policy decision. A settlement was necessary because of the overall impact this was having on the health and welfare of the citizens of Memphis."

The first meeting between the union and the mayor's representatives with Miles as mediator was set for 10:00 A.M., March 23. Two assistant city attorneys, Thomas R. Prewitt and Myron Halle, and Councilman Tom Todd represented the mayor; P. J. Ciampa, T. O. Jones, and Bill Lucy, another International representative, represented the union. James M. Manire, assistant city attorney, later joined the City's negotiators, and Dr. Ralph Jackson joined the union's negotiators. The union asked Dr. Jackson to come in as a representative of the Negro community. One city official said of the Mayor's representatives, "It was a poor choice; they were from the don't-give'em-an-inch school." Todd was described by the same official as being antiunion, anti-government help, anti-anything dealing with poverty. Fellow Council member, Mrs. Gwen Awsumb, said of Todd later, "He never explains things; he just votes. I have taken the trouble to go around and ask him, but he doesn't project himself into an interchange of ideas like the rest of us do. When we go to vote, we pretty well know how people are going to vote. But you never know about Todd."[20]

The mayor's representatives also were unfamiliar with labor negotiation procedures and tactics and seem to have lacked coordination in their initial approaches to the negotiations. The first meeting on March 23, therefore, broke down when the mayor's representatives

20. *The Commercial Appeal Mid-South Magazine*, May 11, 1969, p. 7.

questioned the legality of meeting with members of the union's committee who were affected by the Chancery Court's decision holding them in contempt of the Court's injunction. The question was finally resolved on March 25 when Chancellor Hoffman clarified the legal implications with the City agreeing not to press the legality issue any further.

When the meetings resumed March 25, discussion turned to what form the agreement, if any, would take. Frank Miles suggested the use of a "memorandum of understanding." This, Miles said, was a technique he had often used as a mediator, i.e., to get the parties to set out a memorandum of understanding of the issues as the mediator understood them. He proposed that if agreement was reached at the meeting, he would present the memorandum to the City Council and ask them to adopt it by resolution. This procedure, which was acceptable for exploration to both parties, would have given the union a written agreement approved by the legislative arm of the City. Unless the mayor refused to cooperate, it could be a very meaningful solution to the dispute.

Negotiations then moved to the issue of recognition. Miles commented: "We were on recognition Monday and Tuesday. Wednesday, March 27, we were still on recognition." He noted, "I find that when a word presents a particular problem, I can often get around it by defining it and using the definition in its place." Recognition means that the parties agree to meet periodically to discuss wages, hours, and conditions of employment for a specific group of people. The City was willing to agree to this language, including a statement that such discussion could lead to meaningful agreements, but [Dr. Jackson] a member of the union team objected to it. He felt very strongly that the word "recognition" should be used because of its racial connotations in this case. Dr. Jackson was particularly concerned about recognition of the Union's right to represent the workers and the black man's right to speak for himself.

When agreement could not be reached over the exact language to be used in a statement on recognition, the union accused the city's negotiating team of failing to negotiate in good faith, and asked that the meeting be recessed. Added to this charge was a statement by the union accusing the City of "leaking" to the press information about what had been going on in the negotiating sessions. "We knew that we couldn't negotiate in a fish bowl, i.e., the public media," said Epps. This had been what Loeb wanted from the beginning. "It was for this reason and the unwillingness to put recognition in writing that we accused the City of not bargaining in good faith."

Some members of the union team were restless because they were supposed to be at a meeting planning for the march to be led by Dr. Martin Luther King, Jr. the following day, March 28, so the meeting was adjourned with the understanding that they would meet again when called together by Miles. The union attached the condition that whenever the City was ready to sit down and negotiate in good faith they would be ready to meet. That evening, over local television, the union again charged the City with a failure to bargain in good faith.

The atmosphere for negotiations was exacerbated when the march the following day was broken up by window-breaking and looting. Dr. King's aides took him to the Rivermont Hotel for safety. Memphis city police, Shelby County sheriff's deputies, and Tennessee highway patrolmen reacted quickly and violently as they had in an earlier march on February 23. Charges of "police brutality" by marchers and observers were later investigated by a closed session of the United States Civil Rights Commission. The Commission concluded that beyond doubt there was police misconduct.

Miles said that his first reaction was to let things cool down a bit before calling the parties together again. On the following Monday, April 1, he called the City and union representatives and set up a meeting for the following Friday, April 5. The meeting never took place because Dr. King was assassinated Thursday evening, April 4. Although the violence in Memphis following Dr. King's death was relatively minor, other cities, especially in the Northeast, experienced widespread disorder.

Federal Intervention

Following the assassination, President Johnson sent Undersecretary of Labor James Reynolds to Memphis. Reynolds reported that he was in his office on April 5 when President Johnson called him.

He asked me why I wasn't down in Memphis trying to settle that strike. I explained to him that the Department of Labor doesn't normally get involved with a strike unless both parties request this, and then it is the Federal Mediation and Conciliation Service that would be involved. The only other cause for the federal government to get involved would be a national emergency. He then told me, "I regard this as a matter of great danger having implications far beyond the strike itself. The urban problems facing our nation could be enlarged by the events of Dr. King's death. I want you to get down there and help settle that thing."

Before leaving for Memphis, Reynolds called Governor Buford Ellington of Tennessee and explained to him the President's directive. Governor Ellington welcomed Reynolds' entrance into the dispute and promised his cooperation. After arriving on Friday evening, April 5, Reynolds contacted Mayor Loeb, who was too tired to see him that evening and suggested a meeting the following morning. Reynolds told the mayor that he "wasn't here to impose a solution or to circumvent his position, but . . . was here to try to bring the parties to some form of agreement they could live with." That evening, Reynolds met with Frank Miles and with union representatives. Reynolds and Miles discussed the plan of action they would use when the parties were asked to meet again. The next morning Mayor Loeb agreed to Reynold's entry into the case after the undersecretary explained that "this thing *had* to be settled."

After the mayor agreed to his mediation efforts, Reynolds and Miles called a meeting of city and union representatives for 3:00 P.M., April 6. The two sides met with the mediators until early the next morning, and adjourned until later in the day. The second meeting carried into early Monday morning, at which time the mayor and Jerry Wurf were called in. "Enough progress had been made in the language of the agreement, including the issues of recognition and dues checkoff," said Miles, "so that the issues were narrowed down to one: wages."

Resolution of the Checkoff Issue

The dues-checkoff issue was resolved by establishing a collection procedure through the independent employees' credit union. "This took time to accomplish," said Miles. "We had to get approval from the executive board of the credit union and also from its Washington headquarters since it was federally chartered, but the time was well spent, for this was a very critical issue. James Reynolds was extremely helpful in cutting red tape. He knew the right people in Washington to call to get this through for us."

Resolution of the Wage Issue

The wage issue remained to be solved. Miles reported that the City was in real financial trouble at the time. Loeb made a presentation of the City's fiscal position which indicated that the City was in no position to grant even a token wage increase. Both Reynolds and Miles were impressed by the mayor's grasp of the City's fiscal problems after three months in office.

The mayor wanted to wait till the beginning of the City's fiscal year in July to grant a wage increase. Miles said, "We knew members of the union would never stand for this; they wanted an increase immediately." The mayor was offering an increase of eight cents an hour, and the union was asking for considerably more. The union had support from some members of the City Council who suggested an increase of fifteen cents an hour. "With this support," said Miles, "I knew it was going to be difficult to get the union to settle for anything less than fifteen cents." The wage issue was therefore twofold. A means of compromise had to be provided on the amount as well as the timing of any wage increase.

The sessions were adjourned Monday, April 8, for the King Memorial March and Tuesday, April 9, for Dr. King's funeral. The parties met again on April 10 and each day thereafter until agreement on the wage issue was reached on April 16.

The settlement was reached with the union members receiving a wage increase of ten cents an hour, effective May 1, and another increase of five cents an hour to become effective September 1. The key to the solution was finding a means for the City to pay for a wage increase until June 30, the end of the fiscal year. The City had already indicated that a wage increase could be written into the budget for the new fiscal year beginning July 1. The compromise finally reached on this issue was the result of behind-the-scenes work by Frank Miles and other interested third parties. "An anonymous benefactor and longtime friend of this city provided our solution," said Miles. This individual contacted Miles offering to supply $60,-000 of his own money to finance the wage increase for the remaining months of May and June in the old fiscal year. The City agreed to accept the offer. "The solution to the wage issue would have been extremely difficult without this gesture," commented Miles.

THE FINAL SETTLEMENT

A merit promotion plan, a no-strike clause, a no-discrimination clause, and a grievance procedure were added to the agreement. (See appendix F.) The grievance procedure provided for nonbinding arbitration by a panel of three persons. The City and the union would each select one member of the panel, and the third member, who would be chairman, would be jointly selected by the appointees of the union and the City. The final power to resolve a grievance remained with the mayor. "It would be unlikely," said Miles, "that the mayor could justify rejecting any decision reached by an impartial arbitrator."

The final memorandum of understanding was presented to the City Council and passed by a 12–1 margin on April 16, 1968, after a strike of 64 days. It provided a working agreement between the union and the City through June 30, 1969. The one dissenting vote was cast by Tom Todd, who, as a member of the City's negotiating team, remained adamant against the union. The union voted unanimously to accept the agreement.

ELEMENTS LEADING TO A SOLUTION

The "Memphis formula" can be reduced to a set of six variables, each with a number of supporting factors, that significantly affected the agreement reached by the AFSCME and the City of Memphis. These are unified Negro support of the strike, articulate Negro leaders, coercive pressures from the Negro community, support of organized labor and national civil rights leaders, communication through mediation and neutral third parties, and a factor which can be described as the "Memphis image."

Support of Negro Community

At any given time, one or more of these variables may have taken precedence over another. However, the continued unified support in the Negro community for the strikers was crucial to the success of the union in negotiations with the City. Earlier failure to mount strong support for the union during the Ingram Administration underscores the importance of this factor. Mayor Loeb was convinced he could break the strike by the use of strikebreakers to provide limited garbage pickup, but he considerably underestimated the cohesiveness of the strikers and their supporters, a cohesiveness strengthened by the Mayor's antiunion and anti-Negro image.

Negro Leadership

The presence of articulate Negro leaders was important in providing coordination for coercive pressures upon the City. Memphis Negro ministers generally had no record of being outspoken to the white establishment. Dr. Ralph Jackson, director of the Department of Minimum Salary of the African Methodist Episcopal Church, who became an active spokesman for the Negro community during the strike was a case in point. Following a City Council meeting on February 23, which had refused to hear a Public Works Committee Resolution supporting the strikers, Dr. Jackson participated in a march by union members and supporters down Main street. Even though a friend of Mayor Loeb, Dr. Jackson was maced by police along with other bystanders when a disturbance broke out between marchers and the police. After this incident, he became an activist in support of the strikers. Following the macing incident, Dr. Jackson and others went to a meeting in the Mason Temple where they were given the details involved in the sanitation strike and "the inhumane conditions under which they were working at that time. . . . From that, a vast source of information was brought out about the overall conditions in the city. . . . I had become . . . unaware of conditions in trying to make it under the system. We had really gotten away from the things that go on and the conditions under which people live and work, the types of wages and salaries they receive, the types of homes they live in. All of these things were unfolded to us, and we had to look at these and the sanitation strike in the light of the needs of the folk. The need for a commitment to change these things is what actually got me involved." At a mass meeting of strike supporters shortly thereafter, Dr. Jackson said, "I have a confession to make. For 30 years, I have been training to hold myself in check. I couldn't understand what made some people lose control of themselves and fly off the handle. I never thought it would happen to me. But I lost 30 years of training in just 5 minutes last Friday [February 23]."[21]

The Public Works Committee hearing February 22, followed on February 23 by the macing incident, was also the turning point for Reverend James Lawson, who had supported the strike but had not been actively involved until that time. At first the Public Works Committee had refused to hear Reverend Lawson and other black ministers, but later had passed a resolution supporting the strikers after what resembled a sit-in by union members took place. Lawson was infuriated because he thought the Public Works Committee hearing's chairman, a black member of the City Council, "was trying to coddle to Loeb and the white establishment." C.O.M.E. was organized after the macing incident demonstrated that the police did not discriminate in their treatment of Negro marchers. The strength of black identity as an issue could be clearly seen at this point. Led by Reverend Lawson, C.O.M.E. directed the coercive pressures from the Negro community, and the ministers' congregations provided an important source of funds for the strikers. Ministers from C.O.M.E. also participated in discussions with the mayor.

The strength of these Negro leaders lay in their demonstrated ability to apply coercive pressures on the City. When the City Council rebuffed the ministers on February 23 by refusing to hear a Public Works Committee resolution calling for recognition of the union and some form of dues checkoff, the ministers took to their pulpits and called for the boycott of all downtown stores, the daily newspapers, and all Loeb businesses. The boycott was successful. Business showed a marked decline downtown. Negroes did not shop there, white customers shopped out East in the shopping centers, and rural trade stayed away. The *New York Times*[22] reported on March 18, "The boycott is generally conceded to be hurting business although there are no really reliable estimates of how much. One source said business had fallen more than 35 percent in the downtown area." According to W. T. Ross, the boycott's success caused businessmen to place pressure on the mayor to settle the dispute.

Coercion

Included in the set of coercive pressures from the Negro community was the implicit threat of increasing militancy among young-

21. Stanfield, *In Memphis: More Than A Garbage Strike*, p. 33.
22. *New York Times*, March 18, 1968, p. 28.

er Negroes. Such groups as the Black Knights and Invaders, whether militant in their beginnings or not, were so labeled by the daily newspapers. Members of these groups had spoken at one or more of the meetings supporting the strikers. Edwin Stanfield[23] reports one such incident when a young man spoke to a mass meeting.

"I'm a radical," the young man began. "I'll tell you just like that I'm a radical. . . . Before Henry Loeb will listen, the garbage has to be in the street, . . . not in your back yard. As long as those trucks are allowed to roll, they can keep it picked up wherever they want it picked up. . . ."

"Preaching and money raising are fine. Somebody has to do it. But there are some *men* out there; we've got to do some *fighting.* Not marching—fighting."

"And when you talk about fighting a city with as many cops as this city's got, you better have some guns! You're gonna need 'em before it's over!"

Most Negro leaders subscribed to Dr. King's philosophy of non-violence, but when met with white indifference to their pleas for justice for the strikers, they talked about "going fishing." This implied a threat of leaving things in the hands of the militants.

The white community through its police, newspapers, and other public media established a policy of alienation of these young Negroes. It never sought to work with them but chose instead to work against them. Although the young people who might be labeled "militant" remained a very small minority, the City's policies of alienation, condemnation, and force applied by police did not diminish their numbers. "The looting and breaking of windows during the march led by Dr. King, March 28, was what really awoke the community to what was happening," said Frank Miles. "It was at this point that the City realized this thing had to be settled before it got further out of hand." Although its importance was exaggerated in the press, the threat of violence produced movement behind the scenes to settle the dispute. There was, however, an apparent difference in the meaning of "militant" as used by Negroes and whites.

23. Stanfield, *In Memphis: More Than A Garbage Strike,* pp. 43-44.

Whites interpreted militant as meaning force and violence, while blacks interpreted it as meaning unrelenting direct nonviolent action to achieve their ends. Probably because they wanted to justify their own violent response to the demonstrations, the white community and the press exaggerated the significance of those in the black community who advocated violence. However, Negro leaders such as Dr. Jackson and the Reverend Mr. Lawson minimize the importance of radicals. According to Lawson, "they never got past rhetoric. They bragged a lot about what they were going to do, but they never did it. We've got pictures of the disturbances, and we *know* who was in on it. . . . In fact, they discredited themselves in the black community by failing to go beyond their rhetoric. . . . I don't see that they really did bring in white support. It was really Martin's death that was the drawing point for whites." Dr. Jackson said, "Memphis has never really had a real violent effort here. Even that first march that was broken up; half a dozen windows were broken. When Martin was killed, less damage was done in Memphis than anywhere . . . largely because of the influence of leadership . . . which comes from the ministers." Dr. Jackson thought that the creation of radicals by whites "was the newspaper and the power structure method and effort of developing this thing. This was another way of solidifying the racism in the white community against what was being done. As long as they could show that Memphis had some of those folk . . . you were reading about in those other towns, then this gave them the reason to use force to put it down."

Labor and Civil Rights Support

The coalition of organized labor and the Negro community provided the civil rights movement with a new power base. The acceptance of the cause by local white unions was not immediate, however. "The insertion of race as an issue," said one union observer, "couldn't help but make it difficult to get widespread local white union support." Two locals, the Rubber Workers and the Retail Clerks, offered immediate support. Newsletters from the AFL-CIO Committee on Political Education (COPE) were sent to union locals outlining the economic issues of the dispute. (See appendix G.) In addition, resolutions from the AFL-CIO Labor Council in support of the strikers' demands were presented to the mayor. Absent at first, however, was the financial support of organized labor and the presence of its members in the daily marches on City Hall.

The entrance of national personalities such as Bayard Rustin, Roy Wilkins, and Dr. King during the fourth week of the strike attracted national publicity and with this came financial support from several international unions. The entry of these well known national leaders also broke the local news "freeze" on the activities of the Negro-union coalition and focused national attention on the dispute. This attention attracted support for the strikers and criticism of Memphis and its leaders.

A significant force for settlement was the desire by local union leaders and the white power structure to emphasize the trade-union rather than the racial aspects of the conflict. These white attitudes strengthened the effectiveness of racial demonstrations, especially after national publicity was focused on the dispute. The threat to "go fishing" by the Negro ministers and leave things in the hands of the militants strengthened efforts by local white union leaders to refocus on the trade union aspects of the strike in order to obtain local white unionist support. A march of nearly 500 white union members on March 4 was organized by Tommy Powell, head of the Memphis AFL-CIO Labor Council. "Morale toward the middle of the strike," said Baxton Bryant, "became a real problem as did the lack of money." The presence of white support could not help but lift the morale of the strikers while it reinforced the position of those seeking to restructure existing white institutions over those wishing to destroy these institutions. It deemphasized racial aspects of the strike and underscored for the mayor the fact that he was dealing with trade-union issues affecting both blacks and whites.

AFSCME was an important vehicle of change. It provided the common ground around which the Negro community closed ranks. The presence of the International officers provided prestige and know-how for the collective bargaining process while not usurping local control of the dispute. The coalition of the civil rights movement and organized labor was a significant element leading to settlement of the dispute.

Third Parties

The role of communication through neutral third parties and the mediation process also provided an important component in the eventual agreement. Memphis is perhaps unique in that it possessed a substantial number of white citizens who were capable of acting as third parties. This could have been a product of its early efforts at desegregation of public facilities and the subsequent creation of dialogue between the white and black communities. Their failure to bring the dispute to an early settlement was no reflection on their efforts. The continuation of dialogue between the City and the union was vital to any hope for settlement of the dispute at a minimum cost to all concerned.

Mediation took the dispute from the public media and placed it back at the bargaining table. It replaced the growing emphasis on racial issues with reemphasis of the economic issues. In view of the absence of a precedent for recognition of public-employee unions and the newness of the city administration, the use of mediation took on special significance. It provided an arena for orderly discussion where the union could negotiate as an equal with city government. This level of participation was significant when viewed in light of black identity as an issue.

Mediation relies on communication, and the selection of a mediator who could effectively perform this function was important. In discussing Frank Miles, James Reynolds said, "He was respected by all concerned and had access to everyone. Having someone like this with a professional labor background is something for us to think about in other municipalities."

The Memphis case suggested that professional skills were more important than personal identification, though the latter cannot be totally disregarded. Frank Miles was, without a doubt, a member of the white establishment. He was a friend of the mayor and for a decade had been employed as a member of management. But he brought to the negotiation process a long record as a professional mediator and a highly refined understanding of labor-management problems.

James Reynolds brought to the negotiations the prestige of the President and federal interest. His role was important for this reason alone, but the real groundwork for the agreement was laid by Frank Miles. Miles's imaginative attacks upon the economic issues and the skill with which he and James Reynolds handled the negotiations were important elements leading to agreement by the parties.

The "Memphis Image"

Another factor leading to the settlement was the "Memphis image." The "Memphis image" is an undefined element that led to growing pressure on the mayor from members of the white community for a resolution to the dispute. Memphis, which captions itself as the "place of good abode," suddenly found this epithet challenged by violence and the assassination of Dr. King. The national publicity given Memphis focused the attention of the nation and the world on it. "When *Time* magazine, following the assassination of Dr. King, described Memphis as a 'decadent river town,' " said John T. Fisher, a prominent local businessman, "some people really got their feathers ruffled and started doing things." Businessmen were the ones to benefit or lose most from the "image," not only because they lost sales immediately because of the boycott, but also because of the fear that social turmoil would impede the city's economic development. Businessmen consequently placed increased pressure on the city administration during the last three weeks of the strike. Just as the strike drew the attention of middle-class Negroes to the problems confronting black workers, it also revealed those problems for the first time to many whites whose understanding of race relations previously had been restricted to conversations with their servants.

Of course, Dr. King's assassination had a profound effect on the white as well as the black community. His assassination revealed to many whites the consequences of race hatred and stimulated fears that nonviolence would die with him. A number of white citizens who were deeply concerned about Memphis' race image therefore placed pressure on the mayor to settle with the union.

CONCLUSIONS

The confrontation in Memphis took the form of a labor dispute around which deeper racial issues converged. Negotiation brought a resolution to the dispute, but not before loss of human lives and destruction of property. The presence of a political structure with a leader who remained insensitive to the racial issues surrounding the dispute contributed significantly to the conflict that followed.

The Memphis case demonstrates the value of negotiations in resolving racial conflict. The emergence of a power base provided by the coalition of organized labor and the Negro community gave new life to the old civil rights movement. The inclusion of organized labor provided a vehicle for the institutionalization of racial conflict. In addition, the contribution made by black identity as an issue to the nonviolent restructuring of the white-dominated institutions provides some evidence of its positive potential.

The confrontation between Negroes and the white power structure demonstrated the positive and negative aspects of many of the factors in the constellation of forces which led to the conflict. Racial discrimination, both overt and institutionalized, played an important role in creating the problems which led to this conflict. Racial prejudice and the fear of its consequences also caused many whites, especially white trade unionists and ministers, to be reluctant to support the black strikers openly. Racism also undoubtedly influenced the vigor of the white power structure's resistance to sharing decision-making power with the black sanitation workers through collective bargaining.

On the other hand, the obvious influence of racism and the forceful resistance to change by the white power structure, operating through the mayor and his police, tended to solidify the Negro community behind the strikers, giving them power they would not have had in a purely economic contest with the City, which, but for the support of the Negro community, could have crushed the strike in a matter of hours. The City's vulnerability on the race aspect of the dispute caused some leaders to attempt to minimize publicity given the strike and to emphasize legal and economic questions instead of the race and moral issues involved. However, the City's vulnerability on the racial matters was strategically very important to the ministers and civil rights leaders involved in the conflict. By a willingness to settle the collective bargaining issues, the City was able to prevent racial issues from dominating the conflict.

SUBSEQUENT EVENTS
POSTSCRIPT—THE 1969 NEGOTIATIONS

Events subsequent to the 1968 strike afford some additional insights into the impact of that conflict on the parties involved in it. It is especially instructive to look at the three-year settlement between Memphis and Local 1733 reached on June 25, 1969 without open conflict but with an obvious threat that the 1968 events might be repeated if a settlement could not be reached through negotiations.

The 1969 Issues

The issues in the 1969 negotiations centered on changes in the *product* of the white-dominated power structure as opposed to the *process-oriented* changes demanded by the union in 1968. While economic issues were less important than recognition in 1968, at a press conference less than a month before the threatened strike in 1969, Jesse Epps, chief negotiator for the union and special assistant to the president of the AFSCME, noted that wages will be "one of the keys to whether or not there will be a strike July 1."[24] The union demanded a $2.00 an hour minimum wage, which was an increase of $.40 over the current minimum wage. Other issues included a payroll dues checkoff, a no-strike clause, binding arbitration, duration of contract, and various fringe benefits.

The 1969 Negotiations

Although there were a few similarities between the 1968 negotiations and those which began in January 1969, there also were many differences. The City Council again assumed the position that collective bargaining negotiations were an executive function, but, in contrast with 1968, many councilmen actively worked behind the scenes to reach a settlement. The City's negotiating team was headed by Jerrod Moore, the City's chief administrative officer; the mayor did not take an active part in negotiations but remained "available." The City's negotiators took a much more professional approach to negotiations. Both the union and the City indicated a "willingness" to bargain, and each refused to assume a position from which they could not easily retreat as the mayor had done in 1968. Both sides refused to negotiate in the press as they had done during the first five weeks of the 1968 strike. Jerrod Moore stated, "My position is that I am not going to negotiate in the newspapers."[25] Racial issues were minimized, and negotiations were carried out in a mature col-

24. *The Commercial Appeal Mid-South Magazine,* June 14, 1969, p. 17.
25. *Ibid.* June 4, 1969, p. 11.

lective bargaining atmosphere. No mediator was used during the negotiations.

The settlement reached June 25 included compromises from both sides. The union accepted an immediate wage increase of $.18. A minimum wage of $2.00 an hour was to begin on July 1, 1970. The $2.00 minimum wage was to be raised 15 cents on July 1, 1971, to $2.15 plus a cost-of-living increase. The union gave up its demand for a two-year contract and accepted a three-year agreement which would extend past the administration of Mayor Loeb. The union also accepted nonbinding arbitration, but with Jerrod Moore as the ultimate authority instead of Mayor Loeb as in 1968. The City agreed to a direct dues checkoff instead of a checkoff through the employees' credit union. This issue was a major obstacle to the 1968 settlement. The union also obtained additional concessions from the City on overtime, hazardous duty pay, and medical treatment.

Elements Leading to a Solution (1969)

Many of the factors leading to the 1968 agreement were present in 1969. They were interlaced, however, with a new set of factors which combined with the old to bring about a settlement. The presence of Negro leaders, the involvement of the Negro community, and the threat of coercive pressures were again available to the union. Pressure from the white business community for settlement also was felt by the City. This was supplemented by concern from a new group of white citizens and the white press. By 1969 the City was no longer negotiating with a union of approximately 1,300 members, but with one whose membership had grown to nearly 4,000. Added to this was the threat of a simultaneous strike of 1,700 city-employee members of Local 1288 of the International Brotherhood of Electrical Workers (IBEW).

The power base built by the civil rights movement and organized labor in 1968 remained intact in 1969. As a strike loomed nearer, Jesse Epps began mobilizing support in the Negro community. "We've got to get the preachers lined up, and I've got to get out with the folk,"[26] Epps said. In 1969 C.O.M.E., organized by ministers to support the 1968 strike, was still active and available to coordinate support for the union members from the Negro community.

26. *Ibid.*, p. 1.

As noted earlier, pressure for settlement of the dispute by the white business community increased during the last three weeks of the 1968 strike. The downtown business community suffered heavily during the 1968 boycott by the Negro community and were eager to avoid a repetition in 1969. Following the 1968 strike, the Chamber of Commerce had completed pledges of four million dollars to a "Greater Memphis" campaign designed to enhance the city's "image", seek new industry and develop new business leadership in the community. Although begun prior to the strike, the campaign was reported to be lagging by one prominent businessman. The death of Dr. King and ensuing unfavorable national publicity combined to renew interest in the drive and enabled it to reach its goals. Members of the white business community weren't willing to jeopardize this investment through another costly strike.

Additional support for the union came from a group of white women in affluent East Memphis. This support was an unexpected product of a "spread the misery" campaign conducted by Local 1733 and its supporters in East Memphis shopping centers during the first week in June. The campaign involved visits by the union group to various stores in the shopping centers where they tried on clothing or moved articles about but made no purchases. "Our trips," said Epps, "to Popular Plaza . . . out East . . . [and] to Justine's this week are not an attempt to be impudent, brazen, or vulgar in our actions, but our way of asking, 'Help us; share the comfort in which you live with us.' "[27]

Lester A. Rosen, chairman of the Memphis and Shelby County Human Relations Commission, suggested that an alternative to the demonstrations be found as a means of cooling pressure being built by the campaign in the white community. Jesse Epps suggested a visit by East Memphis women to homes of city employees. Following a tour of the homes by a group of 75 women, the women formed a pressure group called Concerned Women of Memphis and Shelby County, which made several appearances before the City Council requesting action on a broad front to eliminate the poverty they found in the homes of city employees.

Pressure for a settlement in 1969 also came from the white press. In 1968 the two daily newspapers were accused of racist reporting

27. *Ibid.*, p. 11.

and biased coverage of the strike and therefore were boycotted by the Negro community. In 1969, one paper, the *Commercial Appeal,* called for "a fair solution to Memphis's labor problems—reasonable on both sides, and fair to every person residing in this city." It encouraged the use of a mediator, if negotiations became stymied, pointing out that "we can ill-afford a drift into the treacherous waters ahead."[28]

The union also gathered new strength from its successful organizing drive among employees of the automobile inspection stations, the city hospitals, the Board of Education, and the Memphis Housing Authority, which more than doubled the local's 1968 membership. The size of the union with the extensive coverage of a threatened strike made the potential loss to the community even greater.

The City's potential loss was magnified by the threat of a simultaneous strike by nearly 1700 IBEW Local 1288 members employed by the Memphis Light, Gas, and Water Company. The combined strike threat of the two locals meant that nearly 5700 city employees would be on strike.

As we concluded at the end of the 1968 analysis, the inclusion of organized labor provides a vehicle for the institutionalization of racial conflict. The settlement of 1969 offered further evidence that the racial issues surrounding the 1968 dispute had found an avenue for negotiated change in Memphis through organized labor. The willingness of the City to negotiate and the presence of a framework for negotiations provides some optimism for the use of a negotiation process to resolve racial conflict where the conflict centers on such permanent relationships as employment. The Memphis case shows how broad Negro community support can be used to strengthen the bargaining power of a group who, because of low skills, otherwise would not have enough power to force an employer, especially a government entity, to recognize and share power with them.

28. *Ibid.,* June 5, 1969, p. 6.

PART 4

The Strike by Cleveland Water Works Employees

JAMES E. BLACKWELL
MARIE R. HAUG

Editors' Introduction

THIS is the second of the analytical case studies here presented. It too concerns a dispute between public employees and city officials. Like Memphis the workers were organized (indeed, the same international union was involved), the membership was predominantly black, and the racial factors appeared to be of considerable importance. Thus it permits some degree of comparability to the Memphis situation. In contrast, however, are its northern location, the incumbency of a black mayor seeking reelection, and the fact that it deals with a grievance rather than with a wage demand. On the methodological side, this Cleveland study was handled by a black-white team of sociologists, in contrast to Memphis, which was done by a pair of white economists.

More importantly, this case was selected because it afforded an opportunity to study the mediation process in a racial dispute. This mediation process which was so crucial to the final settlement was carried out by Willoughby Abner, director of the National Center for Dispute Settlement of the American Arbitration Association. Thus we were provided with an unusual opportunity for examining a dispute in which the protesters were black, the establishment included blacks and whites, and the successful mediation was effected by a black. The intra- and interunion relationships in a racial context are added items of interest.

In any case involving an established labor union within the context of union-management relations, the identification of racial factors and the determination of their significance is difficult. It is unfortunate that it was not possible to make available to the reader the interview material used by the scholars in putting together this report. In those interviews there are differing judgments on the relevance and importance of race in the incident described. The perceptions on this point tended to be clearly related to role and, less clearly, to race. Thus white unionists at the International level and white management representatives tended to see the issue in union-management rather than race terms. Black protesters tended to see more of race both in their own actions and perceptions and in those of the city establishment. We are impressed with the insights of our independent scholars and, further, believe that in such cases the *perception* of race as a factor is as important as the *fact* of demonstrable racist actions.

James E. Blackwell has lived and worked in Cleveland and had an intimate knowledge of the city and its functioning. An added dimension was derived from the fact that as a black he was able to obtain and interpret information from black participants and observers who were otherwise unwilling to discuss the case, particularly in its racial aspects.

Marie R. Haug also had a close knowledge of the city and brought to the study a special knowledge of labor unions deriving from her prior experience in that area.

The Strike by Cleveland Water Works Employees*

ON a hot Thursday morning, August 14, 1969, Clarence King, Black union steward in the Water Works of the City of Cleveland, stopped a city truck from leaving the premises because of a dispute over whether a member of his union, AFSCME (American Federation of State, County, and Municipal Employees), or a Teamsters' union member should be driving it. John Minder, white, chief engineer at the Water Works, dismissed King, long considered a troublemaker because of his militancy. Although the jurisdictional argument was quickly settled by the business agents of the two unions, King's dismissal still stood, at the insistence of the city utilities director, Ben Stefanski, also white. The following day a wildcat work stoppage began, with the union demanding King's reinstatement. Mayor Carl Stokes, first Black mayor of a major city, then just embarking on the primary campaign for his reelection, came out to the Works to talk to the men, nearly all of whom were Black. He urged negotiations and brought the antagonists down to City Hall to talk, but no agreement was reached, as Stefanski was determined to maintain discipline and demonstrate that management was in control.

During the following week, the strikers, who formed only one segment of Local 100 of AFSCME, sent groups to other installations in the city urging their fellow members to walk out also. Some threats were used, and the city administration invoked the State Riot Control Act, arresting several of the union leaders. Willoughby Abner, a Black, was called in as a mediator, but there was still no progress in negotiations. On Friday, August 22, Local 100 held a well-attended membership meeting which voted overwhelmingly to strike, and

* Data on which this analysis is based were derived primarily from extended interviews with the major parties involved on both sides. Black respondents were interviewed by the Black scholar and white respondents by the white scholar. The interview material was given on a confidential basis and is, therefore, not included. Additionally, the authors had access to a great deal of documentary material.

on Tuesday, August 26, many city offices and work locations were picketed. The local secured official labor support from the AFL-CIO central labor body executive board, but Robert Duvin, city labor relations attorney and a white, persuaded other unions dealing with Cleveland *not* to respect the picket lines. Jerry Wurf, white, international president of AFSCME, came into the negotiations in the middle of the week, and in a marathon session with Stokes and Abner, a settlement was reached in which the union pledged no more wildcat strikes and accepted a 30-day suspension for King. This was ratified by the local on August 28.

There are four questions to be investigated in analyzing this dispute:

1. To what extent did race play a role in the development of the strike and to what extent was it a factor in the outcome?

2. Was the presence of a Black mediator useful in reaching a settlement in a situation where Blacks were on both sides of the bargaining table, and, if so, why?

3. What were the relative weights of economic interest and racial solidarities in the power struggle represented by the strike and its political implications?

4. What are the implications for other disputes involving Blacks and whites on both sides of a confrontation?

In order to suggest answers for these questions, detailed statements are necessary on the historical background of the dispute, the precipitating incident itself, the forces at work in the confrontation, the course of negotiations and settlements, and various post-settlement events.

BACKGROUND

The Cleveland Political Situation

During and immediately following the First World War, the city of Cleveland began to experience an unprecedented influx of Black Americans. As with most migrants, the Blacks were pulled to Cleveland by the promise of a better life characterized by unlimited economic opportunity, political freedom, and first-class educational development.

Most of the Black people who migrated to Cleveland were from the southern states of Alabama, Mississippi, Arkansas, Georgia, Florida, and Tennessee and the border state of Kentucky. They came for jobs, better schools, better housing, a higher standard of living, and to increase their chances of being culturally and structurally assimilated into the mainstream of American life. The level of aspiration was high and partially realized each time a Black man became a "racial first" in some new dimension of life previously unavailable to Black people.

Cleveland gradually found itself enjoying a reputation as a liberal city. Black men could be elected members of the City Council, although from predominantly Black wards. Black men could be elected or appointed municipal judges, and a few could rise to key political positions in City Hall. However, the attainment of such positions in the political structure was significantly related to the increasing voting power among the Black people. In spite of the liberal image, dubious at best, Black people in Cleveland tended to be concentrated in the inner city, rarely comprising a significant proportion of the suburban population. A distinct pattern of ecological succession became discernible over the years in which Blacks tended to follow the residential path of the Jews. Otherwise, restrictive barriers operated to contain Black people in a distinctly Black ghetto. Several Black ghettos developed in the inner city, many of which came to represent a cross section of the Black social class structure: the urban poor, a Black bourgeoisie, and a Black elite.

The poor increased their numbers through a larger birth rate and a high rate of migration to Cleveland. Not able to realize their expectations and faced with mounting forces of discrimination and de facto segregation, the Blacks in Cleveland became disenchanted, disillusioned, and alienated from the white power structure which had not been responsive to their needs. A sense of powerlessness and a feeling of oppression by the "system" developed among the Black ghetto dwellers, whether in the Black slum or in the Black middle-class neighborhood. By 1966 Black people comprised in excess of 30 percent of Cleveland's population. Most of the Black voters were Democrats.

The Stokes Administration

In 1967 the Black community joined forces with certain white citizens who were disenchanted with the lackluster leadership of the incumbent city administration to elect Carl Stokes as the first Black man to become mayor of a large city in the United States. The Black community gave the mayor approximately 99 percent of its votes, which was unquestionably the deciding factor in his being elected.

The election of a Black Mayor of Cleveland was symbolic of the new mood among Black people and actual evidence of the potential of Black political power. This election also served once again to raise expectations of the Black masses as well as to generate hope that a Black mayor would create a more equitable opportunity structure for the alienated and powerless segments in the Black community. New and Black faces appeared in City Hall. Black technicians and administrators emerged; some effort was made to bridge the gap between the city government and its people through the involvement of local leaders in diverse government-sponsored community development projects.

The Council of Economic Opportunity, the Neighborhood Development Corporation, PATH, (Plan of Action for Tomorrow's Housing), and other formal organizations were developed as structural mechanisms for realizing rising expectations. However, the resultant era of good feeling was to be short-lived. Charges that the new "Fat Cats", (Black *and* white) were exploiting the citizenry, an unresponsive City Council, limited job opportunities following the completion of lengthy training programs, and other difficulties precipitated doubt in some quarters concerning the degree of commitment of the new city administration toward rectifying old ills.

For example, segments of the Black Nationalists questioned the sincerity of the administration or charged it could not operate independently of the invisible white power structure which allegedly financed the successful bid for election. In this view, white industrialists and the white corporation elite, who form the core of the power structure which controls the city, had successfully surrounded the new mayor with their own functionaries.

Whatever the politics of their appointment, the new staff recruited by the administration tended to be bright, young, upwardly mobile, and aggressive. They managed to circumvent the dictates of slow-moving old-line bureaucrats who had formerly controlled the decision-making process in the city government. The new decision makers and advisors established their authority and their primacy in determining, inter alia, accessibility to the mayor and in advising him on crucial decisions affecting the revitalization and growth of the city. Gossip claimed that several of them served as a direct pipeline between the city administration and the white power structure. The new style of work was vigorous but divisive, demoralizing some who had been in positions of trust, confidence, and decision-making for several years. Several resigned; some were demoted while others remained in their positions but were stripped of power and prestige.

The new "managers and administrators" tightened their control over the internal structure of the city government, but not without conflict with the City Council. Promayor and antimayor forces quickly became apparent within this legislative body. Most of the mayor's support was among his political friends from the East side of the city and among the more liberal elements within the Council. He also had the backing of part of the white corporate elite, who needed his ability to "keep Cleveland cool" in order to protect their control over economic institutions.

The antimayor forces were concentrated largely among the ethnic representatives from the West side, led by Council president James Stanton, who had systematically constructed a personal power base of his own. The antimayor forces occasionally seemed motivated by political considerations to block a program sponsored by promayor groups and designed to promote the general welfare of the population. As a result of this type of internecine warfare, many promises of improved living conditions were unfulfilled at the conclusion of the mayor's first term in office. The City's relations with various labor unions deteriorated rapidly.

It is in the context of the complex relationship between a city governed by a Black mayor, allegedly indebted to an invisible but powerful white power structure, the uncertainty of political support from the white ethnics on the West side, the divisiveness which characterized the City Council, and the disillusionment among many of the Black community that the labor dispute under study here must be understood. As a final complication, the dispute erupted just six weeks before the primary election in which the mayor was opposed by a white racist candidate of his own party, with the potential of a general election thereafter in which he would face a popular representative of the white ethnic community as the standard bearer of the opposition party.

Union Organization and the City of Cleveland

Employees of the City of Cleveland are currently represented by 14 unions, among which three are of major importance because of their size. Local 244 of the Teamsters covers municipal and county drivers, chiefly of garbage trucks. Local 1099 of the Laborers Union, AFL-CIO, includes municipal and county laborers, some of whom work with the garbage drivers. Local 100 of AFSCME, AFL-CIO, has a wider jurisdiction, covering not only the Water Works personnel, blue collar and white collar, but also employees in a number of other city departments. The major blue collar segment of the union is in the Water Works; these workers comprise about half the membership.

In each of these unions, the membership is largely or substantially Black, while the paid leadership is or has been white. This is, in part, a reflection of the changing racial composition of city workers. The business agent of the Teamsters Local, who has been in office 17 years, is James Trusso, a white of Italian extraction. A similar situation obtains in the Laborers Union, where the key business agent is an elderly Italian, Joseph Farinacci.

In Local 100 of AFSCME, the membership is more nearly racially balanced, but the business agent is Tony Stalteri, a younger white of Italian background, and, until recently, the president was Nick Jablonski, a young man from the Polish section of the city. An indication of the changing composition of the work force can be seen in the history of the Water Department's blue collar component. These men used to be mainly foreign born, and were, in fact, called the "wooden shoe gang." During the last decade as this group retired, it was gradually replaced by Blacks as a result of the changing population and political pattern of the city. Since applicants needed a reference from their councilman, these jobs became a source of political patronage for the increasing number of Black city councilmen who were elected to office from the spreading ghetto area. However, the Water Department workers, formerly in the Plumbers and Pipe Fitters Union, only voted to join Local 100 about six years ago. This happened at about the time the racial mix was changing and has produced a situation in which most Blacks in the local are blue collar, and most whites are white collar. Thus Local 100 is split on race-class lines.

Up until the administration of Mayor Stokes, none of these 14 unions had written labor contracts with the City. There was a hodge-podge of gentlemen's agreements, under-the-table deals, and "past practices." Business agents would meet over dinner and drinks with the commissioners to settle grievances or do each other favors. Problems were dealt with on a political basis, and Local 100 functioned in some ways like a political club rather than a labor union. Membership included supervisors and executives; even the water commissioner was a member. Former leaders in the union used it as a springboard to run for political office or gain political favors. One former officer secured a desirable spot on the Board of Elections, for example. Overtime allowances were used to pay off favorites or as substitutes for wage increases. Thefts of tools and pipes from the Water Department were often of large proportions, and these "fringe benefits" were allowed to continue, sometimes without reports being made to the police.

Particularly during the last few years, however, this situation had been changing. Frequent stoppages were staged by the militant Blacks in the Water Department and a number of written memoranda of settlement negotiated. Because some Local 100 members were growing weary of the continual loss of earnings involved in these confrontation techniques and also because there was a general national movement toward written labor contracts with government bodies, Local 100 made a formal demand for a negotiated contract in 1967. There is some indication that the new city administration wished to move in the same direction because of the stabilization of relationships which would ensue. In any case, when the Teamsters called a "sick call strike" in 1968, one of the bases of the settlement was that a labor agreement would be worked out.

Shortly thereafter, the mayor announced in a press conference that contract talks with all 14 city unions would begin. In these talks, the City was represented by Robert Duvin, a white labor relations attorney, who is chief company bargaining spokesman for the big food chains and a member of the law firm which also includes a former Democratic mayor, Thomas Burke. At the first session Local 100 separated itself from the joint talks. By this time under the leadership of Robert Brindza, a former UAW member, Local 100 insisted on separate talks, as did the Operating Engineers, because it did not want to be held back by the footdragging of the other unions, who were very reluctant to abandon their former political wheeling and dealing. Also, the local was emerging as the most militant of the city unions and undoubtedly hoped to make a name for itself and win prestige and additional membership by "beating the pattern" and exceeding the settlement made by the other 13 unions. These other organizations, on the other hand, had a history of working together, having formed a joint council several years before with Trusso of the Teamsters as president and Farinacci of the Laborers as secretary. Local 100 had preferred to go it alone even then, claiming it would gain nothing and merely have to fork over per capita payments. Apparently there were also some hard feelings over jurisdictional differences and possible raiding.

In any event, in the early summer of 1968, 25-month agreements were drawn up for the 13 unions in the joint council and signed by Stokes and Duvin for the city. Each contract provided a wage increase, grievance procedure, no-strike clause, revisions in the progression schedule, and other benefits. However, on the whole these contracts were management oriented, with a strong management-rights clause. Furthermore, the legal status of the contracts was somewhat cloudy. Some persons in the City Law Department theorized that the entire contract would never stand up in court because its provisions went contrary to civil service rules and because there was no charter authorization for the mayor to act on behalf of the City in labor negotiations.

Local 100 refused to accept the same contract terms as the other unions, holding out for more. The negotiating committee at the time included Clarence King (Black), steward in the Water Works, and a union militant who consistently refused to compromise on contract issues. The first tentative settlement was rejected by a vote of the local, and, even after the City made a few more concessions, it was rejected again with King leading the opposition. At this point the

City, on Duvin's recommendation, was preparing for a strike and was determined to take on Local 100 rather than give in any further. But then "Glenville happened": the pitched battle between police and Black militants in which seven people were killed in the Cleveland ghetto, followed by rioting and the calling in of the National Guard. Neither side wanted a strike at this juncture, and it was agreed to submit the unresolved issues to arbitration, a procedure which King was instrumental in persuading the membership to accept on the basis that any settlement would be retroactive. The arbitration produced additional individual adjustments, specifically for white collar workers in the Water Department.[1]

The Local 100 signing did not bring labor peace. Grievances began to mount up, some involving continuation of past practices and others concerning disciplinary actions. The union was demanding full compliance with the terms of the agreement. Lower level management of the City, on the other hand, which had no part in the negotiations and did not understand or perhaps had never even bothered to read the contract, insisted on carrying on in the old way. Furthermore the old ways of winning concessions at the Water Works also continued. There were a series of confrontations and disputes, grievances and arbitrations, with the City frequently taking an inflexible stand, twice getting an injunction against the union, and the union calling wildcat strikes and threatening to strike. King, who had been suspended during the negotiations for heading a stoppage but then reinstated, was active in attempts to enforce the agreement. The parties were on a collision course, with hostility building up in the context of a power struggle.

In the meantime, another element complicating the situation was the determination of Stokes and his advisors to bring new, trained leadership into the city administration and reestablish efficient operations in the various city departments. According to at least one informant, when Stokes came into office he found city government in a shambles. In some cases, departments were under the direction of elderly individuals, some of whom had serious health problems. The Water Commissioner, Thomas Stanton, had had several strokes and was close to retirement age. Much of the routine business of his department was being handled by his long-time office secretary, a

1. See Appendix I.

former Local 100 officer. The deterioration of management pervaded the city operations; it had been the practice to avoid decision-making, to smooth things over rather than solve problems, and to keep the peace rather than maintain discipline. As a result, it was almost impossible to get fired from a city job, at least that was the folklore; even the worst infraction of rules was apt to bring no more than a week's layoff.

The new city utilities director appointed by Stokes was Ben Stefanski, a young attorney whose father owned a large bank in the Polish community, one of the largest ethnic sections of the city. Although plainly a political appointee, Stefanski apparently took his new duties seriously. He replaced the Water Works superintendent, a former salesman without technical training, with a white engineer, John Minder, who had been recruited through an executive search firm used by the City to find capable staff. Minder, although an experienced engineer, had no background in labor relations.

In short, at the same time that Local 100 was attempting to enforce a new labor agreement providing protection for its members, the city administration was trying to eliminate old favoritism and irregularities and establish discipline, efficiency, and scientific management in the city departments.

THE STRIKE AND NEGOTIATIONS*

The August 1969 strike of AFSCME Local 100 was precipitated by a series of incidents which occurred August 14 and 15, 1969, at the Harvard Water Yards in Southeast Cleveland. The issue was a question of jurisdiction concerning who should be the driver of a water truck which was about to leave Harvard Yards. The union claimed that a water truck was stripped down and converted into a supply and delivery truck. In this sense, a new job was being created by the City. Changing the jurisdiction of the truck fell within the realm of negotiation. At 8:30 A.M. on August 14, as the truck was about to leave the Yard, Clarence King noticed that a Teamster was on the truck as the "driver" with a water service man as a "helper." King took the position that if the City had decided to reclassify the jobs on the truck, the union should have been notified. It was degrading

* See Appendix H for chronology of the strike.

to force a water service man to ride on a delivery truck as a helper. Apparently the decision had been made by the City to reclassify the positions on the truck approximately two weeks prior to August 14, but according to the union the change had never been formally communicated as required under the terms of the 1968 contract between the City and the union.[2] King claims to have inadvertently discovered the City's intentions through a conversation with a fellow worker. The Teamsters, however, had learned of the change two weeks prior to the Harvard Yards incident through formal channels of communication. Minder claims that King, knowing of the change, had already boasted to his men of his plans to handle the matter before the incident at the yard.

King questioned John Minder about the new arrangements and reverse roles on the truck. His objective was to make immediate adjustments in the job assignment consistent with union guarantees granted under the 1968 agreement. The Teamster's steward also participated in these initial discussions. Minder's decision was that the Teamster would be the driver, and the water service man should be the helper. Clarence King disagreed with this decision, stopped the truck, was given the keys, and physically prevented it from leaving Harvard Yards. King telephoned Kenneth Worwood, director of District Council 78 to apprise him of the incident. Worwood was at Highland View Hospital attempting to settle an issue involving the hospital workers and the County; however, he telephoned Anthony Stalteri, Business Manager of Local 100, to apprise him of developments. Clarence King contacted Stalteri immediately after the Worwood-Stalteri conversation and was told by Stalteri to "hold everything until I get there." This statement was interpreted by King to "stop the operation" which is precisely what King proceeded to do.

When King was given the keys from the truck after stopping it from leaving Harvard Yards, Minder telephoned the Law Department of the City of Cleveland, and was advised to order King to return the keys and leave the premises. He also called Utilities Director Ben Stefanski, who additionally advised that if King refused to comply he be suspended. Minder then learned that the keys had been returned, and he ordered the driver to go out on the job, but King physically prevented the truck from moving by standing

2. See Appendix I, sections 48 and 49.

in the exit. He argued that Stalteri and Worwood would soon arrive to discuss the issues involved. Minder reports that he warned King for the second time that he faced suspension if he continued to interfere with the operations of the truck. King insisted that they should at least wait to discuss the matter with the business agent. It is well to keep in mind that when King initiated the work stoppage he was technically off duty. He had completed his night shift. Charles Coulter, a Black supervisor, talked with King, trying to cool the situation. Minder, who had been on this job for approximately two months, may have originally attempted to play down the incident to his superiors to create the impression that he was in control of the situation. Initially, he took the position that there would be some repercussions, but he did not anticipate a "work stoppage." The day before the incident occurred, Minder had discussed his work at Harvard Yards with Charles Sandor and Charles Bednar, two of Stefanski's assistants, informing them that "things were going smoothly." There is some inkling that the City was using the interval between the telephoned notification from Minder and the arrival of the business agents and union representatives to plan its strategy. Stefanski, for example, who had been openly antagonistic to King during and after the 1968 negotiations, apparently considered that he now had King in a position where he could be discharged.

The two business agents, Anthony Stalteri of Local 100 and James Trusso of the Teamsters Local 244, arrived shortly and discussed the issues with Minder and King. Minder offered to put a laborer on the job, which was an acceptable alternative to Local 100. Trusso, on the other hand, argued that the man presently working on the job should not be reclassified as a laborer since this would reduce his pay rate. A more equitable and acceptable solution would be to retain his water service classification, which would preclude a reduction in pay. Trusso and Stalteri also conversed privately before reaching the agreement that the truck was to be driven by a Teamster union member and that his helper would be a man from the water service department. The helper position was to be viewed as a reclassification and a new job which, from the union perspective, was a satisfactory arrangement.

Contradictory information was provided concerning what happened next. There is consistency in the statements of the union people that once the agreement was reached between Trusso and Stalteri and this was related to Minder the matter was about to be considered closed when Minder received a telephone call. Following this conversation, Minder is reported to have said that "all bets are off, and King is suspended now." The union leadership believes that Ben Stefanski, after conferring with several people in City Hall, ordered Minder to suspend King on the spot. Minder denies that this was the nature of his conversation and claims that he informed Stalteri and Trusso that the suspension still stood since the matter was now in the hands of the "higher-ups." By this term, he apparently was referring to the legal department and the director of utilities. The reaction of the union representatives of Local 100 was one of intensified anger coupled with loss of faith in the City's commitment to abide by the terms of the labor agreement.

Harvard Yards continued to operate for the balance of August 14. During the day, however, several meetings occurred both among the labor forces and the management personnel, and there was some interaction between the two groups.

On August 15, work stopped completely at Harvard Yards. Representatives of Local 100, under the leadership of the chief steward, successfully prevented all trucks from leaving the premises. At approximately 11:00 A.M., Walter Burks, a Black, personnel director for Cleveland, went to the Yards to assess the work stoppage after hearing from Ben Stefanski that Clarence King had thrown up a picket line there. While he was there, Kenneth Worwood and Anthony Stalteri arrived. Burks discussed the work stoppage with Worwood and Stalteri as well as with John Minder and other supervisory personnel. Burks claims that he requested King to vacate the Harvard Yards inasmuch as he was violating laws since he was suspended and no longer in the employ of the City. King's argument was that, as a chief steward, he had a right and a responsibility to remain at the Yards. The union claims that Burks's behavior at the Yards was indicative of the intransigent and vindictive stance that the City was to take in subsequent meetings. Burks is reported to have said to Worwood, for example, that "You've gone too far this time. We're going to break your union." The implication of this remark was that the City planned to exploit this incident to destroy the power and weight of the union.

Walter Burks left Harvard Yards and, accompanied by John Minder, went to Newburgh Heights to inform Chief of Police Novak of an impending strike by Local 100 and of the existing conditions. Later Burks returned to the Yards where he was met by two representatives from the City Law Department, attorneys Loeb and Moore, who had brought the official suspension papers with them.

The suspension papers (a formal letter), were officially served on Clarence King at Harvard Yards at approximately 12:30 P.M. on August 15. King was charged with violating Civil Service Rule 9.10 in the following respects:

1. conduct unbecoming an employee in the public service;
2. disorderly or immoral conduct while on duty;
3. insubordination;
4. willful violation of any of the provisions of law governing the Civil Service or rules or regulations of the Commission; and,
5. failure of good behavior, which is detrimental to the service.

The letter of suspension also cited as evidence against King: (1) unauthorized removal of city property, to wit, keys to a City of Cleveland truck; (2) unlawfully preventing "the egress of City of Cleveland trucks and the orderly operation of the Harvard Facility; and (3) refusing a lawful order from his superior to remove himself and desist in obstructing the operation of the Harvard facility."

Notification of a hearing before the Civil Service referee scheduled for August 19, 1969, in Room 335 of City Hall at 2:00 P.M. was stated in the suspension order. King was also apprised of his right to be represented by a counsel of his choice at the hearing.

Minder then attempted to reestablish services at Harvard Yards, but King, with the assistance of approximately 50 union members, blocked the exit of trucks from the premises. An argument ensued, but the chiefs of police from Newburgh Heights and Cuyahoga Heights arrived in time to force King aside. A brief scuffle followed during which a truck inadvertently ran over the foot of Walter Harris, a water serviceman. He claimed that it was deliberate, but the matter was dropped. Burks and unidentified members of the Cleveland Law Department then went to the Municipal Court of Garfield Heights in whose jurisdiction the Yards are located, to seek an order of arrest against Clarence King. However, this was to no avail since the prosecutor of this small suburban municipality could not be found. The weather was very hot, and the situation quite tense.

During the early afternoon of August 15, Mayor Stokes arrived at the Harvard Yards to determine what he could do in a personal way to terminate the work stoppage. One informant said that "the mayor turned on his charm, and within five minutes he had all the workers in the palm of his hand." The workers stated that they would be willing to return to work immediately if the City reinstated Clarence King, their chief steward. Some of the rank and file had already expressed grave concern over the "double-talk" they had received in the past from the city administration. To the rank and file, a critical issue was the symbolic value and the actual meaning of Black leadership as epitomized by Clarence King. Others perceived the suspension of Clarence King as a deliberate effort of the City administration to "bust the union." This position is based upon the fact that a chief steward is elected by the members and is charged with clear and precise mandates to be their representative on all matters concerning the welfare of the union members. Within this framework, the behavior of King was consistent with his responsibility to union members and involved the execution of what was considered his duty. To remove him forcibly was tantamount to union-busting.

The mayor expressed the belief that the problem was not insurmountable and that it could be settled quickly if union leaders were to go to City Hall to discuss the matter calmly. The mayor left after obtaining a commitment from the union officials and the city representatives that they would meet at City Hall on that day.

There are those who questioned the wisdom of the mayor's becoming involved in the problem at that stage. They viewed his intervention as giving credence to the position that the issues involved were potentially explosive unless resolved immediately and said that this provided encouragement for some to become intransigent in reaching a solution. Albeit, once at City Hall and meeting in the Tapestry Room, the Mayor stated that the problem was a simple one which did not warrant his participation, and he left the matter in charge of the director of utilities, with whom the union could find an equitable solution through free discussion.

The union was represented at this meeting by Kenneth Worwood, William Petite (assistant director of District 78), Anthony Stalteri, and Ola Hinsley (chief steward of the Clerical Department in the union). The City was represented by Walter Burks, John Little (an executive assistant to the mayor), and Ben Stefanski. Before the mayor left the meeting, Worwood pointed out to him that the meeting would produce nothing if Stefanski were left in charge. That argument was to no avail, and the mayor left after about 15 minutes of discussion with both management and labor representatives. Stefanski and his staff conferred privately at this point and decided that they should stand firm. In retrospect, some are convinced that the issues would have been resolved had Robert Duvin, the city labor counsel, been present. It is believed that he would have managed sufficient objectivity to move the opposing sides from the impasse.

At this stage in the development, the union's position was that Clarence King should not be discharged and that the City's dictatorial methods of dealing with union matters had to be curtailed. On the other hand, the City remained adamant in its stance that King was to remain suspended, that the authority of the City had to be respected, and that the matter would come before the Civil Service. Within five minutes after the Mayor left, the meeting came to an abrupt end.

The union questioned the necessity of taking the issue to the Civil Service for a number of reasons. The letter of suspension presented to Clarence King did not specify the limits of the suspension. However, under the terms of the Agreement of Understanding (also called the Contract of 1968), any decision to suspend a member of the union for a period of 30 days or more would be a Civil Service matter.[3] If the suspension is for less than 30 days, the union could take the matter directly to arbitration as a grievance. A very basic and fundamental factor operating at this juncture was the union's distrust of the Civil Service. This distrust is based upon the widespread belief that the Civil Service is no more than an instrument of the city administration and does not perform useful services for city employees. The Civil Service commissioners are appointed by

3. See Appendix I, sections 76 and 77.

the mayor and have been accused in the past of being discriminatory, especially in the appointment of Black people to high positions. The union claims that the Civil Service has often used its prerogative of selecting one of the three top candidates who score highest on a competitive examination to discriminate against Black Americans. It is claimed that even when a Black man scored highest on objective tests, the Civil Service passed over him for "qualitative reasons." It is in this context that the apprehension over allowing King's fate to be left in the hands of the Civil Service must be viewed.

The union maintained its picket lines at Harvard Yards throughout the weekend, and a limited strike began on August 16, 1969. Conversations continued on August 17 between Burks and Worwood on possible methods of resolving the dispute. They agreed by telephone on a ten-day suspension for King. However, that agreement was abrogated that evening as a result of a televised statement by Nick Jablonski, president of Local 100, in which he denounced Ben Stefanski and demanded his removal from office. It is significant that Worwood, the director of the District Council, was totally unaware of the fact that the president of the local was to be interviewed and that his statements were to be publicly aired. This episode is the first major evidence of the leadership and communications difficulties which became pervasive factors in the ensuing period of the strike and mediation. Burks and Worwood discussed the situation again following the televised interview with Jablonski. Burks, however, returned to the City's initial position that King would be dismissed from public service.

Although the pickets continued throughout the week, efforts were being made to settle the basic problems. However, these efforts were complicated by a series of events and crises which forced each side into a harder line toward the other. For example, policemen from Newburgh Heights were charged by union workers and officials with "invading Harvard Yards like the Gestapo" on August 18 and with acts deliberately designed to provoke the union people into incidents which would result in mass arrests. On the same day the City charged that union representatives were harassing supervisory personnel at Harvard Yards. Parenthetically, supervisory personnel are viewed as management personnel by the City and must remain on the job in situations of this sort. The City had taken deliberate steps to remove supervisors from union jurisdiction.[4] This was viewed by the union as designed to weaken its strength, but by the City as a way to differentiate between the management level and the employee level of responsibility.

The City charged the union with additional acts of threats and intimidation of city employees as a result of incidents which occurred at various buildings and plants where members of Local 100 worked. It was claimed that these incidents were intended to coerce reluctant members to walk out or to refuse to cross the picket line, either at the Gilman Building or at the Southerly and Westerly Sewage Plants. The City claimed that Black Nationalists were used to force all but two employees to leave the Gilman Building. This charge is denied by Harlell Jones, leader of the Afro-Set, a Black Nationalist group, and was denied to Burks in his office during the dispute. However, it can be safely assumed that it was because of the reported violence and threats of physical abuse of workers who wished to cross the picket lines that, on August 19, Clarence King was arrested, and the mayor appeared on the three city television networks to denounce the violence and intimidation allegedly perpetrated by members of Local 100 with outside assistance. King was charged with violating the State Riot Control Act, a matter which will be discussed later in this report.

On the day of King's arrest, he, Kenneth Worwood, Nick Jablonski, and Anthony Stalteri went to City Hall for the hearing with the Civil Service referee, Mary Hutchings. They claim that the site of the meeting was changed without their knowledge, and, consequently, they were 25 minutes late in getting to it. In that interim, Miss Hutchings had entered a plea of "not guilty" in King's behalf. The six witnesses for the City who were present included Mr. Minder, Chandler Taylor (a truck driver), Charles Coulter (the supervisor), William Podloger (a water serviceman), William McKnight (chief counsel for the City), and Jay Loeb and William Moore (city attorneys.)

The use of the referee system is to avoid many of the time-consuming features involved in disciplinary actions against City employees. The primary responsibility of the referee is to collect facts and to refer these facts to the commissioner. The facts in this case were never

4. See the letter from T. E. Stanton in Appendix J.

actually heard by the referee because of three postponements of the hearing and because a settlement was reached before the last date established for the preliminary hearing. On the first date, Worwood was not permitted to represent King at the hearing on the ground that he was not a lawyer. When he and other union associates walked out of the meeting, King was arrested. Later that day, Jablonski and Stalteri were also arrested on the charge of violating the State Riot Control Act.

Arresting union officials on State Riot Control Act charges has been questioned by many. It is assumed that the City's prime motivation was to end the stoppage by silencing its leadership. It is argued by some that, since this act was enacted over strong labor reservations and objections and with the declaration that it would never be used against labor, the City, in using it, was running the risk of alienating labor. This could have been particularly deleterious to the mayor since he was seeking renomination within six weeks. On the other hand, had the city resorted to an injunction, it might have escalated the conflict further. Also some claim that it would have validated certain rights for the union that it was inadvisable to legitimize. The authority of the City to enter into a contractual relationship with organized labor and to grant exclusive rights to a particular union was at issue. Granting the rights to a specific union as in the Memorandum of Agreement of 1968 was viewed by some members of the city's legal department as potentially vitiating the Civil Service and denying the proposition that a person is not required to be a member of a union in order to be hired and advanced in his job. It was argued that Cleveland's city charter protects the employment rights of every citizen and that these cannot be abridged by a mayor's signature. Therefore, resorting to the State Riot Control Act was an act of expediency designed to abate the efforts of the union to spread the work stoppage into an all-out strike against the City without going into court to demand enforcement of a contract the legality of which could be questioned.

Another significant meeting involved Eugene Burns, executive administrator for the county commissioners. How this meeting occurred is clouded in contradiction. Worwood maintains that he was approached by Eugene Burns at Harvard Yards in the early evening of August 19, and the two of them decided to go someplace for a drink to talk over the situation. According to this version, they went to a bar about two blocks from the Yards for that purpose. Burns is reported to have said that he was to play a major role in the mayor's forthcoming campaign for nomination and reelection and that it was in everyone's best interest to settle the situation as expeditiously as possible. Worwood stated that the union would settle for a five-day suspension of Clarence King. Burns agreed to this and stated that he would set up a meeting at City Hall for 9:00 the same evening. The City claims that Worwood called Burns on August 20 in an effort to set up such a meeting and that a meeting of no longer than three minutes took place at 3:00 P.M. that same day. Worwood reports that the meeting involved himself, Burns, and Sidney Spector, another political advisor close to Major Stokes. Spector stated, to the chagrin of all, that his hands were tied and that he could not alter decisions previously made by Burks and Stefanski. Burns replied that he had been deceived; the rug had been pulled from under him. Consequently, there was no change in the situation.

FORCES AT WORK IN THE DISPUTE

The pattern of forces at work was more complex than in the ordinary labor dispute. In all labor-management conflict settlements, the goals of management and those of the union must be accommodated, and, often, the interests of other unions must be taken into account as well. There are, on occasion, personality clashes which must be side-stepped or resolved. All these familiar ingredients were present in the Local 100-City of Cleveland confrontation. In addition, however, there were critical political objectives to be considered in this dispute, involving the reelection campaign of the first Black mayor of a major American city; this, in turn, brought the goals of the Black community into the picture. Furthermore, the presence of Black and white on both sides of the bargaining table added a racial component to the situation.

The goals of management in the dispute were relatively clear-cut. Discipline had to be established in the operation of the city water facilities in order to assure efficient, orderly operation. The supervisors had to be recognized by the workers as being in control. It had to be clear who was boss. There is some indication that the new management team, and specifically Stefanski, threatened to quit if the city administration did not hold firm and back them up. Stokes could ill afford the loss of his Polish utilities director just before a primary election. To the management people, it was a test of will, for which they had been prepared psychologically by the abrasive relations of the past year. The particular issue, King's discharge, was important only as a symbol, just as King himself was a symbol of the intransigence of the union and its refusal to recognize management's right to govern. Although Duvin, the City's spokesman in negotiations, agreed with those who felt the issue had been misunderstood at the outset, he considered it important to establish the integrity of the union no-strike clause and, in this sense, also supported the disciplinary goals of the City's managers.

The union took the position that the problem with Clarence King was only symptomatic of broader concerns such as developing some sort of formal structure which would prevent the City from "running rampant over its employees." Obtaining more specific commitments from the City that the grievances of the union would indeed be acted upon quickly and judiciously was also of primary concern.

Another crucial issue involved the "militancy of the union" and the symbolic meaning of "manhood" for a union whose constituency at the Water Works was 85 percent Black. The crux of this issue lay in the timing. Local 100 began its militancy in 1966, which significantly was the same time that the "new militancy in the Black Revolution" began. This militancy is expressed by such slogans as "Black Power" and "Black is Beautiful." Local 100, it can be hypothesized, was caught up in the new mood among Black people, as distinguished from hyphenated Negro-Americans, to establish their identity and a self-realization of manhood. The uncompromising stance of the City and its specific attack on Clarence King, a man regarded as a fighter for the rights of his men, were conceptualized in terms of the white power structure's persistence in suffocating any Black man who dared buck the system. King's followers regarded the City's actions as intolerable and untenable.

There is also some support for the assertion that the union sought to utilize not only the more up-to-date management policies of the new administration but also the understanding and sympathy of a

Black mayor for an organized group of Black laborers who were attempting to "make it" in a racist society. Local 100 made notable gains in the three-year period, 1966-69, in terms of improved wage scales for its members who fell into an extremely large number of minutely distinguished job classifications. Considerable gains had been made in working hours, overtime pay, holidays, and general working conditions. Nevertheless, the union's goal of full respect for the dignity of its members, as intangible and elusive a quality as that may be, was not yet realized, although still considered attainable. As in social movements generally, the closer the proponents of change get to their articulated goals, the more impatient they become, the more persistent they become, and the more likely to expand the original goals into increasingly diffuse objectives. This is based on the premise that the original goals may have been too limited, and the possibility of attaining them may have been underestimated.

As members of the Black community of Cleveland, many union members had raised their hopes and the level of their expectations with the election of a Black man as Mayor. They felt that it was their near-unanimous support which elected him; therefore, the mayor was politically and morally obligated to reciprocate by maximizing benefits for Black people while he was in the position of leadership. In spite of what had been accomplished toward this end, some segments of the Black people concluded that what had been done was tantamount to tokenism. They claimed much more could be done for Black people than attempting to placate a dissident group or "keeping the lid on in a potentially explosive city" while the white power structure was allowed a continued monopoly on lucrative city contracts, political payoffs, and rich investments. In the view of this group, the mayor should not permit himself to be co-opted by the ruling white power structure but should offer Blacks the biggest "piece of the action." For them, impartiality was not enough.

The other 13 unions dealing with the City, particularly the Teamsters and the Laborers, had different goals. In the first year of their formal contracts with the City, their expressed goals were to protect the integrity of their agreements and not to submit their membership to financial hardship by walking out in sympathy. However, it has been claimed that some of these unions had not wanted contracts in the first place since formal agreements restricted their freedom to deal politically. Their real goal was to break Local 100 to end the threat to their jurisdiction from this industrial union operating in the midst of a group of craft bailiwicks. With Local 100 defeated, it would be possible to split up the membership among the old-line unions and dispose of a serious rival, which in recent months had conducted successful raids by offering greater benefits in insurance coverage, grievance settlements, militancy, and the like. Further, these other unions, with their predominantly Black memberships, had to avoid the development of racial solidarity with Local 100 if the jurisdictional competition was to be dealt with.

On the other hand, the goals of the AFL-CIO were to get the strike settled without upsetting the generally good relations between the central labor body and the city administration. Also, the ties of the AFL-CIO to Democratic Party politics spurred the leadership to avoid any outcome which would produce a Republican city administration in the pending elections. A further problem was the danger of an upset in the endorsement procedures of the AFL-CIO. Failure of the council rank and file to go along with formal support of the mayor for reelection would have surfaced a deepseated split among the members, at least some of whom were Wallaceites. Such a public revelation of differences would have embarrassed the Federation by exposing this division, weakening its political clout.

Personality Factors

The negotiations and the mediation process can be better understood by shedding some light on the prime role that personality played. Early in the process, it became apparent that this factor was critical since clashes between antagonists militated against immediate settlement.

There is no unequivocal and uniform perception of the mayor cutting across political lines, except that he is highly regarded for his personal charisma and for his persuasive powers, with the added reputation for being a tough negotiator who is unlikely to bend when he feels that his cause is right and just.

Clarence King is the personification of the "John Henry" type, standing more than six feet tall, a muscular man in a solidly constructed frame. He is volatile, prone to intersperse his conversation with flavored and emotionally packed four, five, and polysyllabic expletives, and at the same time, compassionately protective of the men under his supervision. He is a street fighter and well versed in the dynamics of brinkmanship in negotiation. He rarely sits still in meetings but effectively employs the technique of strutting about as if in complete confidence of himself and of the position he is expounding. He is argumentative, boisterous, and dominates the situation he is in by brute force. It should also be pointed out that, although he appears to be genuinely committed to gains for union members, another motive may be his recognition that this success can be used to strengthen and solidify his own power base within the union structure. But, he is honest and claims to be above payoffs. He barks and boasts that it is he who has brought in more union members than anyone else, which may be the source of the raiding charges against him.

Kenneth Worwood is mild-mannered, soft-spoken, and polite. Rather than asserting his power and the authority incumbent in his position as the director of the District Council, he seeks to reason and persuade.

Nick Jablonski is almost universally regarded as an opportunist, who viewed this situation as a means of undercutting the utilities director, Ben Stefanski, and of entrenching himself with the mayor's political opponents. It is claimed that he campaigned actively on the West side of Cleveland for the Republican candidate for mayor, Ralph Perk, and provided Perk data from the utilities director's office. This did not put him in good standing with the union, and he resigned from the presidency of Local 100 four months after the settlement was reached, ostensibly to take a better position elsewhere.

Ben Stefanski, the director of utilities, is regarded as youthful, handsome, and well-meaning, but still green in human-relations techniques. He is politically important to the mayor as a link with the Polish community. To Stefanski, King's refusal to comply and play the subservient role was unforgivable because it threatened his newly acquired managerial authority. In some opinions, he became so angered as to carry out a personal vendetta against King. In any event he was excluded from all but the earliest negotiations.

Walter Burks is perceived as a dedicated, hardworking, and "fiercely-loyal-to-the-mayor type" but naive about union activities inasmuch as he had neither experience nor formal training in the labor-management field. He had worked in City Hall for approximately 20 years but was appointed director of personnel only a few months before the 1969 strike.

Robert Duvin is a bright, articulate attorney who seemed caught in an ethic of loyalty to his client, the City, and cognitive of certain rights which should be granted to the union under the terms of the Agreement of 1968. At the same time, he appears to have been insensitive to some of the nuances of race relations and to the importance of "pride and manhood" among the new breed of Black Americans.

Further Racial Issues

In further discussing the racial component and its impact on the forces at work in the dispute, it is important to distinguish between attitudinal and institutional racism and race differences as situational inputs. Attitudinal racism can be defined as a socially stereotyped imputation of inferiority or superiority to people on the basis of externally visible biological characteristics; institutional racism as the crystallization of these attitudes into social structures and formal institutions. In these terms, one can discern manifestations of racist attitudes on the part of all parties to the dispute and can attribute the consistent miscalculations of the chief protagonists as to the actions of the others to these attitudes. Institutionalized racism, on the other hand, characterized large areas of the social context of the controversy.

The management side, as represented by Stefanski, Duvin, Minder, Bednar (Stefanski's assistant), and Spector (the mayor's assistant), rejected racism on the surface, and, indeed, all of these men had accepted employment under a Black mayor and claimed they admired him. On the other hand, these officials undoubtedly underestimated lower-class Blacks, tending to view them as hotheaded, emotional, easily led, lacking in good sense, and the like. At least, Clarence King was frequently described in pejorative terms, i.e., big, black, brutish, prepsychotic, intransigent, etc. While such stereotypes might also be used to describe workers in general, certain slips in language during the interviews, particularly of the top officials, suggested a profound lack of respect and depersonalizing of the Blacks.

The underrating of their antagonists was one reason why management made the error of thinking that King and his following would not strike over the suspension and that King could be gotten rid of with impunity. An additional variable was the sensitivity of the mayor, in the context of widespread overt and covert institutional racism, to pressure by whites. Stokes is said to have reacted bitterly to expectable union threats as if they were racist-inspired rather than part of a labor conflict strategy.

Leadership of the other unions shared the management's attitudes, at least with respect to viewing their Black membership as a group to be manipulated and controlled rather than consulted to an even greater degree than they did their white membership. As for the AFL-CIO leadership, leaving aside their own views, they were faced with the pockets of racism and of Wallace support among their white membership. They were aware that during the 1968 election, large blocks of Cleveland racist votes could only have come from their white constituencies. This was a threat to the political plans of the AFL-CIO with respect to the city election campaign. Thus, racism, institutionalized in the political realm, affected the deliberations and maneuvering of the AFL-CIO leadership.

Racism on the Local 100 side played a somewhat more subtle role. It is difficult to assess the extent to which white office-worker members of the Local resisted support of the stoppage on racial grounds because the color line was confounded with the manual/non-manual division in the Local and with antagonism toward the Water Department workers for their militancy. On the other hand, King and his group of supporters miscalculated the extent to which racial solidarity would move the mayor to settle in favor of the union, despite the other forces he had to contend with in the situation. Also, King consistently interpreted various stages in the development of the dispute in terms of his own dignity as a Black man, rather than in terms of labor-management give and take, and, in this respect, was reacting to racist beliefs and behavior in his environment.

Both sides in the dispute had to take racial differences into account in planning their tactics because of the constant presence of institutionalized racism. Thus, race differences affected the planning of Local 100, other segments of the labor movement, and the city administration. Local 100 had to swing the white 50 percent of its membership into backing its Black 50 percent by stressing the need to support union leadership under fire, even though many recognized that the stoppage was a violation of the newly-made contract, and the confrontation had escalated into an unnecessary and essentially dangerous test of strength. Other unions having contracts with the City had to stress the sanctity of their agreements in order to control their restive Black memberships. The AFL-CIO Council had to endorse an awkward strike in order not to give ammunition to certain affiliates who opposed support of a Black mayor and were ready to charge the AFL-CIO with a sellout. The city administration, keenly aware of the closeness of the coming municipal election, needed more than the support of the Black community; it also needed the endorsement of labor and votes from a segment of the various ethnic communities in order to squeeze out a victory—all this in the framework of a cry for "law and order." Race differences were a major input in that the city managers directly involved in the dispute were the mayor's chief political link to the ethnic neighborhoods, with the general labor side only a weak link to these areas. The specific union involved was, however, a potentially powerful influence on the mayor's major Black base. It was a situation where the city administration could not afford to have either side win, but also could not afford to have either side lose.

THE MEDIATION

In the late afternoon of August 20, management and union representatives realized the necessity of third-party intervention in order to reach an acceptable solution to the strike. Willoughby Abner of the National Center for Dispute Settlement of the American Arbitration Association was brought in as the mediator. Mr. Abner is a Black man and was acceptable to both sides largely because of his reputation for objectivity and fairness in the mediation process and especially acceptable to the union because he had a reputation for past militancy.

Both sides agreed that there would be no taking of notes during the mediation sessions other than an informal transmission of personal notes across the table. Each side presented its points of view

and its proposals to which the opposing side responded and presented counterproposals.

The first meeting with Abner was held on Thursday, August 21.
The City presented a proposal that King be suspended for 30 days
and be reassigned to another location for the balance of 1969. At the
end of that period of time, King would return to Harvard Yards.
This proposal, although it involved a retreat from firing King, was
rejected by the union.

The union made a counter proposal that King be suspended for a
period of 90 days on paper but only two weeks in actuality. The
union also proposed that King be placed on probation for the remaining days of the suspension.

During this first meeting, the City was represented by Robert
Duvin, Walter Burks, Philip Curd, and Donald Insul; the latter two
are associates of Duvin's law firm. The union was represented by
Worwood, Petite, Stalteri, King, and Robert Brindza, regional director of AFSCME.

This meeting lasted for approximately 11 hours without any sign
of alteration in what appeared to be irreconcilable positions on each
side. At one point in the meeting, Duvin made a statement to the
effect that King should learn to control his tongue. This precipitated
an outburst from King in which Duvin was accused of attacking his
manhood, and King expressed his determination to return to Harvard Yards to continue business as usual even if the City dared to fire
him. The Black mediator saw the compelling urgency of forcing both
sides to understand the meaning of such an outburst—the misinter-
pretation of Duvin's remarks, which he viewed as concerning the
union's response to the Agreement, and the insensitivity of Duvin
to the connotations of these remarks for a Black person. In separate
caucuses with the concerned parties, Abner was effective in creating
this understanding and enabled King to grasp the significance of
his behavior at Harvard Yards during the preceding week in weakening the integrity of the union contract. Duvin made another tacti-
cal error by suggesting that Local 100 not put King on the payroll
during the period of his suspension. This was taken as further evidence that the City was seeking to destroy King.

The second meeting occurred on August 22, and lasted some 12
hours, with each side holding firmly to its position. That night, the

union held a large membership meeting and voted to back the Water Works stoppage by calling a strike of the entire Local. The third mediation session lasted some ten hours—from 1:00 P.M. to 11:00 P.M. on August 23. Robert Duvin, chief negotiator for the City, had left town for other business, and the City was represented by Walter Burks. Since the City had already backed away from the position of firing King in its first proposal, which had been rejected by the union, the mediator's major effort here was directed toward creating a situation in which the focus of the negotiations would be exclusively on the number of days that King would be suspended. To accomplish this, it would be necessary for the City to withdraw its demand that King be transferred from Harvard Yards. The question of the transfer had now become important to the union. Neither question was resolved on Saturday, and the mediator agreed to remain in Cleveland through Sunday, August 24.

The mediator met with representatives of the city administration for a two-hour period on Sunday, August 24, before departing for Washington. Abner's position was that various incidents by representatives of the administration had undercut and vitiated the effectiveness of the City's negotiators. One way of restoring confidence in the authority and power of the City's negotiators was to permit them to place the issue of a 90-day suspension on the table as a *bargaining* position. A framework for resolution of the conflict could then be provided.

Within one hour after the mediator left Cleveland, the Executive Committee of Local 100 met. In a news conference at 9:00 P.M., the union issued an ultimatum that if the dispute was not settled by Monday, August 25, the City would face an officially sanctioned strike by 8:00 A.M. on Tuesday, August 26. This was an implementation of the formal strike vote of the Local the previous Friday night.

It should be pointed out here that the support for the strike among the 1,300 members of Local 100 was not unanimous. The lack of unanimity is evidenced by the number of persons who crossed the picket lines each day. This number varied between two hundred and four hundred although more stayed out after the stoppage became an official strike. There were those people who objected to tremendous personal financial losses over what to them was a power play by Clarence King. There were those who felt that King was forcing the rank and file to pay for his "grandstanding" while he, in all likelihood, would not suffer financially. Some union members resented not being consulted before the initial work stoppage occurred, and others were weary of the wildcat strikes which had been called by Local 100 during the preceding year. Nevertheless, the strike seemed to have had the support of at least three-quarters of the union members and of the members of the Executive Committee. Some members of the Executive Committee felt that the union had got itself into a bind and that outward solidarity was imperative in order to achieve success.

The fourth meeting of the mediator with the representatives of the union and of the City was continued for a nine-hour period beginning at 4:30 P.M. on August 25 and ending at 1:35 A.M. on August 26. The City restated its offer of August 23 of a 90-day suspension, and the union again rejected it. The union presented the same counter proposal which had been presented in the previous meeting: a two-week suspension, beginning on the day of the dispute. If this had been accepted, King would have had three days remaining under suspension. The City rejected the offer. At this point, the City still felt that it had backed the union into a corner and that it could possibly win the case. At the same time, some members of the City's negotiating team realized that a mistake had been made in charging King with insubordination and with other charges that could not be supported by concrete evidence. The mediator sensed that the impasse could only be broken if the mayor met with the international president of the union, Jerry Wurf.

While negotiations were in progress, both sides were attempting to get general labor support in the city. Local 100 officers went to the top leadership of the AFL-CIO to request formal endorsement for the strike after it had officially been called by the local membership meeting. They were informed that the AFL-CIO Executive Board and the larger AFL-CIO Delegate Council endorsed a strike only if it was sanctioned by the parent international union of the local involved. Furthermore, it was the policy of the Board *not* to ask the members of nonstriking unions to respect picket lines of striking unions at a common work location since this could mean hardship for large numbers of uninvolved workers. However, it was the international unions which decided how their locals should respond to picket lines. Often, workers were permitted to cross the lines but urged to refuse to do the work of strikers. Thus according to the AFL-CIO it could not press the other unions to aid the Local 100 strikers by also going out on strike. Apparently, the AFL-CIO officials contacted Jerry Wurf, president of the AFSCME international and, learning that the strike was sanctioned, adopted an Executive Board motion to support the strikers by a majority but not a unanimous vote.

In the meantime, the administration was seeking returns for past and potential favors from the other unions doing business with the City. When it became clear that the AFL-CIO would endorse the strike, it was not at all obvious what the other city unions would do. Already the Teamsters at the Water Works itself had refused to cross the picket lines on the grounds that the situation was too hot, and they might get hurt. Therefore the City's labor relations attorney and the personnel director called a meeting of the business agents of the other 13 unions. In the context of some unions' fears of raiding by Local 100 and their desire to get rid of the pocket of militancy which was upsetting the applecart with their own members, the city representatives were able to elicit pledges that the unions would support the City in the dispute and not honor the picket lines. The rhetoric used to support this position was the need to maintain the sanctity of the union contract and its no-strike clause.[5] The City interpreted this action as loyalty to the mayor. It could be more accurately described, at least with reference to some unions, as preferring to destroy a union rival to getting rid of a Black mayor.

During the second and last week of the stoppage, the AFL-CIO was also putting pressure on both the City and the union, behind the scenes. The mayor was being reminded of the political liability of an antilabor stand and that King's suspension was not worth it, while Local 100 and King were being told that if they failed to accept a compromise agreement, the AFL-CIO could not implement its support further. It was in the context of all these cross-pressures that the final settlement was made.

The local-wide strike began officially at 8:00 A.M. on Tuesday,

5. See the letter from Walter Burks in Appendix J for an example of this position.

August 26, when more than 1000 members of Local 100 remained
off their jobs and/or participated in the picket lines where they
worked throughout the city. Burks ordered that they be "marked
A.W.O.L." This expansion of the strike exacerbated an already
tense situation between the union and the City. It was evidence of
the weak leadership in the union inasmuch as the District Council's
director could not persuade the Local to desist in its intent to broad-
en the base of the strike. In effect the strike was expanded without
the approval of the International's president, according to one
source. A further complication was the mediator's threat to discontinue the sessions if no agreement was reached quickly and if the
union expanded the strike. This was a ploy which backfired inasmuch as both the union and the City were psychologically prepared
to continue the conflict, if necessary.

The mediator met with the mayor on the day the strike expanded
and gave him his assessment of the situation. Although some city
officials had recommended against a meeting between the mayor and
the international president of AFSCME, Abner insisted just as strongly that such a meeting was the only recourse remaining. The City
officials thought that the mayor should not be involved for political
reasons and also that it would endanger the future effectiveness of
the City's negotiators if the mayor went over their heads. However,
Duvin realized the bind the City was in and urged a top-level meeting under appropriate conditions. In the end, Abner was instrumental in persuading the mayor to participate in a private session
with Wurf on the grounds that the mayor's personal presence was
needed and that Wurf was essential to back up the union leadership
in enforcing any agreement reached in the mediation process. In
short, for a variety of reasons, a meeting at the highest decision-
making level was vital if a workable solution to the strike and related issues was to be obtained.

The mediator also drew up the discussion agenda for the meeting
between the mayor and Jerry Wurf. The proposals for discussion
called for the union to move from its insistence on a two-week suspension for King to a 30-day suspension. It also called for the City
to retrench from a 90-day to a 60-day suspension, and, if no agreement was reached, an arbitrator would decide between the alternatives.

The secret meeting between the mayor and Jerry Wurf was a stormy and lengthy one, held in Willoughby Abner's hotel room on the night of August 27. Both men possessed powerful egos, and each was adamant in his position. The Mayor was accompanied by Robert Duvin, and Wurf by an assistant from outside Cleveland.

After several hours an agreement was reached which consisted of the following essential items:

1. King was to be suspended for 30 days, retroactive to the first day of the work stoppage.

2. The City withdrew its demands that King be transferred to another plant.

3. The union guaranteed that no further work stoppages would occur for the duration of the Agreement period[6] (essentially a commitment to honor the no-strike clause in the Agreement).

4. If a work stoppage occurred, the District Council would be placed in a trusteeship, the district director would be replaced, and, possibly, the entire staff would be dismissed.

5. Wurf agreed to make a public statement on television to put the force of the International behind the no-strike pledge and to save face for the mayor who had denounced wildcat strikes as intolerable and disruptive to the City.

On Friday, August 29, some 900 members of Local 100 met and ratified the terms of the settlement. During this meeting King rose to express his support of the terms and accused the rank and file of playing into the hands of the City by crossing the picket lines or by not remaining on the picket lines. Nevertheless, his expression of support was sufficiently persuasive to permit ratification, and the strike was officially settled.

ELEMENTS LEADING TO A SOLUTION

Several factors account for the settlement which was reached at that time: of crucial importance was the role played by the Black mediator. It is generally agreed that he was particularly effective in this complex situation which pitted a predominantly Black union, fighting for the dignity of its Black chief steward, against an administration headed by a Black mayor. Quite early in the mediation

6. See the Agreement in Appendix J.

process, the value of the Black mediator became apparent. It is highly doubtful that anyone other than an effective Black mediator would have been able to deal with the "dignity-manhood issue" symbolized by King's position. There is reason to believe that he won the respect of the mayor by his ability to stick with the issues and because of the commonality of color.

Of equal significance was the political factor. The City was confronted with a mayoralty primary within six weeks after the inception of the work stoppage. Failure to settle the strike loomed large as a viable campaign issue which could have been exploited by the mayor's opponent. The continued escalation of the strike could have been politically disastrous for the mayor.

The mayor and his staff saw the political necessity of maintaining the support of organized labor in this election. Their concern was not so much for the financial support of labor as for the endorsement of labor for the mayor's reelection. A prolonged strike could have alienated labor from the city administration.

Another political factor was the danger of erosion of support from the Black electorate. Although the degree of support in the Black community for King and the union could not be accurately measured, the mayor could not afford the risk of gambling with the emotions of a group which had given him almost 100-percent support in the previous election. A refusal to settle the dispute could have raised alarms of co-optation and a sellout to the white power structure which could have triggered anti-Stokes sentiment among the highly vocal Black Nationalist segment of the Black community. The reality of this problem had been vividly portrayed in the City's involvement in another conflict, between the McDonald restaurant chain and 14 organizations comprising a Black Unity Group. In short, the mayor could not gamble on a low Black turnout in the elections.

The union was ready to settle the strike primarily because it would have been bankrupt had the strike continued for many additional days. From the Local's perspective, finding a quick solution was an economic necessity. Many union people, officials and rank and file, did not wish to see the mayor injured politically by a prolonged strike. There was also the possibility that rank-and-file support was diminishing significantly and rapidly. The International wanted to extricate itself from a "sticky issue," involving abrogation of a newly signed contract.

SUBSEQUENT EVENTS

Local 100's relations with the City have not been altogether smooth since the end of the stoppage. The utilities director feels that the situation is now under control and that King has learned his limitations. The chief engineer at the Water Works shows a certain respect for King as a worthy adversary with whom he can get along. However, the antagonisms are not entirely dead. King received a large amount of overtime during the winter because of an arrangement for having a steward on duty at all times, and this was leaked to the newspapers and received some publicity. Since it occurred shortly after the director had ordered the elimination of all overtime as an economy measure, there was apparently some resentment among other Water Works employees. On at least one occasion there was a brief stoppage which resulted in a few days suspension for King, which he accepted without protest. There is evidence that the City is building a written record on King's "misdeeds" on the job.

In other city departments where Local 100 has members, there have been stoppages, brief sitdowns, delegations to City Hall and other actions. The Local's Executive Board has had some internal disputes on the right way to handle these events, and there has even been some talk of splitting the Water Works off as a special subdivision of the local. In the meantime, it is not certain whether the Local has grown stronger or weaker since the stoppage. The City claims that several hundred members have dropped out while the union claims it has gained hundreds of new members. Negotiations for a new contract are scheduled to begin in a few weeks from the time of this writing, and the possibility of continued conflict is very real.

CONCLUSIONS

This paper has attempted to analyze some of the crucial issues connected with a strike of Local 100 of the AFSCME, which occurred during the last two weeks of August, 1969, in Cleveland. Specific attention was devoted to the significance of race as a factor at critical stages in the strike and negotiations for its settlement, including the utilization of a Black mediator. The racial issue has been treated in relation to cross-pressures from economic interests, political implications, and general ethnic solidarity.

The following conclusions are drawn from this investigation:

1. In a study of this sort, it is not fruitful to focus only on the specific period during which the strike occurred if one is serious about understanding the dynamics of social change. Such a focus would be entirely too parsimonious and of limited utility in grasping the diverse perspectives which are likely to be revealed during the strike and to influence the negotiating process. This position is embodied in the earlier discussion of the patterns of union-management relationships developed over a long period of time.

2. Race and racism are crucial variables to be considered in labor disputes involving different racial groups regardless of whether these groups are exclusively management or labor or internal to each. The Cleveland situation is sufficiently complex that analytical distinctions must be made between levels of racism and the consequent impact of racial differences. In conceptualizing racism in the terms expressed in this paper, it is clear that the representatives of management rejected "white racism," at least on the surface. It is also clear from the behavior of management, as evidenced in slips of the tongue when dealing with lower-class Black union members, that the internalization of racist notions may be so complete as to govern subconscious dimensions of behavior. Inadvertently, racist attitudes surface in periods of crisis and Black-white confrontation and exacerbate existing personality incompatibilities. It is the inability to handle racist notions at the cognitive level and to behave according to new definitions of the situation that confounds efforts to mediate disputes involving diverse racial groups.

3. Successful mediation is considerably more difficult to achieve when the race issue is complicated by the pressures of political factors and economic uncertainties. The attainment of a settlement was a function of the ability to deal effectively with these complex issues. For example, political considerations included the relationship between the mayor and labor, the Black community, the white ethnics, the white liberals, and the white power structure. Each of these elements had to emerge unscarred from the efforts to solve the dispute.

It was also politically imperative for the mayor to reestablish the authority of the city administration over its employees and to extract from the Local a further commitment to respect the integrity of the Agreement signed in 1968.

4. A Black mediator can be of inestimable value in mediating racial disputes; however, this seems to be a function of the convergence of the man's ability, personalities involved, and the forces of social change which provide the context in which the dispute occurs. It has been suggested in this study that the success of the Black mediator in the Cleveland case should be viewed in the context of the interplay of all such forces. In addition to this generalization, it can be stated with some degree of specificity that his sensitivity to the weaknesses in the communications system between the opposing forces as well as within each of the antagonistic groups and his awareness of the power struggles within these groups helped to establish a framework for successful mediation at the highest levels.

5. It should be obvious that the fact that both management and labor are Black does not preclude the emergence of the usual labor-management conflicts. Nor does such a condition assure expeditious solutions to these conflicts. The management-labor roles may or may not be altered by color; in fact, the issues may become more complex by the introduction of color as a variable in addition to economic factors. Indeed, at certain stages in a dispute, the economic variables may become paramount, superseding the significance of race. It is suggested that this outcome will be more likely when private industry rather than a government entity is involved as the management side because of the lesser salience of race differences in a less political context.

April 1970

APPENDIX A

Bibliography to Part 2

"Answer to Riots—The Rochester Plan," *U.S. News and World Report,* August 4, 1969.

Berube, Maurice B., and Marilyn Gittell. *Confrontation at Ocean Hill-Brownsville.* New York: Frederick A. Praeger: Publishers, 1969.

Bird, Robert S. *Ten Negroes.* New York: *New York Herald Tribune,* 1963.

Boggs, James. "The Myth and Irrationality of Black Capitalism." New York: Interreligious Foundation for Community Organization, 1969 (mimeographed).

Booker, Simeon. "What Nixon Plans for Blacks: None Offered Cabinet Posts," *Jet,* December 26, 1968.

Boulding, Kenneth E. *Conflict and Defense: A General Theory.* New York: Harper and Row, 1962, Chapter 15.

Bradley, Valery Jo. "Integrationist Superintendent Fired Despite 'Opposition,'" *Jet,* July 10, 1969.

Brager, George A. and Jorrin. "Bargaining: A Method in Community Change," *Social Work,* XIV:4 (October, 1969), 73-83.

Brown, Judith. "Toward a Female Liberation Movement, Part II." Gainesville, Fla.: SSOC/SDS Chapter, 1969 (mimeographed).

Carmichael, Stokely. "What We Want," *New York Review of Books,* III:5 (September 22, 1969).

Campbell, Leslie. "The Difference," *Negro Teachers Forum,* I (December, 1966).

Chalmers, W. Ellison. *Racial Negotiations—A Project Statement.* Ann Arbor: Institute of Labor and Industrial Relations, 1968.

————. *Racial Negotiations Project: Preliminary Report to the Ford Foundation.* Ann Arbor: Institute for Labor and Industrial Relations, The University of Michigan-Wayne State University, 1969.

———— and Gerald W. Cormick. "Collective Bargaining in Racial Disputes?" *Issues in Industrial Society,* I:3 (1970), 8-16.

"Coming Together, Texas Style," *Time,* March 7, 1969, p. 67.

"Confrontation and Response." New York: High School Principals Association, 1969 (mimeographed).

Cooper, Ralph (narrator of recording). *The March on Washington: A Chronological History of Negro Contributions.*

Coser, Lewis. *The Functions of Social Conflict.* New York: The Free Press of Glencoe, 1956.

Coulson, Robert. *How to Stay Out of Court.* New York: Crown Publishers, Inc., 1968.

Cruse, Harold. *Rebellion and Revolution.* New York: William Morrow and Co., Inc., 1969.

"Discussion Guide for Citizens' School Seminars, Nov. 10-21, 1969," Dayton: Dayton Public Schools, 1969.

"Draft Model Contract to be Negotiated with Schools and Local School Boards." New York: New Coalition, 1969 (mimeographed).

Edwards, E. Babette. "The Black Professional—Judas in the Living Room?," *Kweli,* June, 1969, pp. 1-2.

Fantini, Mario D. "Participation, Decentralization, Community Control, and Quality Education," *Teachers College Record,* LXXI (September, 1969).

Farber, Jerry. "Students as Nigger," *Renewal,* IX:5 (May, 1969).

Featherstone, Joseph. "The Albany Stranglers: Choking off Community Schools," *New Republic,* July 19, 1969.

"Flaring Again: Racial Violence," *U.S. News and World Report,* August 4, 1969.

Forman, James. "The Black Manifesto." New York: Interreligious Foundation for Community Organization, 1969 (mimeographed).

Gittell, Marilyn. *Participants and Participation: A Study of School Policy in New York City.* New York: Frederick A. Praeger: Publishers, 1967.

————, and Alan G. Hevesi. *The Politics of Urban Education.* New York: Frederick A. Praeger: Publishers, 1969.

Haddad, William F. "The Establishment," *Manhattan Tribune,* May 3, 1969, p. 13.

Halisi, Clyde, and James Mtume. *The Quotable Karenga.* Los Angeles: U.S. Organization, 1967.

Handlin, Oscar. *The Newcomers: Negroes and Puerto Ricans in a Changing Society.* Garden City, N.Y.: Doubleday and Co., 1959.

Hash, Howard. "Collective Bargaining In Voluntary Agencies," *Social Casework,* L:4 (April, 1969).

Havrilesky, Catherine. "Re-tooling of the Obsolete White Liberal." New York: Afram Associates, Inc., 1968 (mimeographed).

———— and Preston Wilcox. "A Selected Bibliography on White Institutional Racism." New York: Afram Associates, Inc., 1969 (mimeographed).

Hentoff, Nat. *Our Children Are Dying*. New York: Viking Press, 1966.

Kheel, Theodore W. "Can We Stand Strikes by Teachers, Police, Garbage-men, Etc.," *Readers Digest,* August, 1969, pp. 99-103.

Kihss, Peter. "Kheel Forms Panel to Aid City in Crisis," *New York Times,* March 18, 1969.

————. "2 Panels Set Up to Counter Threat of Community Disputes," *New York Times,* January 7, 1970.

King, Martin Luther, Jr. *Letter from a Birmingham Jail*. New York: Fellowship of Reconciliation, 1963.

————. *Where Do We Go from Here: Chaos or Community?* New York: Bantam Books, 1968.

Kinney, Monta. "Statement Presented Before the State Board of Education." New York: Afram Associates, Inc., 1969 (mimeographed).

Levin, Henry M. *Community Control of Schools*. Washington, D.C.: The Brookings Institution, 1970.

Lomax, Louis E. *To Kill a Black Man*. Los Angeles: Holloway House Publishing Co., 1968.

McSurely, Alan. *How to Negotiate*. Louisville: Southern Conference Educational Fund, 1967.

Mahome, Othello. "Incident at Cornell," *Liberator,* IX (June, 1969).

Montgomery, M. Lee. "The Concept of Victory." Philadelphia: Center for Urban Affairs, Temple University, 1970 (mimeographed).

"Negotiations: A Tool for Change." New York: Scholarship, Education, and Defense Fund for Racial Equality, 1968.

Nierenberg, Gerald I. *The Art of Negotiating: Psychological Strategies for Gaining Advantageous Bargains*. New York: Hawthorn Books, Inc., 1968.

1969 National Conference of Black School Board Members, January 30–February 2, 1969. New York: Scholarship, Education and Defense Fund for Racial Equality, 1969.

Oppenheimer, Martin, and George Lakey. *A Manual for Direct Ac-*

tion: Strategy and Tactics for Civil Rights and All Other Non-violent Protest Movements. Chicago: Quadrangle Books, Inc., 1964-65.

Pentecoste, Joseph. "Black Psychology," *Black Liberator,* V (June 1969).

Phillips, McCandlish. "Groups in Harlem Plan a Coalition," *New York Times,* July 14, 1969.

Piven, Frances Fox. "Disensus Politics: A Strategy for Winning Economic Rights," *New Republic,* April 20. 1968.

_____. "Militant Civil Servants in New York City," *Trans-Action,* VII (November, 1969).

_____ and Richard A. Cloward. "Rent Strike: Disrupting the System," *New Republic,* December 2, 1967.

Poussaint, Alvin F. and Linda R. McLean. "Black Roadblocks to Black Unity," *Negro Digest,* November, 1968.

Protest and Its Handling: Do's and Don'ts and What If's. Trenton: New Jersey Education Association, 1969.

"Race Makes a Difference: An Analysis of Sentence Disparity Among Black and White Offenders in Southern Prisons," *Special Report.* Atlanta: Southern Regional Council.

Report of the National Advisory Commission on Civil Disorders. New York: E. P. Dutton and Co., Inc., 1969.

Rogers, David. *110 Livingston St.: Politics and Bureaucracy in the New York City School System.* New York: Random House, 1968.

Rubinstein, Annette T. (ed.) *Schools Against Children: The Case for Community Control.* New York: Monthly Review Press, 1970.

Seaver, Ted. "The Care and Feeding of Southern Welfare Departments." Washington, D.C.: Poverty/Rights Action Center, 1966 (mimeographed) .

"Seek Twp. Poverty HQ for Blacks, Puerto Ricans," *New York Post,* December 19, 1969, p. 17.

Selznick, Philip. *TVA and the Grass Roots: A Study in the Sociology of Formal Organizations.* New York: Harper and Row, 1966.

Simms, Gregory, and Enrique Arnyo. "Report of the Conference Proceedings of the Borough Presidents of Manhattan and the Bronx Held on December 9, 1967." Trenton: New Jersey Community Action Training Institute, Inc., 1968.

Skolnick, Jerome H. *The Politics of Protest.* New York: Ballantine Books, 1969.

"Southern Campuses in Crisis," New South, XXIV (Spring, 1969).

"State of the Southern States," *New South.* XXIV (Spring, 1969).

"Student—Teacher Relations." Washington, D.C.: D.C. Teachers Union, 1969. (mimeographed)

"The Five Demands Go Through Changes," *Observation Post,* (City College of New York), VLI:1 (September 4, 1969), 4 (see appendix B).

Urban America, Inc. and The Urban Coalition. *One Year Later.* New York: Frederick A. Praeger, 1969.

U.S. Department of Labor. *Brief History of the American Labor Movement.* Washington, D.C.: U.S. Government Printing Office, 1957.

Walls, Dwayne. "Fayette County, Tennessee: Tragedy and Confrontation," *Special Reports.* Atlanta: Southern Regional Council, 1969.

Walton, Sidney F., Jr. "End of the Use of the Word 'Negro' when Referring to Biologically Black Persons." New York: Afram Associates, Inc., 1969 (mimeographed).

Wilcox, Preston. "So You Want to Be Black." New York: Afram Associates, Inc., 1967 (mimeographed).

_____. "The Crisis Over Who Shall Control the Schools: A Bibliography." New York: Afram Associates, Inc., 1968.

_____. "Black Studies As An Academic Discipline: Toward a Definition. New York: Afram Associates, Inc., 1969 (mimeographed).

_____. *Education for Black Humanism.* New York: Afram Associates, Inc., 1969.

_____. *Integration or Separatism in Education: K-12.* New York: Afram Associates, Inc., 1969.

_____. "It's Not a Replica of the White Agenda," *College Dilemmas,* Spring, 1969, pp. 6-10.

_____. *Models for Local Affiliate Structures: Issues and Dilemmas.* New York: National Association for African-American Education, 1969.

_____. "Observations on the Transition from Centralization to Decentralization," *Foresight,* I (August, 1969), 7-8.

_____. "The Community-Centered School," *The School House in The City.* New York: Praeger and Company, 1969.

Wright, Richard. *White Man, Listen.* Garden City, N.Y.: Anchor Books, 1964.

Yancey, A. H. *Interpositionullification.* New York: American Press, 1959.

APPENDIX B

Interracial Negotiations at City College of New York

The Five Demands go through Changes*

Demand of Black and Puerto Rican Students	*Negotiated Settlement*
1. A degree-granting School of Black and Puerto Rican Studies.	1. Proposed "School of Urban and Third World Studies" to be opened in September 1969.
2. Separate orientation for Black and Puerto Rican freshman.	2. Proposed separate program with a special director. Director to be nominated by Black and Puerto Rican students.
3. Student voice in the SEEK program including the hiring and firing of personnel.	3. Recommended SEEK become separate department headed by director appointed by President. Students would have indirect voice in department. Pre-Bac council to be formed with budget derived from SEEK student activities fee.
4. Racial composition of entering classes reflect the Black and Puerto Rican population of the city high schools.	4. Dual admission policy adopted. 300 additional freshmen for SEEK to be admitted in September 1969. By February 1970 60% of freshmen would enter by competitive exam and 40% would be selected by special criteria.
5. Spanish and Black and Puerto Rican history be required of all education majors.	5. Adopted.

* Source: The City College *Observation Post,* Sept. 4, 1969, p. 4.

156

Recommendation of Faculty Senate	*Action by Board of Higher Education*
1. Reaffirmed its position that a program should be established but asked President Copeland to create a commission to study details and report back in September 1969.	1. Rejected separate school. Set forth guidelines for "interdisciplinary degree programs, institutes or departments."
2. Urged orientation be open and voluntary for all, and asked the Department of Student Personnel Services to establish special orientation programs for any group of 100 or more students who wish such a program.	2. Considered freshman orientation "to be a matter falling under the jurisdiction of each college." No action taken.
3. Recommended that the Pre-Bac program become a department in the College of Liberal Arts & Science with student participation in the departmental curriculum committee as well as other committees.	3. Each senior college directed to establish department which includes counsellors from SEEK. SEEK "should not offer credit courses" but accelerate those in it to begin study in regular college. . . ." Authorized transferring jurisdiction of Central SEEK program to College from Hotel Alamac.
4. Recommended a long term policy of open admissions, University-wide. For the short run, the Senate asked for the admission of as many as 400 students per year (for the next two years) on the selected high school basis, with no decrease in the number of students admitted by the currently used methods.	4. Moved Master Plan up five years to provide place for every NYC high school graduate, in September 1970, to some unit of the University. Rejected dual admissions.
5. The Board approved these requirements on May 5, 1969, so the Senate did not act.	5. Passed. Takes effect this fall.

Afram Associates Materials

ACTION STIMULATOR #6: THE COMMUNITY
TAKES A STAND!

DECLARATION   Dayton Model Cities Planning Council
    OF   Education Committee
INDEPENDENCE: Joint Community School Council
                (Sept. 13, 1969)

On August 14, 1969, the Dayton Board of Education signed an agreement with the Model Cities Planning Council stating:

"The Board and the Council will determine the qualifications for the selection of the Project Director. . . .

"Recognizing the importance of close liaison between this position and the Education Committee in the appointment or termination of the Project Director, recommendations of the Planning Council will be sought and considered. Termination of the employment of the Project Director shall be consummated only upon the concurrence of the Board and the Council. . . ."

In issuing his directive of September 9, 1969, relieving Arthur Thomas from administrative responsibilities in any school and directing him to "refrain from entering any school or grounds other than his office at Louise Troy," Dr. Wayne Carle acted outside the limitations of his authority. Dr. Carle usurped the prerogatives of both the Model Cities Planning Council and the Dayton Board of Education. Dr. Carle is clearly out of order.

The Model Cities Planning Council's Education Committee and the Joint Community School Council instruct Arthur E. Thomas, the Project Director of the Model Cities Education Component, to continue to report to work and to carry out his regular duties.

Mr. Arthur E. Thomas is instructed that if he is called to report to the Superintendent of Schools or any of his subordinates he is to report this information to the Chairman of the Education Committee of the Model Cities Planning Council for further instructions.

Since our major concern is the education of our children, the Education Committee and the Joint Community School Council wish to announce that schools will be open on Monday, September 15, 1969, and operating fully under the Model Cities Education Component.

We demand that the Superintendent of Schools and the Board of Education and the law enforcement agencies of the City of Dayton fulfill their responsibilities in insuring the safety of all Model Cities children attending schools inside and outside the target area.

For clarification and further information, call the Model Cities Planning Council, 224-7422, 1100 W. Fifth St.—our center of communication.

COMMUNITY SCHOOL CHAIRMEN:

Mrs. Juanita Johnson, Dunbar

Mr. Hoarace Kelly, Edison

Mrs. Sudie Allen, Grace A. Greene

Mr. Peter Hill, Irving

Miss Barbara Dennis, Louise Troy

Mrs. Lillian Walker, Macfarlane

Mr. Augustus Beal, Miami Chapel

Mr. Robert Allen, Roosevelt

Mrs. Ida Page, Acting Chr. Weaver

Mr. Levoyd Thomas, Whittier

Mr. George Self, St. James

(Prepared after 5 hours of discussion at a joint meeting, Sat. Sept. 13, 1969, Dunbar High School.)

AFRAM ASSOCIATES, INCORPORATED

103 East 125 Street   Harlem, New York 10035

THOUGHT STIMULATOR #6: DIFFERENTIAL ETHNIC GROUP REACTIONS TO DUAL CAUCUS EXPERIENCES

A. DIFFERENTIAL RESPONSES TO CAUCUS EXPERIENCES: BLACKS VS. WHITES.

BLACKS	*WHITES*
1) Feelings of togetherness and cohesiveness.	1) Feelings of rejection.
2) Class and color differences are subordinated in interest of group cohesiveness.	2) Class and ethnic differences are heightened.
3) Task-orientation.	3) Emotion-laden.
4) Sense of belonging develops.	4) Divisiveness develops.

B. DIFFERENTIAL RESPONSES: MIXED GROUP ACTION
   VERSUS MULTI-RACIAL ACTION (1)

	BLACKS	*WHITES*
1) *Mixed Group Action:*	Divided by white togetherness.	Cohesiveness of whites directed against Blacks.
2) *Multi-racial* Action:	Togetherness based on prior preparation.	Divided through reaction to Black rejection of subservient roles.

(1) Multi-racial action is differentiated from "mixed group" action
    in that in the latter instances the Blacks and whites met together
    to discuss the subject issues. In the former instances, the Blacks
    met alone as did the whites, *before* they came together for multi-
    racial action.

SUMMARY AND ANALYSIS

These data were collected by observing participant behavior in several Problem-Solving Encounters. It is based on observations and experiences reported by the participants after having participated in
caucuses, mixed, and multi-racial groups. The data are based on reactions to initial participation in such experiences. This paper does
not purport to make statements about participant behavior over a
long period of time. In each instance, the subject under discussion
was of a Black-white nature.

One can posit from the above findings that:

(1) Black togetherness develops as a reaction to the sanction to meet
    alone. Black togetherness develops as a consequence of a *delib-
    erately planned effort.*

(2) Whites are *automatically* organized against Black togetherness.
    White togetherness is automatic as long as it is anti-Black. With-
    out Blacks to reject, white in-group divisiveness comes to the
    surface.

Chronology of Events, Part 3 (Memphis)

October 13, 1964	Local 1733 received its charter from AFSCME.
1965	Effort to strike for recognition by Local 1733 thwarted by an injunction obtained by the City.
November 2, 1967	Henry Loeb elected mayor in a runoff election against William Ingram.
January 1, 1968	City government changed form—commission to mayor-council form.
January 31, 1968	Origin of sewer workers' grievance.
February 1, 1968	Meeting of P. J. Ciampa, international union field staff director, with Charles Blackburn, director of public works, City of Memphis, to outline the union's request for recognition, a dues checkoff, a grievance procedure, and a nondiscrimination clause for union members.
February 8, 1968	Letter from P. J. Ciampa to Charles Blackburn reiterated the union's request made February 1.
February 11, 1968	Meeting of Local 1733 following unsatisfactory settlement of sewer workers' grievance
February 12, 1968	Walkout of 1,375 employees of the Department of Public Works.
February 13, 1968	Meeting of mayor with strikers in Ellis Auditorium from which he walked out.
February 14, 1968	Meeting of P.J. Ciampa and Mayor Loeb in the mayor's office. Meeting broken up by a heated exchange of words. The mayor said he would not talk with the union until the men went back to work.
February 16, 1968	NAACP threatened massive demonstrations.
February 18, 1968	First informal negotiations began between city and union officials, sponsored by a group of predominantly white ministers.
February 19, 1968	Second meeting of City and union officials

	while NAACP and strikers picketed City Hall.
February 22, 1968	Sit-in at Public Works Committee hearing by 700 sanitation workers. The committee passed a resolution to be read to the City Council the following day calling for recognition of the union and a form of dues checkoff.
February 23, 1968	Passing of a substitute resolution by City Council which called for acceptance of all strikers' demands except recognition and dues checkoff. Refusal to hear citizens. March along Main Street after City Council meeting by union members broken up by police with force after incidents involving marchers and a police car.
February 24, 1968	City got Chancery Court injunction against striking and picketing. Participants in strategy meeting of Negro ministers incensed by police treatment and refusal of City Council to hear their demands.
February 25, 1968	Negro ministers called for a boycott of downtown stores, two daily newspapers, and every establishment doing business under the name "Loeb."
February 26, 1968	Daily marches began downtown.
February 27, 1968	Union official cited for contempt of court along with other union officials, thereby delaying his appearance at a hearing before the City Council.
March 1, 1968	Hearing on contempt cases postponed until March 5, 1968.
March 4, 1968	White union members, 500 strong, marched with strikers. First open support of strike by organized labor.
March 5, 1968	Union leaders sentenced to 10 days in jail and $50 fine in state court, and freed pending appeal.

March 9, 1968	Three thousand Tennessee National Guardsmen bivouacked in Memphis without incident.
March 18, 1968	Dr. King addressed 15,000 people in Memphis's Mason Temple.
March 23, 1968	Nonbinding mediation begun by Frank Miles.
March 27, 1968	Mediation sessions recessed until further notice by Miles.
March 28, 1968	March led by Dr. King brutally broken up by police after youngsters started looting. Dr. King taken away for safety. Four thousand Tennessee National Guardsmen were called in and a curfew placed on Memphis.
March 29, 1968	March of two or three hundred adult Negroes from Clayborn Temple to City Hall and back under heavy armored guard.
April 3, 1968	Temporary restraining order against marches by Dr. King issued by Federal District Court Judge Bailey Brown. Dr. King labeled it a basic denial of First Amendment privileges. Dr. King addressed 2,000 people at Mason Temple. His last public speech.
April 4, 1968	Assassination of Dr. Martin Luther King, Jr., at the Lorraine Motel.
April 5, 1968	Mayor Loeb's resignation called for by the Memphis Central Labor Council, AFL-CIO, and Baxton Bryant, executive director of Tennessee Council on Human Rights. Undersecretary of Labor James Reynolds arrived to serve as mediator, sent by President Johnson. March on mayor's office by 150 ministers, mostly white, called for recognition of the union and dues checkoff.
April 6, 1968	Mediation sessions between City and union begun again by Frank Miles with James Reynolds.

April 7, 1968	Mediation sessions continued until early morning, April 8, recessing for memorial march and funeral.
April 8, 1968	King memorial march led by Mrs. King and other dignitaries.
April 9, 1968	Dr. King's funeral in Atlanta, Georgia.
April 10, 1968	Mediation sessions continued daily through April 16.
April 16, 1968	Agreement reached settling the strike.

APPENDIX E

Excerpts from Selected Interviews (Memphis)

INTERVIEW WITH JESSE EPPS
SPECIAL ASSISTANT TO THE PRESIDENT
AFSCME
JULY 8, 1969

What was the International's reaction at first to Local 1733's going out on strike?

There was a large group of men in Memphis who were fed up with problems they were facing. They had been promised this and proised that, but never received anything. Every year they saw the police and firemen get the raises, and they were just tired of this sort of thing. When the International learned of the strike, it was at first concerned about the amount of support the men would give it. If you're going to have a strike, you've got to have preparation. We weren't sure whether all the men were together. This had been the problem in 1965. There was no hesitancy on the part of the International to support the strike, only concern as to whether the men were properly organized to go out on strike. The International wanted to send in a team to settle the strike as fast as possible.

How did you see the Memphis strike as affecting your southern organizational efforts? (As seen from the beginning of the strike.)

We did not think it would escalate as it did. Thus, we didn't see it originally as having an impact on southern organization. I came into the strike on the second day. In the second week, we saw the City's position harden. We saw the strike growing and becoming important in our plans for southern organization.

The strike should not have occurred in February. If we had planned it, we wouldn't have called it then because you want garbage to pile up in the hot months, not the cold ones. As the City began to hire strikebreakers, some of whom were Negroes, we saw that we had to go to the Negro community to present our problem and encourage their support so as to protect the jobs of the men against strikebreakers from their own community.

Had there been any plan on the part of the union to make this a race issue?

By no means! It was a race issue by the nature of the situation. We had to react to the situation as we found it. Loeb insisted on championing the white racists who elected him. He always insisted he wanted to be a mayor of "all the people," but when it came down to it, he admitted he had no obligation to the Negro community because they had not helped elect him. Dr. H. Ralph Jackson got the Negro ministers together and asked the mayor to meet with them. He did, but instead of listening to the ministers plead for his support, he asked them to support his side. When the ministers refused, he became angry and vowed to "get even" with them and the union before he left office. This occurred in the second or third week of the strike.

In the trilogue, as it has been described by Baxton Bryant, that took place between you, the mayor, and members of the Ministerial Alliance on February 18, what happened? What prompted the cool atmosphere between the union and the city? Was there any meaningful understanding reached through these talks?

On February 14, the mayor had said that he would not meet with the union anymore. He considered the strike to be illegal, and for him to talk with the union would be in violation of the law. Thus, he used the moderator to address the union rather than communicating directly with us. It was against his *principle* to talk with the union at this point.

There were four or five of these meetings all told. From the meetings, the mayor at least got it very clear that he was dealing with a union which had professional skills. The issues were brought out so that all present understood them. In fact, the ministers' comprehension of these issues was the basis for their eventual march on Loeb's office following King's assassination. The white ministers' support was rare though they sympathized with us. By and large, there was no visible white ministerial support.

What compromises were offered by the union?

There was one issue which we considered nonnegotiable, and that was the recognition of the dignity of the workers' right to determine their own destiny. We were willing to accept any form of this recognition just so long as the City gave the workers recognition. We were willing to find ways to help the mayor back away from his stand and save face. As you know, the art of negotiation is compromise, and we were willing to do this in any way feasible. We suggested a check-off of dues through the credit union, and we also suggested an exchange of letters as a means for recognition.

Who were the union's representatives at the bargaining table?

P. J. Ciampa, Bill Lucy, T. O. Jones, and, later, myself and Dr. H. Ralph Jackson. In a discussion of the chronology of the mediation sessions, the first session broke down March 23 when one of the city negotiators brought up the legality issue. It was true that Loeb had agreed not to bring this up, and he later apologized to Frank Miles for this having happened. On Sunday, March 24, we did not meet, but both parties talked with Frank Miles, who worked out an agreement such that the legality issue would be bypassed. We met again on March 25. We first discussed the form that the agreement would take and then turned to discussion of recognition.

Discussion on recognition continued through March 27. Dr. Jackson was the one who didn't want to leave out the word "recognition" in the agreement. He wanted to be certain that the City really gave the men the recognition they wanted. Finally, an agreement was worked out to spell out the meaning of recognition in the contract as a substitute for the use of the word. Dr. Jackson finally accepted this compromise.

When we came down to the point where we would write this out, the City refused. They were willing to agree to recognition verbally but did not want to reduce this to writing. This, they said, would compromise their original position. This was violating the common law which said that strikes were illegal. For them to agree, they said, would be a violation of the law.

This was the point at which we accused them of failing to bargain in good faith. This was compounded by the appearance in the afternoon's *Press Scimitar* of what had been going on in the negotiation sessions which were supposed to be closed to all. We felt the City had done this and that it was just another means of the City to make publicity. We knew we could not negotiate with them in a fish bowl, that is, the public media. This had been what Loeb wanted, and we felt that this particular leak to the press was just another example of this policy. It was for this reason and the unwillingness to put recognition in writing that we accused the City of not bargaining in good faith. We also did this later that night (March 27) on television.

On the wage issue: How was the settlement reached? What were the respective positions? Who said what to get the settlement? How much power did the parties have?

The mayor was very convincing about his budget presentation. He convinced everyone that the City didn't have the money. He offered to make money available next fiscal year. Actually, the City ended up the year with a two-million-dollar surplus. Money was only part of the total picture for us. If we could just have gotten a modicum, it would have been sufficient.

The compromise that was worked out was due to some behind-the-scenes work of several interested third parties such as Ned Cook, President of E. L. Bruce & Co., and Abe Plough, President of Plough Inc. At this point in the strike, they were the only ones who could communicate with the mayor. They were his friends, and he admired them for their position in the community. These parties attempted to bridge the gap between the mayor and Jerry Wurf as the mayor tried to save face. These men and others brought about the agreement on wages which the union accepted reluctantly on the basis of the mayor's presentation of the City's fiscal problems.

What, if anything, did you learn about organizing from the Memphis case?

It brought to light a whole new concept of "maximum involvement." In order to be successful, you have to have an informed citizenry and an involved citizenry. We had to bring the issues to those who would be involved and affected by the strike to insure their participation. In Memphis, this group was the Negro community.

What difficulties, if any, were incurred in getting the full support of local organized labor? What finally brought about the visible support of local white union members? What financial support was offered by organized labor, both local and national?

At first we got little support, and, even in the end, we didn't get much support. Tommy Powell was the main local union leader who gave us support. The building trades didn't help us. The industrial unions did help with financial contributions. When we invited outside civil rights leaders such as Bayard Rustin, Roy Wilkins, and Dr. King, we began to get national publicity for the strike and with it some financial support from other international unions.

All the while, white unionists did not join in our marches to offer visible support. We went to them and told them that this was a trade-union issue, and we needed their support to show Loeb. Powell was with us through all of this. He helped organize a march of white unionists March 4. This was the only case, however, of mass local white unionist support in the marches downtown. Even in this lone instance, the white unionists would not start the march with us at Clayborn Temple but chose instead to start from their meeting hall blocks away. They also didn't mingle with our men but more or less marched to themselves.

The United Rubber Workers first offered support in the form of free use of their meeting hall as long as we needed it. The president of the Retail Clerks was a good friend of T. O. Jones and also a political supporter of the mayor. He thought he could have some influence on the mayor but quickly found out that he couldn't. This local had more or less been the parent organizer of Local 1733 when it was first formed. There was some support from the UAW as they also offered the use of their meeting hall.

INTERVIEW WITH DR. H. RALPH JACKSON
DIRECTOR OF THE DEPARTMENT OF MINIMUM SALARY
AFRICAN METHODIST EPISCOPAL CHURCH
JULY 21, 1969

How did you become involved in the dispute?

The dispute to start with was really between the sanitation workers through their union and the City. I was contacted for permission to use my name as a member of the community on the committee to raise funds for the strikers. I stated that they could use more than my name; I would be out of town, but when I got back I would also actively help them raise funds for that purpose. When I returned, I found out that they were to have a meeting with the City Council. When we got to this meeting, instead of a meeting, the City Council came in and read a statement that they would have nothing to do with it, and they were leaving it in the hands of the mayor and adjourned the meeting without giving anybody a chance to say anything. The union officers decided that all the members representing the union and some of the community would return to Mason Temple where they would hold a meeting and discuss where they were going to go from there.

We started marching for Mason Temple and were told that if we marched on the right hand side of the center line we could go in the street. Within about two blocks, a disturbance started behind me. There was a debate as to what started it, but, anyway, the police started indiscriminately to mace the folks in the line, including me. This made me mad as it did several others. We then went to Mason Temple where we got all of the details involved with the sanitation strike and the workers' grievances. Once we had heard their grievances and the inhumane conditions under which they were working at that time, it was a natural sequence that we decided that this was something that we had to commit ourselves to obtain fully. From that, a vast source of information was brought out about the overall conditions in the city. It had been so easy for all of us to lose sight of what was happening around us. I and others had become unaware of conditions in trying to make it under the system. We had really gotten away from the things that go on and the conditions under which people live and work, the types of wages and salaries they receive, the types of homes they live in. All of these things were unfolded to us, and we had to look at these and the sanitation strike in light of the needs of the folks. The need for a commitment to change these things is what actually got me involved.

What was the impact of this strike in the black community?

The same day that the strikers marched, or I guess it was the next day, we called the ministers together and explained to them the conditions that the sanitation men faced, and they immediately rallied along with leaders of the city, the NAACP with Mr. Jesse Turner, and members of the community in support of the sanitation workers in their demands for recognition for the union so that the workers would have somebody there really to represent them and try to change these conditions. I think that since the workers are on the low end of the economic scale and could not support themselves, many of us just launched in and tried to help them out.

How were you brought into the negotiations that were conducted by Frank Miles?

When the community became involved with mass meetings, I was elected as finance chairman to raise money for the men. We made speeches at various meetings, and I guess from this that certain ones of us evolved as spokesmen for the community. When it was time for the negotiations, Mr. Wurf, who was president for the International, felt that the community had become so involved then that someone should be in the negotiations representing the community as well as those representing the union. The union officials decided to ask me to sit in on the negotiations. So I went in as a representative of the community.

How did you see the parties in the negotiations? What was your assessment of both parties, the union and the City?

The first item that we had to deal with was recognition. It was obvious to me from the start that the men there who represented the City were not there with the authority to make any kind of a decision. They came there with instructions, and, if anything further had to be done, they had to adjourn and go back and get instructions. To me, the whole thing seemed like a waste of time because we were getting nowhere real fast.

It seemed to me that by this time things were polarized. The City was determined not to recognize the union, to meet the demands of the workers. It was obvious; they were coming in saying we can't do this and we can't do that, the same old malarky they always come up with. So this was what we were confronted with. It was not a case of someone coming in and saying "all right, we have a problem, so let's solve it." It was kind of "we want you to understand our position of why we can't do this or that. We've got a lot of people in the East end of town who are a large number of votes, and they would never understand it or appreciate it if we did this or that. The mayor must save face, and the mayor has a number of telegrams, 200, from folks who want him to stand pat, and he must stand pat because these are the folk who elected him." All of this kind of thing was what we had to face.

The discussion of recognition at this time was dealing with ways of skirting the use of the word recognition. Frank Miles was suggesting that recognition be spelled out, but you objected to this. Why?

I took the position that when we went to the table and the City was on the other side, that until the City recognized who we were there could be no further negotiations. Otherwise, they were talking to us as though we had no name. "We recognize the right of the people to organize," this is what they said; "We recognize the right of the people to organize." But they stopped right there, and they did not say, "We recognize the obligation of the City to recognize and deal with the person that this organization says we want to deal with them." I don't know if that covers too clearly what I was trying to say there, but what I'm trying to say is that it was one thing to say "we recognize the right of people to organize and to select certain persons to speak for them," but that is not saying "we recognize you as the persons selected by these people." That was the point. They were willing to stop right there, and I was not willing to stop until they were ready to say that these people had the right to organize and select someone to represent them, and the City had the obligation to recognize the persons the people had selected. This is recognition. The argument over exclusive recognition was not a problem with me. The agreement that we finally came to satisfied the point that I had raised. Otherwise I would not have agreed to it. I use the illustration to you that if we are not recognized here as representatives of the union, then you might as well say "hey you" and not call my name or say Dr. or Mr. Jackson, but when you say Dr. Jackson or Mr. or whatever you choose, then you recognize me as a person. Until that was done, then there could be no further discussion. They finally got it worded a way that was satisfactory.

At the first meeting held with Mr. Miles, it was pointed out that whatever went on in there was to stay in there. I raised the question immediately that, as a representative of the community, I was a member of the team, but the mayor as representative of the City was not on the team, and if the same restriction would be put on the mayor, then I would keep quiet. But if the mayor went all over town bleeding off at the mouth on what he was going to do, then I was going to answer him. I would not be bound by this agreement under these circumstances. I believe it was after that, once or twice, something came out in the press, and this was a reason for the meetings to break down. But I believe there was another reason. That was because at the same time we were negotiating the other leaders were still having their mass meetings, the union was still meeting, and pressure was building up with people thinking that we, on the inside, were negotiating and that we were going to settle this thing any day now. At the same time we were sitting in there, these city folk were doing nothing but playing games. You would agree on some language in the morning session, and in the afternoon they would have been to City Hall, and what you had been working on in the morning had to be changed. We just weren't getting anywhere in the language. There was no meaningful progress being made. I walked out on the negotiating team feeling that I could be more effective in the community. I was spinning my wheels talking with folk who had no authority to act and who represented folk who had no intention of meeting the demands of the people.

Can you point to any particular pivotal points in the strike as you saw them unfold?

No, I can't. I really consider it a series of pressures which caused the settlement. I couldn't identify any one point beyond Dr. King's assassination that would have any more significance. Of course, the City was very concerned with its image. If there is one thing the white people, the racists, in Memphis are concerned with, it's their image. They're not concerned about doing anything, even today, for the poor or the black. This concern for their image is natural because they want to attract industry, and you can't do this if you've got race trouble or labor force problems.

*What is your evaluation of the impact of radicals on the black com-
munity and their impact as you saw it on the white community?*

I think there is one point that Memphis has that has never been
understood, and that is the tremendous influence upon this community by the nonviolent forces. In spite of what the middle-class white
may say, I am a disciple of nonviolence and what Martin [Luther
King] said. I believe in direct action, but I do not believe in violence.
There was a tremendous amount of pressure both from the young
and the old that the way to bring this strike to an end was to stop
the trucks and to stop the strikebreakers. There was quite a bit of
talk about that, but I really don't feel that Memphis . . . well, Memphis has never really had a real violent effort here. Even that first
march that was broken up, half a dozen windows were broken. When
Martin was killed, less damage was done in Memphis than anywhere,
and I feel this is largely because of the influence of leadership in the
black community, which comes from the ministers. We talked with
the folk the newspaper made militant, bad, and finally had put them
in jail. This was the newspaper and the power structure method
and effort of developing this thing. This was another way of solidifying the racism in the white community against what was being done.
As long as they could show that Memphis had some of those folk
who were doing the same thing just as bad as those folk you were
reading about in these other towns, then this gave them reason to
use force to put it down. They had to have some reason to use all
those police on what was happening here. They proceeded to make
themselves some real bad gangs. I think they've got one fellow down
there in jail named Ferguson. The worst thing he ever did was have
a wooden pistol and point it at some cars. They kept on making him
a villain until they got enough on him to put him in jail.

I really don't think these radicals had any impact on bringing the
strike to a settlement because, you see, they had not built them up
that well at that time. Most of these folk that they had brought
forth as the Invaders . . . the Black Knights have never been considered as militants as the white press uses the word. To them, the
term means burning, looting, and destruction. They developed these
folk. They took out statements that others had said and got them
to comment; e.g., "Dr. Jackson has said what we are going to do is to
march downtown until the merchants lose so much money they have

to close up. What do you think about all this marching?" And they might say, "Well, it's all right to march, but I'd rather burn." The press would go out and quote this person and put his picture in the paper. Well, here would come someone no one had ever heard of until the reporter asked him this question, and now he's got his picture in there, and here comes another reporter, and overnight he has become a spokesman. He would be the great militant. The more he would talk, the more he would be quoted in the newspaper. After he is quoted and quoted as saying all this, they have created him as a leader. It might be a little fellow who was going around doing little odd jobs washing cars for people and doing things like that. He gets quoted; he begins to wear his hair long and to wear beads and a shirt with a gun on the back of it. They take this person and build him up as someone who is out for burning and looting, and so they begin to arrest him and harrass him and intimidate him. They create these folk.

How do you view the support given the black community by or-ganized labor?

This strike went on for a good while, and a lot of money came in here to assist the workers in a relief fund. Hundreds of thousands of dollars were sent to Memphis by organized labor throughout the nation. The local unions on several occasions joined in on marching. There were other unions who followed the old pattern. You must remember that the unions are made up of the people of Memphis, and Memphis is by and large a racist community. So you have racist unions here. Yet, to answer your question, on the whole I think we got fairly good support out of the local unions, and we got real good support out of the internationals. Of course their entrance was due to publicity we got. You see, the reason why Bayard Rustin and Wilkins and Martin King were ever invited into Memphis is im-portant. The local press had put a freeze on our news. We had a strike going on here, demonstrations going on everyday, had mass meetings going every night, and we still had cities around us like Nashville or Little Rock that hardly knew what was going on. They had a press; this was an organized effort. We had tried several ways to break this. We had contacted sources in New York through the National Council of Churches to try to get some kind of aid in here to get news out of the city as to what was going on, and we could not get it. This is the time we were faced with the young radicals you mentioned who were saying "we must escalate; we must bring more pressure." This is what he was saying: "All this marching is not going to do anything for you; you've got to do these other things." This is what the young man was talking about. [Reference back to the young radicals from Stimfield.] We took the position that we would not go that road, and instead we began to invite in national persons so that they would bring the press with them. So now when we said that Bayard Rustin was coming, this was an occasion for national hook-ups to catch on. Naturally, when the strike became national and known, the efforts of these people were able to bring in funds, but as long as it was a local affair and blacked out by the local press and played down, then naturally there was no support coming, but, as soon as these other things happened, support came.

One of the first questions I asked the union when I was talking with them was "where are the local white unions?" This was done when I first got involved, but the point is—and this is the same thing I told you—this is a racist community, and the white unions are made up of the community. This is what you had. It was later when they came up and joined in on the marches and made small contributions. But that by and large was the situation and still is the situation in Memphis with the trade unions and so forth. They still do more talking about moving toward apprenticeship than actually happens.

How do you view the long-range impact that the strike has had on the black community as well as the white community?

I think that the main thing is that, after the strike, the union [AFSCME] began to organize in other fields—hospitals, board of education, county hospital, and all these kinds of things—which really gives the unions now a force of around 7,000 members. Well, 7,000 organized blacks is a moving force in any community. The effect in the white community was that there were several leading business-men who entered into dialogue sessions after the sanitation strike right on up through now. Many of them have breakfast with blacks and other meetings where they discuss conditions in the city, but you must keep in mind that most of these people represent individual citizens who are trying to avoid the conflict we had last time, but these are not city officials. The Chamber of Commerce has a new executive who has come in and attempted to keep some dialogue going on in the black community, but, there again, he has to deal with an executive board down there that he has to always be good God, good Devil. They tried to get out a strong statement commemorating the assassination of Dr. King. We pointed out to them that we were not interested in celebrating his assassination but dedicating ourselves to finishing the work he had started. This would be an annual affair. They never did get a statement up because every time they got one up the executive board that had to approve it kept watering it down so that every time it came out it just didn't mean anything. What I'm really saying in answer to your question is that an organization of 7,000 blacks is a helpful and moving sign in the black community, while in the white community, aside from a few individuals who have attempted to move for betterment in the community, Memphis has made very little real movement or change so far as the city administration and the power structure are concerned.

I think one of the reasons for this is that people in Memphis are hung up over the word "union." "Union" to them really means some executive in Washington running things, telling them what to do in Memphis. In the black community, the word "unions" represents the workers, our brothers, sisters, fathers, and mothers. We are not involved in what happens to the high offices in Washington, but we are involved in what happens to the workers.

How do you assess the impact of black identity on the black community as represented by the sign carried in the march, "I Am A Man"?

The creation of that sign came from this office as we were getting ready for the marches and deciding on the different signs and placards we should have. The sign "I Am A Man" really came up from the idea that this is what the men are really saying when we say these men have the right to plan for what they feel is the best interest of their families. You have to keep in mind that Mayor Loeb was saying that he was fighting the union because he didn't feel it was best for the men. What we were saying was that it was not Loeb's responsibility to decide what was best for a man. If I feel what I should have is an endowment policy for my children, mortgage insurance on my house, whatever I feel is the best way to help me to provide for my family, which is my responsibility as a man, I have that right to decide for myself and not Loeb. These men had the right to decide for themselves what was best, and if they decided that a union was best, even if the union was not the best, they have a right to decide that. And the City had the obligation to recognize that they had this right. This goes back to my original argument about recognition. This is what these men were saying, "I am a man, I don't need any Great White Father. I am a man, this is what I've decided I want in the best interest of my family, and as a man I have the right to make that decision." While the sign was new to a lot of people, it was not new to the black people because this is what we were steadily saying in our speeches at the mass meetings: "This is a man and not a child, and he has the right to decide for himself." So we had built this up, and when the man came out on the street with the sign, this was what he needed, it was backbone for him, and it was instant communication to the black community because we had been discussing it.

The following response was added as an afterthought by Dr. Jackson at the end of the interview when he was asked if there was any additional information he might want to add in light of the other questions that had been posed to him.

The whole thing involved in this sanitation strike should have and could have been solved immediately had the City Council, which we had just set up as a new form of government, been interested in performing their duties without taking dictates from their executive as they did this time. [Reference to the 1969 settlement] This new Council came in just before the strike, and they were only interested in saving face for the mayor rather than assuming their responsibilities. I think this is one thing that has happened in the last year. The council members have become a little more independent in their thinking. I am not too sure that isn't political because, from their action down there, I see two or three potential candidates for mayor, and I wouldn't be surprised if what is happening now is not so much for the good of the community as much as it is for the person in it. I don't think that in writing up the story of the Memphis sanitation strike it should be left out that here you had a bunch of councilmen who acted like cowards and children and refused to stand up. They failed the city far more than the mayor because the mayor stood out there as an individual acting like a little boy saying "I'm stubborn and I'm hardheaded" and always saying "I'm a stubborn man" because to me that was always childish because when I did that as a child I always got a whipping, and I didn't think that was anything in particular to be proud of, but the Council, if it had acted and lived up to its responsibilities, even the mayor couldn't have done these things. While I have no particular grief for Loeb and his action at that time, I certainly think that the council members failed miserably in living up to their responsibilities.

INTERVIEW WITH JAMES MORRIS LAWSON, JR.
PASTOR CENTENARY UNITED METHODIST CHURCH
JULY 21, 1969

How did you become involved in the strike and how did you assess the impact of the strike on the black community as it (the strike) developed?

I had supported the efforts of the union members to organize from the beginning, even before Loeb. T.O. Jones had come to me and sought my support, which I was willing to give. I gave support at the beginning of the strike, however, only from the pulpit as I did not enter directly into the events of the strike.

On the twenty first of February, some friends called me and asked me to come down to City Hall for a Public Works Committee hearing the next day. They were going to listen to the workers' grievances, I was told. Well, from the time I arrived there, I could see that they weren't interested in hearing those of us, the ministers, who were there. The chairman, Fred Davis, and other committee members kept throwing out jibes such as "We don't want to hear from the ministers; we want to hear from the men." Davis was following the same old Loeb line about the leaders not really representing the men. I got on the phone and told T.O. Jones to get his men down there to City Hall as fast as he could. By and by, the chambers began to fill, even the aisles. We told them to keep coming in; all the while the chairman kept saying that the fire marshal had placed the capacity of the chamber at 475. We ignored him.

He began to say "I am here . . ." and I shouted down, "You are here because we elected you!" I kept this up, and it spread throughout the men. Davis said then that he was trying to walk both sides of the street, and I shouted, "You can't do that!" What resembled a sit-in continued until late that afternoon when the Committee finally agreed to present a resolution to the Council the next day calling for recognition of the men.

This was the first time that I had become involved actively. I was infuriated by Davis's trying to coddle to Loeb and the white establishment. The next day the council substituted their own resolution, which supported Loeb's position for the Public Works Committee resolution. They would not hear us ministers and, after passing their resolution, shut the mike off and closed the meeting.

This made me angry. After some conference, the men decided to line up outside the municipal auditorium where the meeting had been held and march back to Mason Temple. We told the police that we could handle the marchers if they left us alone and that our objectives were for a peaceful march. As the march proceeded, we were challenged by some young police officers who apparently were unconcerned with any approval given the march by their superiors. I came up to them and told them that we could handle things if they just wouldn't try to cause any problems. Police cars were driving alongside our column of marchers, forming a barrier on one side with the curb on the other. The march had not gone three blocks when I looked back behind me and saw that a police car had driven into the marchers and that they were rocking it. I ran back trying to stop them, and then the whole police force came with mace, not just at those surrounding the police car, but the whole line of marchers. They began macing all of us, Dr. Jackson, myself, and many bystanders. There's no need to say that this was a turning point for me. We immediately, following this march, began to get together the ministers and our organization, coming from the first meeting, was called Committee on the Move for Equality [C.O.M.E.]. I was chosen as spokesman for this group. As chairman, I was its chief spokesman for everything. We called the next day for the boycott that you know about. Within a few days, blacks completely withdrew from downtown.

What were the major events of import as you saw them, and what was your role in them?

Of course, February 23 was such a pivotal point for all of us, but another point that was crucial for its importance in building morale and gathering support for the strikers was the entrance of national figures, such as Bayard Rustin, Roy Wilkins, and Martin Luther King. The former two came in during the first week in March, and Martin came in March 18.

We had been meeting in Mason Temple, which is the national headquarters of the Church of Christ. It seated about 12,000 in its auditorium and could hold that many more standing. When Rustin and Wilkins came in, there were eight to ten thousand at these meetings. They were somewhat taken aback by the size of the movement. The crowd was enthusiastic, and these men were caught up by it. The publicity they gave the workers was important. When Martin came in on the eighteenth, there were 25,000 there to hear him. They were packed, and I mean packed—in the aisles, everywhere. Yet, in all this sardine atmosphere, no one became agitated. They were there to hear Dr. King. We even took up a collection for the men in this atmosphere with no trouble at all. Martin was visibly shaken by all this, for this kind of support was unprecedented in the Movement. No one had even been able to get these numbers out before.

Before Martin left that night, he agreed to come back and lead a march the next Friday. These mass meetings helped boost the morale of the men, plus it did something for the leaders. It was certainly a traumatic point in the strike.

On Thursday evening before the march planned for the next day, we met with the teachers. Teachers are notorious about not supporting these kinds of issues, but we had 150 teachers together who were ready to support by encouraging students to miss school and support the march. Snow had begun to fall, and by this time we had four or five inches on the ground. And, if you know Memphis, you know the whole city stops when it snows. We had scheduled, in addition to the teachers, another mass meeting which was packed. All this had taken place with the snow having come down. These people were out to support us despite the snow. This was significant in that it emphasized the commitment of the local community in support of the strike.

What was the impact of the militants on the white community, and how were they viewed in the black community?

To me, the crucification of Dr. King was another important event because I did not begin to get calls and mail from the white community offering to help until after Martin's death. You ask about the importance of radicals. To my mind, they never go past rhetoric. They bragged a lot about what they were going to do, but they never did it. We've got pictures of the disturbances, and we *know* who was in on it, and it was not these radicals. In fact, they discredited themselves in the black community by failing to go beyond their rhetoric. To answer your question, I don't see that they really did bring in white support. It was really Martin's death that was the drawing point for whites.

What support was given by the coalition of organized labor and the black community?

As for the coalition of labor and the civil rights movement, we got about as much support as I expected locally. Wurf talked with other international leaders and got them to put pressure for support on the locals here. We got a little money trickling in, but the big support didn't come till we got national publicity. What Epps has said about the visible support of local white union members is true. They marched with us once, but by and large it was hard to get open support from the rank and file. It was the leadership that gave any support at all.

What were the long-range impacts of the strike on the black community?

The long-range impact of the strike is twofold to my mind. There will be an economic uplifting as the union gains a higher wage for its members from the largest employer in Memphis, and, second, the union will come to have a tremendous political impact as the members radicalize. Politicians will have to come to them for their support.

INTERVIEW WITH DANIEL POWELL
DIRECTOR OF AREA NUMBER FIVE
AFL-CIO COMMITTEE ON POLITICAL EDUCATION
JUNE 11, 1969

Why did organized labor wait so long to support the strike openly?

The race issue was the reason. Early in the strike the question came up whether to make it a race issue or a trade-union issue. The strike probably could not have been won had it not been made a race issue because, as a trade-union issue, it probably would not have attracted the full and solid support of the black community.

Another reason is that it took time to attract national support from international unions outside of Memphis. The entrance of national figures such as Roy Wilkins and Dr. King gave the strike publicity and brought national attention.

The union could never have won with Ingram as Mayor, because his popularity in the Negro community would have prevented solidification of the black community.

Some history of the labor movement in Memphis

Union membership numbers 40,000-50,000 today in Shelby County. Growth has taken place from the entrance of new industries, e.g., electrical and IBEW. The UAW has held its own or lost some, but certainly the overall union membership in Memphis has grown in absolute numbers.

INTERVIEW WITH W. T. (BILL) ROSS, JR.
EXECUTIVE SECRETARY
AFL-CIO LABOR COUNCIL, MEMPHIS, TENNESSEE
JUNE 10, 1969

What happened to the 1965 strike? How effective was it?

The *Alcoa Case* was one of the two cases cited by the chancellor in 1965 as precedent against the strike. This case held that it was illegal for municipal employees to strike. The special judge in the Memphis case in 1965 carried the decision one step further to say that it was illegal to strike *and* picket.

The injunction was issued before the strike took place. It, the strike, never got off the ground.

What impact did Ingram's support in the Negro community have on Local 1733's bid for recognition?

The Ingram support among Local 1733 members as well as in the Negro community definitely had an impact in blunting support for a strike in 1965. When this was coupled with the injunction and the lack of organization, the plans for the strike fell through.

What evidence do you have for the effectiveness of the boycott in the 1968 strike?

The boycott was damn effective. Some businessmen say they still haven't recovered from it. I am sure this prompted all the action that the Chamber of Commerce has taken since the strike. It certainly caused the businessmen to place pressure on the mayor to get the strike settled.

Why did the visible support of local white union members not appear until the middle of the strike?

No, there wasn't any visible support or money at first from the majority of local white union members. When their appeal for support was made to other locals, they got a normal response. Locals receive requests for aid almost daily from unions on strike. Overall, I would say they got as much financial support as any other union. The Rubber Workers and Retail Clerks offered immediate support. Other locals gave token support. The Carpenters gave $100 when first asked.

The U.A.W. local at International Harvester did as little as possible. They are a racist group. Reuther didn't do one solitary thing until after Dr. King was assassinated. Then he came down to make a big blow.

The 500 white marchers that showed up at a march in the first week of March were due to efforts of the Labor Council. We wanted to keep this thing a trade-union issue if possible, to keep away from the racist issues. We had to show this kind of support to keep the Negro ministers in it rather than have them turn it over to the militants.

What were the members' feelings when they went out on strike?

They were about as militant group as I had ever seen. Once, when I was talking with P. J. Ciampa by long distance, he asked me to get them to go back to work, and I told him I wasn't fixing to try, why didn't he do it himself?

The January 31 incident was only the straw that broke the camel's back. These men were organized and ready to go before this incident ever occurred.

INTERVIEW WITH BAXTON BRYANT
DIRECTOR
TENNESSEE COUNCIL OF HUMAN RELATIONS
APRIL 28, 1969

Dan Powell, who is director of the Southeastern Division of COPE (Committee on Political Education), is vice-president of the Tennessee Council of Human Relations and lives in Memphis. The second week of the strike, Dan got back to town and called me and said, "We've got a real problem down here, and I wish you would come down." Well, I went to Memphis and became involved. As you know, you use whatever relationships you have, and you start working with those. I attended a meeting when the ministers were trying to negotiate this thing. This was the meeting of Loeb and Ciampa. Early the next day, I talked with some members, white members, of the Tennessee Council of Human Relations there in Memphis and was startled to find that many people in the Council who I knew to be committed to justice and fairness were on the mayor's side.

I discussed this at length with Mrs. Ray Allen, whose husband is dean at Southwestern. You might say that she was shocked to see that I was shocked at her. Finally, after going through the issues as

I understood them . . . to me it was race as much as labor, and this is where I thought there was a lack of honesty on both parts, both the mayor and the union. The union didn't want to act as if it was race because they wanted the involvement of the union movement. From their standpoint, it wasn't race. They wanted the involvement of a lot of other white unions, and the only way you were going to get others involved is on the basis of a labor dispute and rightly so. Now, the mayor didn't want a race situation, and he was denying it had anything to do with race, but when you lay as many people off as they did on that day in January, and these were blacks, and you keep 15 or 20 people, and they are all white, and you give them an extra day's pay and the others who were black received only call-up pay, it's *race,* brother. When you've got a union that's 95 percent black and a city administration that is 98 percent white, there is just no way that the race issue can stay out of it. So I thought they would have gotten somewhere a lot quicker if the mayor and the Council and union had admitted right away that they had a race issue on their hands. This is not to say that the situation didn't have a lot of other components, and components that were basic as far as the union was concerned or the mayor was concerned.

So out of the talk with Mrs. Allen, she asked me if I would be willing to come to her home and talk with a group of her neighbors. This was about the second week. On the following Friday, I went to her home and met there 25 to 30 people. Included in the group was Charley Crump. This meeting was held after the union had called all its members to City Hall and had wound up serving lunch there in the council chambers with all the ensuing mustard on the rugs, etc. I said this was a beautiful thing, and Charles couldn't understand how I could take this attitude and still call myself a responsible citizen. I told him that he was missing the whole thing, that if we ever got anywhere in this thing, black folks had to feel as if it's their City Hall, and up until the other afternoon it had been the white folks' City Hall. Granted, it might have been used for the wrong purpose, but the fact was they were in it, and they were talking about *their* city hall, and they felt at home. I felt it was very important that they feel this way. We had a good meeting here at the Allen home. We tried to dispel a lot of the rumors. One was that this was the international union stirring this up and that the black folks really didn't want it, but they were being forced to. We talked about the issue as being "I Am a Man"; it was self-identity, self-pride.

It was out of this meeting that we set up a lot of the other confrontation groups such as the one at St. Luke's. We had the union come and give their side. This was the first time the union had spoken to public groups outside of union meetings. We had Mayor Loeb come and give the City's side, and I was surprised and shocked that the *man* who gave the mayor the most trouble in asking him why they couldn't recognize the union was Charles Crump. His feelings had swung around against those of the mayor.

We were in on most of the strategy sessions for the marches. I made speech after speech to the union men, especially when morale was low in the middle of the strike. I established contact with the mayor. Someone said that at one time I was the sole contact between the union and the City. I had total access to the mayor from the time I got there to Martin's assassination.

My relationship with the mayor was cordial though I took the side of the union. The day before Dr. King was killed, I was sitting in on the precouncil meeting with the mayor and later went with him to Southwestern where he was to speak. He introduced me from the platform as a very close friend whom he respected but who totally disagreed with him on the sanitation strike. I did set up the meetings between the black ministers and the mayor and later set up meetings between the law enforcement agencies and the march planners for the King memorial march.

My feeling all the way through was to let the mayor know that you appreciated his feelings and his position but to come down hard on the right of these men to say what they wanted. We were never able to put this across. The mayor would always go back that he didn't believe it was what the men wanted, that he had related to them when he was a commissioner . . . and this kind of crap. I tried to get him to go out and speak to the men. I told him, "Mayor, every time I speak to the men I ask them, 'do you want a union,' and they stand 1,200 strong affirming it." You just can't make me believe that men being forced show that much enthusiasm.

The nearest we ever came to getting the mayor to agree to anything was to try, and we did this repeatedly, to get the mayor to see what was happening in the lives of the black men that he believed in and appreciated. The mayor is a very raw-boned person, as you know, hard driving, self-initiative, and this kind of stuff that is guts and stand-up-and-be-a-man. This is what the mayor purports to believe in. What I tried to say was, "Mayor, you have to admire these men. Here it is you've got the whole city administration and you against the little ole sanitation men and they're standing up to you. They are shaking their fists in your face and telling you to go to hell. Now whether you agree to it or not, there ought to be something in you that appreciates this. Here they have been beat down, they've been folk that have scratched their heads and shuffled their feet, and all of a sudden they stand up and decide there are some things they are going to stand for."

Well, the mayor would appreciate this, and I think the nearest the mayor ever came to giving in was two or three weeks before the tragedy. I gave him the parable in the New Testament about the sower who went forth to sow, and he sowed wheat, and that night when he went to sleep the enemy came and sowed tares. When the spring rains came, and all started to come up, there was the wheat and the tares. The workers of the harvest said they would go in and pull up the tares. But the master of the harvest told them not to do this because the roots were all entwined so that you couldn't pull up the tares without pulling up the wheat too. So they should wait for harvest time, and then the master of the harvest would separate the chaff from the wheat. I went ahead to say: "Here these men are. You can't put them down without destroying this that you believe in. You can't put them down without destroying their guts, their backbone, their pride. This is the wheat that you claim you want." Now the tare, as far as the mayor was concerned, was the union. "When you destroy the union, you destroy these men. Now do you want men who have guts; do you want men who have pride?"

You are even dealing with juvenile delinquency. Moynihan[1] in his study of the Negro family talks about the breakdown in respect for the Negro male, and that this is part of the rebellion of Negro youth. There is not a sanitation worker out there today, if he won his rights, not a father out there who couldn't go home tonight and sit down at his table and his kid wouldn't say, "That's my dad." He becomes

1. U. S. Department of Labor, Office of Policy Planning and Research (Daniel P. Moynihan), *The Negro Family: The Case for National Action* (Washington: U. S. Department of Labor, 1965).

someone worthy of respect. The same pride, the same respect, of wanting to be someone tied up with the union also makes a man want to paint his house, to clean up the yard. Now this the mayor came nearer seeing, and you'd get him nearly over, and then I'm sure the conservative elements would get a hold of him, and next time he would be back in the same rut. So these are some of the things I did. As far as the negotiations, I didn't do anything. I think Mr. Reynolds is one of the most delightful, hard-working men I've ever met. I'm sure Frank Miles did all that he could do. I think the mayor had all kinds of opportunities. To me, it's one of the most tragic things I've ever been under. The mayor was most certainly the dominant fixture in the strike. The two major issues as I saw them were recognition and wages. Recognition was nearly the sole thing because we had indications numbers of times that the small pay increase could be taken care of. The big issue was recognition.

Why did the mayor take the position he did on this issue?

I think it's his whole background, his total inability to perceive, to understand. He had arrogance, pride; he took a position rather quickly. He had made a lot of statements about unions, probably that were untrue but that he himself felt were true. Maybe he found out they were untrue. But his total stand was antiunion. . . . we heard it kicked around quite a bit that he would not be the first mayor in the South to recognize a public employees' union. Legal precedent was not a real issue; it was only a facade.

How did the white community stand in support of the mayor? What segment supported him?

Oh, I would say throughout he had a majority. Because, you see, most people in the last year, . . . their attitude toward public unions was you just don't strike against the city. You just don't strike against the state, the national government. Sanitation workers shouldn't strike at all; they're not too important people. We don't say that in white society; we don't say it in words; we just don't distress ourselves too much in white society on this issue.

What was the state of the Negro community prior to the strike and then after the beginning of the strike?

Well, of course, there never has been a more divided community than the Negro community with its factions. The Crump machine had depended on the Negro vote, and then you've got a Negro community that had just been prostituted politically by Mayor Ingram. He was judge before he was mayor, and he was probably the first judge to ever give the Negro a fair shake in the police courts. Someone suggested, and I don't really know how true it is, that he really didn't like the Negro, but he hated the police more. Therefore, he did do a lot of things and, rightly so, won the respect of the Negro community because he at least would make the police force do their job legally. On this basis, he won their support for mayor. The interesting thing was they never stopped to ask what kind of man he was or what he felt. So Ingram had prostituted this vote. Leob had none of this vote, less than 2 percent.

I visited with Mayor Loeb before he was mayor, and he purported at that time to want to be mayor of *all* the folk. But, you see, the tragedy of Mayor Loeb and other Mayor Loebs like him is that they want to be fair, but he has his own definition of fairness, and his definition comes out of white middle-class society, and his fairness is related to how he judges things. The inability to go to the gut of issues, to the cause, is the real tragedy.

But to return to the state of the Negro community, you've got the many church groups in the community, and I think the churches are still the best organized groups day in and day out in the Negro community. All of these have their own little thing, and they are all very competitive for membership, and sometimes they aren't too ethical. So you had all of this. Then you've got people that cut across all of these groups. You've got people that are trying to get in white society. They accept the white man's values and deny every bit of their blackness. Then there were those who were very aware of their blackness, such as Jim Lawson. You've also got those who had given up. So you had a very fragmented black community before the strike.

After the strike began, it became the issue around which blackness came to be appreciated, and I think the best symbol of that is Dr. Ralph Jackson. As Ed Stanfield reports, Dr. Jackson became militant overnight when he was maced by the police. With one spray from a policeman's mace, Ralph Jackson was turned from a Tomish black who wanted to be white. It changed him for an eternity and helped him find his identity as a black man. He is an activist, not violent though, as a result. The sanitation worker was an underdog. This became in the black community a rallying point. I think there was a solidarity in the black community that had never been seen.

Contrast in importance the economic issues of the strike versus the underlying issues of human dignity.

I think the human dignity issue would override five to one. I don't think the economic issues . . . this is where the mayor made his bad mistake, he didn't see this thing for what it was. This business of "I'm a Man" I think is one of the most marvelous things. The picture I saw happen illustrates this. The day after Martin was assassinated, and you had the tanks rolling down the street, there was this little black man picketing with a sign "I Am a Man" walking on the sidewalk with a big old tank with all armaments down. This was all you could see, this little man and the tank. I think it was one of the most beautiful things I've ever seen. Here something had happened to this little man that this tank with all its size and guns didn't scare him. To me, this was the overriding issue. The others were important, but they would never have been settled, and neither will they in America until the first issue is settled—the dignity and acceptance of the individual.

How do you feel the Negro in Memphis evaluated the role of the union in public employment.

Well, I think Memphis probably made the public employees' union. I think it will become the dominant union in America because of its identification with the black man and with Martin King and also its ability to do some things. I think they see the union as a far bigger hope than the church. They see the union as a place where they can recognize some benefit. They saw some togetherness, and they saw it not bend and break under stress and crisis. It is a tribute to Jerry Wurf, Jesse Epps, Bill Lucy, and P. J. Ciampa that they gave this kind of hope that was needed so desperately.

How do you feel the Negro community stands related to the union on a post-strike basis?

Divided, terribly divided. They won a little prosperity, and now all the old ties are coming up. Jealousy and things of this sort are again present. But there are signs in Memphis. Even though I don't think you can get away from these other divisions, the union is the place where more of the old divisions are finding a common identity. A lot of those who supported various political people and those in the various churches are in the union. The union holds a lot of hope as a unifying force. Even more than that, it has given a whole group of powerless people some power and a sense of direction.

One of the tragedies of Memphis is how little the white community did to get involved, how they could see something like this coming and just stand on the side and watch a tragedy develop. But now the Chamber of Commerce has become involved. There are probably more new starts in Memphis by more new groups: employment, housing, confrontation, sensitivity groups, training groups. Everywhere you turn, there is something happening. It's too early to see, but it could be the downfall for Memphis because what they've got to realize now is that you've got to be for real. It's not going to be enough to have a facade. That may be all right for a start. There has to be a commitment of the heart to the issue. If this commitment goes no further than a facade, then Memphis is in for a lot of trouble.

I think one of the greatest Americans we have today is living in Memphis in the person of Jim Lawson. He probably has one of the best minds in America, and I don't know of anyone who has more commitment of character. Now to the extent that the white community can recognize black leadership that relates to the needs of the Negro, they will not miss the real needs of the black community.

INTERVIEW WITH FRANK B. MILES
CO-MEDIATOR, MEMPHIS SANITATION STRIKE
APRIL 21, 1969

I've been in the labor movement for a good number of years, approximately five years with the Federal Mediation and Conciliation Service and several years in management. I've been representing management for the past 11 or 12 years in the field of industrial relations. I'd been assistant to the director of industrial relations of Plough Inc. about six or seven years before I came here. Since 1965, I've been director of industrial relations, manager of transportation, and was elected vice-president of this company [E. L. Bruce] in December, 1968.

Last year in February when this situation developed with the city and the sanitation workers, I was involved only to the extent that I discussed it with some people who *were* involved, and I probably made some observations at the time. I was asked by one party to call the mayor and discuss certain aspects of the strike that we were concerned about. That concern was that, at the beginning of this dispute, which was purely and simply a labor dispute, if the dispute was not controlled to the point that it could be settled as a labor dispute, then it was liable to spill over into racial conflict. About this time, everyone in the city was becoming more and more concerned about it. Consequently, you had a lot of volunteers in the Ministerial Association and other groups of people becoming concerned. The City was getting a lot of advice and counsel from a lot of people. This was after the strike had been going on two or three weeks, I guess.

My concern began to develop in the first ten days when I saw that the City was hiring replacements. Anyone who is familiar with a strike situation in industrial relations knows that when an employer begins to hire replacements, every replacement hired constitutes one more issue. If there were five issues to begin with, for every replacement you hire for an old employee, you've got one more issue. In the final analysis, the union cannot end the strike, or will not as a general rule, by capitulating and sacrificing all the people out on strike who have been replaced. They will go on and on and keep the strike going indefinitely. And then some of the replacements they were hiring were white, and almost all people out on strike were Negro. This is one of the concerns I had. So my discussion at this stage of it in the first two or three weeks was really just voicing some concern and hoping that I could find some way to resolve the dispute. I made a couple of suggestions which served no purpose at the time. One of these suggestions was to see if the City could not stop hiring replacements until such time as they could resolve the question. The mayor acted on one of the suggestions, but the union didn't buy it, and I could understand why they wouldn't, but it *was* made by the mayor in good faith.

About this time [February 18], the ministers had gotten into it, and they called the city officials, including the mayor, and the union officials together, and they had a dialogue which was rather a three-way dialogue from the union to the moderator to the City. This three-way communication was going on although all three were sitting in the same room right across from one another. A table was running down this way, and a table was running down that way, I understand, and that doesn't make for very good collective bargaining negotiations. As I recall it, they were in sort of a V shape.

The ministers served as moderators and took turns at this. Rabbi Wax was one of them who served as a moderator at one time, and I've forgotten the other ministers. There were priests and ministers; almost all faiths were involved. They were making a sincere and honest effort to try to bring about a dialogue between the parties in the dispute. At this time, the international union's president, Jerry Wurf, entered the picture for the first time, and he participated in those discussions. Without getting the newspaper file out, it's a little difficult to remember all the incidents and the order they took place in, and you may have some information from these other people such as Baxton Bryant on this subject.

The mayor himself participated in these discussions. These lasted about a week, and, from that time on, there was very little discussion and practically no meetings between representatives of the City and representatives of the union until I called them together in these mediation sessions that I started.

At this point, he reviewed my calendar of events. Some of the discussion that followed re-hashes earlier discussion.

My best recollection of this time table as I see it here on this calendar of events . . . [is that] after the initial walkout on February 12, the mayor raised the question of whether the union represented the majority of the employees. So, the union took them up on that and brought the whole crew down to City Hall. Some thousand people were there; there may have been more than that. They asked him for a meeting, and he came over to the auditorium and met with them. Then, after that, he met with the representatives of the union. Mr. Ciampa and Mr. T. O. Jones I know were there. . . . Bill Lucy may have been one of them, but I don't know who the other parties were, but I know especially that Mr. Ciampa was there. They may have met one or two different times. . . . Then on February 17, the

Ministerial Association or at least a group of ministers—I hesitate to say the Ministerial Association, but at least a group of ministers called upon the mayor and asked him if he would participate in dialogue discussions with the union representatives, and they would act as moderators. This started on a Sunday night as I recall it, which my calendar tells me was on February 18. The reason I recall this so vividly is not the exact date as such, but during this first meeting that was held with the ministers, they were hoping that Jerry Wurf, the international president of the union, would get in in time for this meeting. He did. Now, there may have been a meeting held on the seventeenth, but I remember specifically that he came in at 8:00 or 9:00 some time that Sunday night and came into the meeting. They met until 3:00 or 4:00 in the morning as I recall.

I did not sit in and observe these meetings or anything like that, but I understood that it was sort of a three-way dialogue going between the union and the ministers and from the ministers to the mayor's committee. This went on for several days and then broke up and was terminated.

From that time on, there was a series of events that happened, the exact dates of which I am not certain. I see on this calendar of events, and these dates could be right, . . . the entrance of the NAACP, the hearings, and the appearance of the strikers at City Hall. I remember one day in particular when they served sandwiches right in the council chambers down there. This rather shocked everybody when they did this. During this time, there was no direct discussion going on between the union and the City. Representatives of the union appeared before the City Council urging that they take some action on their own to recognize the union. This was the number-one point that the union was concerned about, and that was to gain *recognition*.

There were some people carrying on discussions between the parties, acting as mediators, so to speak, between the City with the mayor's group and the union representatives. It so happens that Ned Cook, who is president of this company, was one of those involved in it. He happens to be a close friend of the mayor's, but he was also interested in the civic life of this community. He established a speaking relationship with the union's committee so that they had a certain degree of confidence in him, such that being a friend of the mayor, he would at least present their side of the case objectively.

He and a young attorney did have the confidence of the union and were working effectively, up to a point. Another attorney, Lucius Burch, worked on this from time to time. He also had the confidence of the union. All of these people were concerned with bringing about some understanding between the City and the union as to what type of agreement they could come up with which would give the union recognition. Once the union was given recognition, they could execute some kind of agreement. The big obstacle was that the City was taking the position that the City could not execute a bargaining agreement with one union exclusively and, from their viewpoint at the time (based upon court decision), rightly so. In other words, they could not grant one union exclusive bargaining rights to represent certain employees working for the City. They had good reason for making this contention, and this was the real problem all the way through it. It boiled down finally to the mayor issuing a letter, and you probably have a record of this if you've got the news clipping on this. It was printed in the *Press Scimatar* right at the top of the page. In this letter, he outlined several points on which he was in agreement with the union. However, he was not willing to grant them exclusive recognition, or checkoff of dues. This rocked along, and all these things happened that you have listed here, possibly on these dates.

Two weeks before March 27, I had participated in some meetings with people such as Lucius Burch, Edmund Orgill, and others who were concerned with bringing about a resolution of this dispute. I had a number of telephone discussions with them over this period of time. It seemed as though every Saturday, somebody had a new idea they wanted to try out to try to resolve this thing. All these attempts were sincere, but I'd have to say they were not realistic in attempting to deal with collective bargaining problems. There had been those who had suggested mediation, those who had suggested arbitration; the papers had even suggested these from time to time. The union was, of course, familiar with the process of mediation. And so again, *without getting into detail as to how I got involved in this,* just let me say that the Council adopted a resolution asking me to act as a mediator on behalf of the Council and to request the mayor's representatives and the union's representatives to meet in mediation sessions. Of course, both parties were in agreement to this before it was actually done.

The first sessions I called together in joint negotiation were in the Claridge Hotel. This represented the first time they had met in a joint conference of this type since the week of February 17. This was March 27. In the very first session, the city raised the question of legality which had to be taken up in the Chancery Court as it relates to this injunction that was granted by Chancellor Hoffmon. As soon as this question was resolved, we sat down and started to deal with the problem. The big problem was to determine just what form or just what approach I as a mediator could make to this situation in order to develop some kind of agreement. I started out on a proposition which I had used many times in mediation, and that was to develop some kind of a memorandum of understanding. I outlined this thought or idea to both parties and told them exactly what I was going to develop. I indicated that I would deal with the various questions they had been discussing and that if I were· successful in setting down a meaningful memorandum of understanding, I would, in making my report to the Council, request the Council adopt this by resolution. This would at least give it some form of legality, and it would be put on the minutes of the City Council records. Unless the mayor just refused to cooperate, it could be a very meaningful resolution of the problem. Both parties agreed to at least explore this.

We found that the biggest problem we had to get over was the key clause in any labor-management-relations problem, collective bargaining agreement, or whatever you want to call it, and that was the recognition clause. The City, of course, spent a good portion of time the first day explaining their position why they could not agree to set forth a "recognition clause" which granted the union exclusive bargaining rights with the City. The City indicated that it would not execute a signed collective bargaining agreement with the union granting it exclusive bargaining rights with this group of employees.

We started our meetings on Monday. We were still on recognition Tuesday and Wednesday. If we could have gotten over that first clause, not all would have been easier, but it would have at least been somewhat easier. We had made *some* progress in agreement as to the form that the memorandum would take. At least it would be something on paper without just being in the form of a letter. All kinds of things had been suggested before, an exchange of letters; you name it, somebody had suggested it. Practically everything except a memorandum of understanding in the context which I was considering.

As we were into the Wednesday meeting, there were members of the union's committee who were supposed to be at union headquarters to plan for the march that Dr. King was going to participate in on Thursday of that week. They were getting quite restless and wanted to leave. We finally got down to that point where we could have gotten over the obstacle of the recognition by spelling out what recognition means. I've found out many times as a mediator that if you have a word that is bothering you, you can get around it by defining it. By using definition rather than the word itself. This was exactly what I was doing, and I was just about to get the parties to agree to this when, without naming the party, one party on the union committee would not go along with it because of the racial implication involved with the use of the word "recognition" and what it meant to him. He felt very strongly that this word should be in the agreement. I was suggesting that, in effect, the City would agree to meet with the union from time to time to discuss wages, hours, and conditions of employment, and this is what recognition means in the final analysis. We also had something else in there that they would try to effect meaningful agreements out of these discussions or something to that effect, but it broke down right at that point.

The union felt that the City was not dealing in good faith, and some information on what had been going on in the meeting was leaked to the newspapers. Thus, there was a good bit of emotional exchange between the two committees. However, both committees agreed to come back whenever I asked them to do so. The union attached a condition to this which I have heard many times: "Whenever the City is ready to sit down and negotiate in good faith, we'll be ready to meet." Of course, the union committee got on television that night and made certain charges which were not too harmful to our negotiations. They were charging that the City's committee was not there with the ability and the authority to negotiate in good faith.

On Thursday, Dr. King came in, and the ruckus which happened on Beale Street transpired in which some of the windows were broken. Dr. King was whisked away from in front of the parade and taken to the hotel.

I allowed this situation to set for a few days so that the whole thing could cool down so that, when I brought them together again, they could come to grips with the problem with less emotion than they would have, under the circumstances, if I had called them right back together, say on Friday, following this parade, march, or demonstration. So, it was the beginning of the next week [April 1] when I started calling the parties to bring them back together. I got an agreement that they could meet Friday, beginning at 10:00 a.m.

Of course, Dr. King was killed on Thursday night [April 4], and, on Friday evening, I began talking with both the union and City relative to setting up a meeting on Saturday or no later than the following Monday. About this same time, James Reynolds, undersecretary of labor, appeared in Memphis and called me. I spent several hours with him down at the hotel on Friday evening discussing the whole thing. We agreed on a plan of action which was that I would call the parties together beginning Saturday afternoon at approximately 2:00 p.m. He had met earlier with the union's committee and went over Saturday morning and met with the mayor.

We started our meetings on Saturday afternoon at 3:00 p.m. and stayed all Saturday afternoon and evening until approximately 3:00 Sunday morning. We met again on Sunday. It was approximately 2:00 on Monday morning before we seemed to be getting somewhere in these discussions. The mayor, representing the City, and Jerry Wurf, international president of the union, were both in Memphis, but neither of them had sat in on Saturday's meetings or Sunday's meetings. Finally, about 2:00 Monday morning, we called for both the parties to come in because, by this time, we had gotten through most of the language of this memorandum of understanding. Incidentally, when we started the meetings on Saturday, I reviewed whatever progress we had made in the first three days, at least the acceptance of the idea of developing the memorandum of understanding with both parties agreeing that this would be a good approach. So, in this context, or the context that a memorandum of understanding would be developed by the panel of mediation consisting of Frank Miles and James Reynolds and that this memorandum would be submitted to the Council as a report, we had begun.

We had made progress through the language of the agreement, even in dealing with the checkoff clause, which was the other real hang-up clause or issue between them, one being the recognition clause, the second being the checkoff clause. And the union had gained acceptance or willingness by the City to allow the City to make deductions through the credit union for union dues. This can be a very complicated process if you want to get into it. We had to have the representatives of the credit union come down here, and their executive board had to meet in session and adopt a resolution whereby they would agree to do this, and then certain other things had to be clarified with the Washington representatives because it is set up under a federal charter. This was time-consuming, but these issues were so important and critical that the time we spent on them was well spent because, at this time, we were narrowing the area of dispute down to the money issue. So, on Monday, . . . well, I think we recessed the meetings until after Dr. King's funeral which was held on Tuesday. I think we came back on Wednesday, and we met on Wednesday, Thursday, Friday, Saturday, Sunday, and again on Monday [April 15]. It was Tuesday morning that I think we finally brought the parties into an area of agreement as far as money was concerned. The issue as far as money was concerned revolved around the City's and the mayor's statement that the City would grant these employees something like 8-cents-an-hour increase, I think. They would recommend this and put it in the budget for the coming year to be paid to these people. But some members of the City Council had proposed increases in excess of this, and one proposal bandied around stated that the employees should receive 10 cents an hour immediately and five cents an hour at some later time, or a total of 15 cents an hour. As I explained to James Reynolds when he came into the picture, that as far as the union's committee was concerned, it was almost a foregone conclusion that, let me say as far as the union's membership was concerned, that it was going to be most difficult ever to get them to agree to settle the money question on something less than 15 cents because they had some support for this from the City Council. This proved to be the case. In fact, the union committee was pressing for much more than 15 cents as we were trying to bring it down to the wire. We finally got acceptance from the union committee that they would recommend 15 cents. We finally got acceptance by the City that they would include this in the budget.

The problem that confronted the City was . . . and the mayor was quite honest, and Mr. Reynolds and I were quite impressed with the mayor's presentation of the City's fiscal problems. They were very real, and he made a very fine presentation of it. The immediate problem that the City was confronted with was that they just did not have the money in the treasury to provide a 10-or 15-cent-an-hour or more, even a 1-cent-an-hour increase as of April 16 or prior to expiration of the fiscal year, which was June 30. So the real problem there was how were we going to bring about an increase of wages, which the union was demanding immediately, prior to this time, prior to June 30. The other question was, we felt, the City was never going to agree to a 15-cent across-the-board increase to be effective immediately. There might be a possibility of their agreeing to a 10-cent-an-hour increase; that is, the 15 cents would be broken up into two segments, one of 10 cents and the second of 5 cents. Without getting into too much detail, we finally came up with the formula that was finally accepted. Instead of any increase becoming effective immediately, it would become effective on May 1, and that would be 10 cents an hour, and then on September 1, there would be a further 5-cents-an-hour increase granted the employees.

We still had the problem of providing the money for May and June. A real good friend of mine and a good friend of the city's contacted me and volunteered to supply the money. I'll say further, without going into any detail about that, that the sum he supplied was $60,000. This was to provide the City with the funds to put the increase into effect. This was a critical point, and this man's volunteering to do this played a significant part in enabling us to bring the strike to a settlement and get these people back to work.

When we finally got this package down, what I'm describing here on money, and we got the language of the agreement worked out where it provided for recognition, a meaningful grievance procedure, a no-strike clause, and the checkoff of dues which would be collected through the credit union, it was all incorporated in this memorandum of understanding. The grievance procedure was one of the real key points in this memorandum, and the no-strike, no-lockout clause is, of course, significant. The grievance procedure has one real significant provision in it, which is that if a dispute is finally submitted to arbitration, the arbitrator's decision would be accepted as advisory arbitration. In other words, the mayor does not have to accept the decision as final and binding. The mayor's decision is final and binding. Of course, the net effect of all this is that if an arbitrator is accepted as an impartial person in hearing a case and makes a recommendation based on something that is equitable, fair, and honest, why more than likely . . . at least the percentages favor the mayor following his advice and decision rendered.

When this memorandum of understanding was completed and being ratified by the union, we took it to the City Council; it was adopted by resolution, and the mayor implemented this resolution by following through with it. Then, for a period of about a week or ten days, I spent at least several hours every other day down there trying to work out some of the details on this thing. The agreement itself almost broke down over a threatened wildcat strike in one of the yards in which the truck drivers refused to take the trucks out. If it hadn't been for the International's representative stepping into the picture, it could have started all over again. Jesse Epps was very instrumental in getting this thing resolved at that point at least. We had a series of meetings after that that served to resolve the problem that they were confronted with. What it boiled down to was that there were just too many people on the job. There were more people that came back to work after the strike than they expected, and this was one of the things I pointed out to you at the beginning that can be a real critical question or problem in any strike in which the employer hires a number of replacements. Thank goodness in that situation they had not hired too many, but, under the circumstances, when they finally called people back to work, there were a few too many, and they had to work this thing out.

The other problem we were involved in was working out the mechanics of this checkoff through the credit union. It finally settled down and, evidently, they have been working under this agreement every since.

The following response was directed to outlining the critical issues and explaining why these issues were critical.

The only reason I refer to the recognition clause as being a real critical question is because, by the very nature of a recognition clause in the framework of a collective bargaining agreement, it sets out very explicitly that the employer recognizes the union as exclusive bargaining agent for a specific group of people or employees. It was not that the City would not recognize this union. They had made it very clear that they would recognize the union, but not as exclusive bargaining representative, and there's a distinction, a very pertinent distinction there, that had to be maintained.

Now the other issue that was most critical was the checkoff clause. I say it was critical because to the union it was highly critical. It was the only means they had in this state where they couldn't have a closed shop or union shop for maintenance of membership. . . . It was a critical question to them of maintaining their membership. It's the only form of union security that you actually have in the State of Tennessee in most collective bargaining agreements. So this was a real critical question with the union. The City had no checkoff system in any form with any of the unions they had relationships with, and they had working relationships with other unions. They had granted recognition to other unions, the painters' union for example, the carpenters' union, the machinists' union, and other unions which have members who were working for the City. But the type of agreement they had was just simply . . . possibly a letter to the City from the union setting forth what the standard, uniform wage rate was for the industry at that time as it would apply to members who worked for the City. The City usually put these rates into effect. Beyond that, there were no written contracts of any kind, not even memorandums of understanding or memorandums of agreement.

The other real important question was, of course, the money.

INTERVIEW WITH JAMES REYNOLDS
FORMER UNDERSECRETARY OF LABOR
CO-MEDIATOR, MEMPHIS SANITATION STRIKE
JUNE 9, 1969

How did you become involved?

After Dr. King's assassination on the fourth, I was in my office on April 5, where I received a phone call from President Johnson. He asked me why I wasn't down in Memphis trying to settle that strike. I explained to him that the Department of Labor doesn't normally get involved with a strike unless both parties request this, and then it is the Federal Mediation and Conciliation Service that would be involved. The only other cause would be a national emergency for the federal government to get involved. Johnson told me, "I regard this as a matter of great danger as it has implications far beyond the issues of the strike. The urban problems facing our nation could be enlarged by the events of Dr. King's death. I want you to get down there and help settle that thing."

I first contacted Governor Buford Ellington of Tennessee and told him that I had been directed by the President to try and bring the strike to a settlement. He welcomed me and offered his cooperation. I caught the first plane out of Washington for Memphis. As the plane took off, I could see fires in Washington from the disturbances there. I arrived in Memphis Friday evening, April 5. I contacted the mayor and explained to him that the President had sent me and why. I told him that I wasn't here to impose a solution or to circumvent his position but that I was here to try and bring the parties to some form of agreement that they could live with. Loeb explained that he was desperately tired from having been up all the previous night and asked if I could come see him the next morning.

I got a pass the next morning so that I could get out on the street. As I approached City Hall, I was met by armed guards. I entered and went up to the mayor's office where I was again met by armed guards. When I saw the mayor, I again explained to him that I recognized his position and responsibility but that this thing *had* to be settled. After discussion, he agreed to my entrance in the case.

What was the state of negotiations when you entered them?

On March 27, the Mayor had gone on television and made some statements about the union and reiterated his position against the union. This made it harder for him to back down. The union also made some charges. Thus, the lines were pretty well drawn.

How well did Leob understand the racial issues?

Loeb really thought he understood the racial issue. He cited his history in business with a predominantly Negro labor staff as a basis for his understanding. His outlook was a part of his whole makeup, which had been the product of generations. He viewed the matter as having been encouraged by radical civil rights people. At heart, he didn't feel the men really wanted the union.

I talked with men on the picket lines who didn't know who I was. I sensed a deep frustration in them. Black dignity was definitely an issue to them.

What was Miles's influence?

Frank Miles had a tremendous impact. He was respected by all concerned and had access to everyone. Having someone like this with a professional labor background is something for us to think about in other municipalities. My coming down enhanced his respectability.

What do you think about current union-City negotiations in Memphis?

Epps is not one of nature's noblemen. When you put him and the mayor together you've got a real powder keg.

Memorandum of Understanding and Attachments (Memphis)

The following memorandum is submitted as the understanding by the mediation panel consisting of Frank Miles and James Reynolds, Undersecretary of Labor, that the City of Memphis, as represented by the executive branch and Local Union 1733, American Federation of State, County and Municipal Employees, AFL-CIO, representing certain employees of the Division of Public Works, have agreed upon the specific matters set forth hereafter.

1.
RECOGNITION

The City of Memphis recognizes the American Federation of State, County and Municipal Employees, AFL-CIO, Local 1733 as the designated representative for certain employees in the Division of Public Works, for the purpose of negotiations on wages, hours and conditions of employment to the full extent and authority provided by the Charter of the City of Memphis and the laws of the State of Tennessee.

The term "certain employees" as used herein places no limitations or restrictions on the right of any employee to belong and be represented by the Union.

2.
PAYMENT OF DUES

In the past it has been the established policy of the City to permit employees to authorize payroll deductions to be paid to their Credit Union. Employees may continue to make arrangements with their Credit Union for the availability of funds for any lawful purpose, including payment of union dues. The manner in which such funds are paid out by the Credit Union is a matter exclusively between the employees and their Credit Union.

The City has no control over the relationship between the employees and their credit union on the disbursements of funds by the credit union.

The City has not in the past and will not in the future attempt to exercise any control over the activities of employees' credit unions, which are wholly separate corporations operating under federal statutes.

Therefore, the City of Memphis recognizes that any employees of the Public Works Division who desire to make arrangements with the credit union in order to pay their dues to Local 1733 may do so and that the City will honor procedures for the deduction of sums payable to the credit union by reason of such arrangements, provided that the arrangement between the credit union and the employee is based upon full compliance with the Federal statutes under which it operates.

3.

PRESENT BENEFITS

The City will formally list the present benefits available and currently in force for unclassified employees, with the understanding that continuing discussion will be held for the purpose of providing for equitable changes therein.

4.

PROMOTIONS

The City shall make promotions on the basis of seniority and competency.

5.

*GRIEVANCE PROCEDURE FOR
THE PUBLIC WORKS DIVISION*

1. The City recognizes and will deal with representatives of the Union in all matters relating to grievances upon request of an aggrieved employee or employees.

2. The representatives of the Union may be the officers of the Union or Union Stewards, provided the Union stewards shall be employees of the City and their names shall be furnished to the City by the Union.

3. Officers of the Union and Union stewards shall be granted reasonable time off during working hours to investigate and settle grievances, upon approval of their immediate supervisor, without loss of pay.

4. The number of stewards and the areas in which they are to be

representatives of the Union shall be determined upon by mutual agreement.

5. Any grievance or misunderstanding which may arise concerning the interpretation or application of City rules and procedure, working conditions, suspension, discharge and discipline, shall be acted upon in the following manner:

Step One—The Union officer or the steward, with the aggrieved employee, shall discuss the grievance or dispute with the immediate supervisor within five (5) working days of the date of the grievance or his knowledge of its occurrence. The immediate supervisor shall attempt to adjust the matter and shall respond to the Union representatives within three (3) working days.

Step Two—If, after a thorough discussion with the immediate supervisor, the grievance has not been satisfactorily resolved, the Union representative and the aggrieved employee shall, after written appeal, discuss the grievance with the Bureau Head within three (3) working days after the immediate supervisor's response is due. The Bureau Head shall respond in writing within three (3) working days thereafter.

Step Three—If, after thorough discussion with the Bureau Head, the grievance has not been satisfactorily resolved, the Union representative, the aggrieved employee and the President of the Local Union shall, after written appeal, discuss the grievance with the Director of the Division of Public Works, within five (5) working days after the Division Head's response is due. The Director of the Division of Public Works shall respond in writing within three (3) working days.

Step Four, Arbitration—If, after receipt of the decision of the Director of the Division of Public Works, the grievance has not been satisfactorily resolved, the Union may request arbitration by writing to the Mayor no later than fifteen (15) working days after the rendering of the decision or the expiration of the time limit for rendering of such decision. The Chairman of the arbitration panel shall hold a hearing within ten (10) working days after the receipt of the request.

The arbitration panel shall have access to all written statements and documents pertaining to the appeals in the grievance.

The arbitration panel shall render its decision based upon a majority vote, no later than thirty (30) calendar days after the conclusion of the final hearing. Such decision shall be reported to the

Mayor and to the Union, shall be a matter of public record, and shall be advisory to the Mayor in order to enable him or his designee to render a final decision.

Selection of the Arbitration Panel—The City shall select one member of the panel, and the Union shall select the other member of the panel. The third member of the panel, who shall be the Chairman, shall be jointly selected by the appointees of the Union and the City.

If, within five (5) days after the request for arbitration is made, the Union and City panelists cannot agree upon the appointment of a third member of the panel, a request will be made to the American Arbitration Association for a list of five (5) arbiters. The Union and City panelists may select one of the list of arbiters or if they still cannot agree, the following procedure shall be followed:

The party presenting the grievance shall be given the first opportunity to strike the name of one of the arbiters contained in said list. The other party may then proceed to strike a name, and this procedure shall continue until one arbiter's name remains. The arbiter whose name remains shall be designated as the third member of the arbitration panel. In the event the arbiter designated declines to act, the procedure of striking names will be reinstated until an arbiter willing to act has been selected.

The arbitration decision shall be in writing and shall set forth the panel's opinion and conclusion on the issues submitted.

The panel shall be without power to make decisions contrary to or inconsistent with or modifying or varying in any way the applicable laws or rules and regulations having the force and effect of law.

The cost of the services of the arbitration chairman shall be shared equally by both parties, but the cost of the services of the other members of the panel shall be borne by the selecting party.

No provision of the above grievance procedure shall be construed in such a manner as to be in conflict with any regulations, ordinances or Charter provision of the City of Memphis.

6.
NO STRIKE CLAUSE

The Union agrees that neither it nor any employee member thereof covered by this Agreement will engage in a strike against the City of Memphis or any Department or Division thereof.

7.
NO DISCRIMINATION

No member of the Union shall be discriminated against or discharged because of the present work stoppage or subsequent Union activities, including the utilization of the grievance procedure outlined herein, and there shall be no discrimination against any employee because of age, sex, marital status, race, religion, national origin, or political affiliation. Nothing herein, however, shall provide immunity of any employee of the Public Works Division for the violation of any law, statute, or ordinance.

April 7, 1968
RESOLUTION

The Public Works Federal Credit Union, Charter No. 15433, authorizes and directs its administrative officers to transmit all union funds so deducted by the City of Memphis to the designated officers of Local 1733, AFSCME, AFL-CIO, after proper authorization from the member of the Public Works Federal Credit Union.

The credit union will issue a check to Local 1733, AFSCME, AFL-CIO, thirty days after receiving the funds.

Acceptance of this resolution is subject to the City submitting a "print-out" and the Credit Union being able to work out the mechanics with the data processing department of the City of Memphis.

JAMES S. CAHILL
President
JAMES E. KNIGHT
Vice President
GEORGE JONES
Treasurer
GEORGE WOOD
Secretary

WALTER F. BAUGHNS
Director
G. T. THOMAS
Secretary C. C.
HUGH M. RICE
Manager

An increase in pay of ten cents (10¢) per hour effective May 1, 1968 will be granted Laborers, Crew Chiefs and Drivers of the Division of Public Works.

Beginning September 1, 1968 the said employees will receive an additional increase in pay of five cents (5¢) per hour.

All striking Employees will return to work Wednesday, April 17, 1968 at the normal reporting hour and Station. Employees failing to return by Wednesday, April 24, 1968 will forfeit right of reinstatement.

———————

American Federation of State, County and Municipal Employees, AFL-CIO

Application for Membership and Authorization for Payroll Deduction

By the City of Memphis to F. C. U. 15433

By—————————————————————— Dept.—————

(Please Print)   Last   First   Middle

Address———————————————————————————

Street   City   State   Zip Code

I, the undersigned, hereby designate the American Federation of State, County, and Municipal Employees, AFL-CIO, as my duly chosen and authorized representative on matters relating to my employment in order to promote and protect my economic welfare; I further request and authorize the deduction from my earnings each payroll period an amount sufficient to provide for the regular payment of the current rate of monthly union dues established by AFSCME Local 1733. The amount shall be so certified. The amount deducted shall be paid to the Treasurer of Local 1733, AFSCME. This authorization may be terminated by me by giving the Treasurer of said Local 1733 a thirty days written notice in advance by registered mail, or upon termination of my employment.

Account No. —————————

Amount —————————

Date —————————

Signed—————————————————

———————

TO: The Comptroller

Dear————————————:

Attached is a list of employees of the Public Works Division setting forth the amounts to be deducted from their regular payroll checks and forwarded to the Credit Union. This office has the written authorization of each named employee for the requested payroll deduction and will notify you at once of the revocation of any employee's authorization.

You will be notified in writing of any deletions or additions to the attached list.

Approved: Signed:

_____   _____

For The City of Memphis   For The Credit Union
                                    F.C.U. Charter No. 15433

APPENDIX G

Selected Documents (Memphis)

WASHINGTON, D.C., FEBRUARY 8, 1968

Mr. Charles Blackburn
Director of Public Works
Room 602
Memphis, Tennessee

DEAR MR. BLACKBURN:

Thank you for the opportunity of meeting with you last Thursday, February 1. I am hopeful that our conversation was fruitful in establishing a relationship between the City of Memphis and our Union. I advised you that a majority of your employees had signed Union authorization and check-off cards.

It was suggested that I send you a letter outlining the Union's requests. Please be advised our requests on behalf of the Public Works Employees who are members of Local 1733 are as follows:

1. Freedom for employees to join the union without fear of discrimination or reprisals because of their membership.
2. A provision for dues deduction when voluntarily authorized by the employee.
3. A mutually agreed upon grievance procedure providing for union representation at all steps with an equitable terminal step.
4. A procedure for continued discussion between designated representatives of the City of Memphis and the union for purposes of further periodic discussion on matters concerning wages, hours, and conditions of employment.

I trust your favorable consideration in this matter will be forthcoming and await your reply. With best regards, I am,

Fraternally,
P. J. CIAMPA
International Union
Field Staff Director

cc: T. O. Jones

RESOLUTION

WHEREAS—Public employees all over Tennessee and the U. S. are now engaged in bargaining collectively with their employers, and

WHEREAS—the Public Works Department in Memphis, Tennessee is now involved in a work stoppage asking to be recognized as a union by the City, and

WHEREAS—Every effort has been made by the American Federation of State, County and Municipal Employees, AFL-CIO to settle the employees disputes in an honest and forthright manner so that these employees can have dignity and justice on the job, and

WHEREAS—The Mayor of the City of Memphis has broken off negotiations and refused to recognize the union elected by the employees and to continue to meet with the Union Representatives, and

WHEREAS—The Memphis AFL-CIO Labor Council and the Tennessee State Labor Council have always spoken out for the working people in Memphis and the State of Tennessee, now therefore be it

Resolved—that the Memphis AFL-CIO Labor Council and the Tennessee State Labor Council along with its more than 100,000 affiliated members give full support and assistance to the efforts of Public Works Department Local Union No. 1733 in their efforts to obtain decency on the job, and be it

Further Resolved—that copies of this Resolution be sent to the Mayor and members of the City Council and to the news media.

TOMMY POWELL
President

Adopted 2/14/68

MEMPHIS, TENNESSEE

TO ALL AFFILIATED LOCALS:

The Public Works Employees are facing their third week in a fight to have the union that they have chosen represent them. This is a fight that many of you have been forced to engage in in years gone by. This basic principle must be recognized by all of organized labor and defended at every opportunity.

There has not been a single one of the employees of the Sanitation Department go back on the job since they went on strike and they are just as determined to win this fight now as they were when they first went out.

Such fearless determination by these people to exercise their right and in so doing attempt to raise their standard of living and preserve their dignity deserves the whole-hearted support of all organized labor.

We are asking for both financial contributions and food and clothing.

Make checks payable to: Citizens Committee to Aid Public Works Employees, 136½ S. Second St., Memphis, Tenn., 38103. Take food and clothing to Church of God in Christ, Mason Temple, 938 Mason St.

> Fraternally Yours,
> W. T. Ross, Jr.

MEMPHIS, TENNESSEE

To ALL AFFILIATED LOCALS:

The Executive Board of the Memphis AFL-CIO Labor Council voted to participate in the economic boycott that the members of Local 1733, State, County and Municipal Employees have been engaged in to strengthen their bargaining position with Mayor Loeb.

The objectives of the boycott are as follows:

1. Stay away from all downtown stores, and their branches; stay away from all establishments connected with members of the City Council; stay away from any business with the name "LOEB" on it!

2. Buy no new clothes for Easter; keep your money in your pocket!

3. Cancel your subscription to the *Commercial Appeal* and the *Press-Scimitar.*

The Council urges all affiliated locals to rigidly adhere to this boycott so that decency and justice can be gained for the Sanitation Department employees.

Fraternally yours,
W. T. Ross, Jr.
Executive Secretary

P.S. A demonstration by organized labor will be held at 4 P.M., Monday, March 4 beginning at the Labor Temple and ending at City Hall. All locals are asked to prepare their own signs and turn out in support of this strike.

Chronology of Events (Cleveland)

August 14, 1969 Morning:	Dispute at Harvard Yards regarding assignment of a truck between AFSCME Local 100 and Teamsters' Local 244.
	Clarence King was given the keys from a truck.
	Clarence King suspended.
	Clarence King stopped trucks from leaving Harvard Yards.
	Jurisdictional dispute settled but King suspension reaffirmed.
August 15, 1969 Morning:	Clarence King refused to allow all trucks to leave Harvard Yards.
	Burks went to Harvard Yards and asked King to allow trucks to leave.
Afternoon:	Suspension papers served on King by attorneys Loeb and Moore of the City's legal department.
	Police Chief of Newburgh Heights and Cuyahoga Heights came to Harvard Yards and asked King to leave. King asked all men at Harvard Yards to block trucks. Approximately 50 men responded.
	City officials went to Garfield Heights Muny Court seeking a warrant for King's arrest.
	Mayor arrived at Harvard Yards and asked for a meeting at City Hall in his office.
	Union and City officials met for two hours.
August 16, 1969	Wildcat strike continued throughout the day. Picketing all day.
August 17, 1969	Picketing continued all day.
Evening:	Conversation between Worwood and Burks about how to resolve the dispute reaches a tentative oral agreement on a ten-day suspension.
	Nick Jablonski appeared on television denouncing Director Stefanski and the city administration and suggesting that Stefan-

	ski be fired, thus abrogating the earlier verbal agreement.
August 18, 1969 Morning:	Mass picketing resumed again at Harvard Yards. Allegations of intimidation of employees made.
Evening:	Additional police (40) required at Harvard Yards.
	Tension mounted to such a degree that Harvard Yards was closed at 10:00 P.M.
August 19, 1969 Morning:	Mass picketing at Harvard Yards resumed. City claims union leaders threatened to bring in Black Nationalists to force cooperation from recalcitrant employees at Gilman Building.
	Mayor Stokes went to the Gilman Building.
Afternoon:	Attempted shutdowns by union officials of southerly and westerly sewage facilities. Some violence reported.
	Westerly facilities closed.
	Scheduled start of suspension hearing of Clarence King in Room 335, Civil Service Commission hearing room at City Hall.
	King, Jablonski, Stalteri arrested on State Riot Control Act charges.
Evening:	Mayor Stokes went on television to denounce the day's violence.
August 20, 1969 Morning:	Pickets appeared at several city facilities including Utilities Building.
	Director Stefanski suggested to Stalteri that a meeting be set.
Afternoon:	Meeting at City Hall between Burns, Worwood, and Spector.
	Union and City agreed upon a mediator. Meeting set for 4:30 P.M., Thursday, August 21, 1969.
August 21, 1969 Morning:	Mass picketing throughout the day.
	Preliminary hearings for King, Stalteri and Jablonski at Garfield Heights Municipal

	Court; defendants pleaded not guilty and asked for a jury trial; $500 bond posted.
Afternoon:	Meeting with union and Willoughby Abner, the mediator.

The City presented a proposal that King be suspended for 30 days and reassigned to another location for the balance of 1969, at which time he would then go back to Harvard Yards. This proposal was rejected by the union.

A counterproposal by the union was that King be suspended for a period of 90 days on paper, but only 2 weeks actual suspension, and that he would be on probation for the remaining days of suspension.

This proposal was rejected by the city Administration.

The meeting lasted from 4:30 P.M. to 3:30 A.M.

August 22, 1969 Morning:	Meeting reconvened with mediator trying to resolve the dispute.
Evening:	Union meeting authorizes official strike action if necessary.
August 23, 1969 Afternoon:	Meeting reconvened at 1:00 P.M. lasted until 11:00 P.M. that day. New proposal submitted by City was 90 days straight suspension.
August 24, 1969 Morning:	The administration met with the mediator. Meeting lasted two hours. New methods were suggested to get a proposal accepted by the union.
Afternoon:	Mediator left the city.
	Union Executive Committee meeting. Strike vote taken.
Evening:	Union called a news conference and announced that if dispute was not settled by Monday, a strike would be officially called at 8:00 A.M., Tuesday, August 26.
August 25, 1969 Morning:	City received reports of alleged union vandalism and intimidations at various sites.
Afternoon:	Meeting held with mediator. City restates its

position of 90-day suspension. Union rejects proposal. Union proposed the same proposal again—2 weeks suspension, beginning the day of the dispute, which left only 3 days suspension remaining for King to serve.

Meeting continued from 4:30 P.M. to 1:35 A.M.

ALL CITY UNIONS NOTIFIED OF THE MEDIATION AND PROPOSALS.

August 26, 1969
Morning:

Strike begins. Pickets at City Hall, all yards and throughout the city.

Approximately 1,000 employees off work due to strike. City marked them A.W.O.L.

Craft workers held meeting and decided to work under emergency conditions.

Afternoon:

Abner meets Mayor concerning inclusion of Wurf in the negotiations.

August 27, 1969
Morning:

Cuyahoga Heights restricted pickets at Harvard Yards.

Local 100 men at Sewer Maintenance forced Crafts to leave West 3rd Street facility.

Local 100 went to AFL-CIO and asked for sanction of strike. Sanction granted.

Afternoon:

At a meeting, business agents of all local unions having written agreements with the City agreed that they would not honor Local 100's picket line.

Numerous reports received all day from various sources concerning threats to employees if they showed up for work on Thursday, August 28. Union called for mass picketing at City Hall on Thursday, August 28, from 11:00 A.M. to 12:15 P.M.

Evening:

Meeting between mayor and Jerry Wurf continued to early hours of Thursday, August 28. Settlement reached.

August 29, 1969
Morning:

Union ratifies the agreement to end the strike.

Memorandum of Understanding (Cleveland)

The attached Memorandum of Understanding covering the terms and conditions of employment of certain employees of the City of Cleveland has been approved this——————————day of September, 1968, by the Committee representing the City and the Committee representing Local 100 and District Council #78, American Federation of State, County and Municipal Employees, AFL-CIO, subject to approval, on the part of the City, by Carl B. Stokes, Mayor, Clarence L. James, Jr., Law Director, and, to the extent required by law, City Council, and subject to ratification, which has already been given, on the part of the Union, by its members.

LOCAL 100
AMERICAN FEDERATION
OF STATE, COUNTY AND
MUNICIPAL EMPLOYEES,
AFL-CIO   CITY OF CLEVELAND

RAY VISH (President)   CARL B. STOKES
LUCILLE BRADY   *Mayor*
ANTHONY DE MARCO
LOUIS DI SANTIS   ROBERT P. DUVIN
ROSE FULTON   *Chief Labor Counsel*
OLA HINSLEY
JAMES HUGES
NICK JABLONSKI
CLARENCE KING
FRANK NOVAK
LUTHER WILSON

DISTRICT COUNCIL #78
AMERICAN FEDERATION OF STATE,
COUNTY AND MUNICIPAL EMPLOYEES,
FL-CIO
AFL-CIO

ROBERT A. BRINDZA   KENNETH WORWOOD
Director   *Staff Representative*

MEMORANDUM OF UNDERSTANDING

PURPOSE

1. This Memorandum is made between the City of Cleveland, hereinafter referred to as the "City," and Local 100 and District Council #78, American Federation of State, County, and Municipal Employees, AFL-CIO, hereinafter referred to as the "Union." The male pronoun or adjective where used herein refers to the female also unless otherwise indicated. The term "employee" or "employees" where used herein refers to all employees in the bargaining unit who are members of the Union in good standing. The purpose of this Memorandum is to provide a fair and responsible method of enabling employees covered by this Memorandum to participate, through union representation, in the establishment of terms and conditions of their employment and to establish a peaceful procedure for the resolution of all differences between the parties, subject to the laws of the United States, the State of Ohio, the City of Cleveland, and all applicable governmental administrative rules and regulations, which have the effect of law.

RECOGNITION

2. The Union is recognized as the sole and exclusive representative for those employees of the City who are members of the Union and in the bargaining unit (as defined later) for the purpose of establishing rates of pay, wages, hours, and other conditions of employment, but excluding all supervisors (as defined in the National Labor Relations Act). The City will accept as proof of Union membership only a dues deduction authorization card in conformity with Paragraph 12 of this Memorandum and only as long as such authorization remains in effect or other satisfactory evidence of Union membership.

3. The Union's bargaining unit includes only the following job classifications:

The City will not recognize any other union as the bargaining representative for any employees within the above bargaining unit.

MANAGEMENT RIGHTS

4. Except as specifically limited by explicit provision of this Memorandum, the City shall have the exclusive right to manage the operations, control the premises, direct the working forces, and maintain efficiency of operations. Specifically, the City's exclusive management rights include, but are not limited to, the sole right to hire, discipline and discharge for cause, lay off, and promote; to promulgate and enforce rules and regulations; to reorganize, discontinue, or enlarge any department or division; to transfer employees (including the assignment and allocation of work) within departments or to other departments; to introduce new and/or improved equipment, methods, and/or facilities, to determine work methods; to determine the size and duties of the work force, the number of shifts required, and work schedules; to establish, modify, consolidate, or abolish jobs (or classifications) ; and to determine staffing patterns, including, but not limited to, assignment of employees, numbers employed, duties to be performed, qualifications required, and areas worked, subject only to the restrictions and regulations governing the exercise of these rights as are expressly provided herein.

NO-STRIKE

5. The Union shall not, directly or indirectly, call, sanction, encourage, finance, and/or assist in any way, nor shall any employee instigate or participate, directly or indirectly, in any strike, slowdown, walkout, concerted "sick" leave or mass resignation, work stoppage, picketing, or interference of any kind at any operation or operations of the City for the duration of this Memorandum.

6. Violations of Paragraph 5 shall be proper cause for discharge or other disciplinary action, but any discharge or suspension of thirty-one (31) days or more for such conduct can be appealed to the Civil Service Commission in accordance with Civil Service rules and regulations, and any suspension of thirty (30) days or less can be appealed through the Grievance Procedure under this Memorandum.

7. The Union shall at all times cooperate with the City in continuing operations in a normal manner and shall actively discourage and endeavor to prevent or terminate any violation of Paragraph 5. In the event any violation of Paragraph 5 occurs, the Union shall

immediately notify all employees that the strike, slowdown, picketing, work stoppage, or other interference at any operation or operations of the City is prohibited and is not in any way sanctioned or approved by the Union. Furthermore, the Union shall also immediately order all employees to return to work at once.

8. In the event that the City claims a violation of Paragraphs 5 and/or 7, the City may, in addition to its remedies at law and/or its remedies under this Memorandum, avail itself of all remedies at equity (including *ex parte* restraining orders) as with the consent of the Union.

9. The City shall not lock out any employees for the duration of this Memorandum.

NON-DISCRIMINATION

10. Both the City and the Union recognize their respective responsibilities under Federal and State civil rights laws, fair employment practice acts, and other similar constitutional and statutory requirements. Therefore, both parties hereby reaffirm their commitments, legal and moral, not to discriminate in any manner relating to employment on the basis of race, color, creed, national origin, or sex.

11. Both the City and the Union recognize the right of all employees and all applicants for employment to be free to join or not to join the Union and to participate in Union or legal concerted activities. Therefore, both parties agree that there shall be no discrimination, interference, restraint, coercion, or reprisal by the City or the Union, or by any agent or representative of either party, against any employee or any applicant for employment because of Union membership or because of any lawful activity in an official capacity on behalf of the Union.

CHECK OFF

12. The City will deduct regular initiation fees and monthly dues from the pay of employees covered by this Memorandum upon receipt from the Union of individual written authorization cards voluntarily executed by an employee for that purpose and bearing his signature. Provided, that— (1) an employee shall have the right to revoke such authorization by giving written notice to the City and

the Union at any time during the months of June and December, and the authorization card shall state clearly on its face the right of the employee to revoke during those months; and (2) the City's obligation to make deductions shall terminate automatically upon timely receipt of revocation of authorization or upon termination of employment or transfer to a job classification outside the bargaining unit.

13. Deductions under Paragraph 12 shall be made during the second pay period of each month, but if an employee's pay for that period is insufficient to cover Union dues, the City will make a deduction from the pay earned during the next pay period.

14. All deductions under Paragraph 12, accompanied by an alphabetical list of all employees for whom deductions have been made, shall be transmitted to the Union no later than the fifteenth (15th) day following the end of the pay period in which the deduction is made, and, upon receipt, the Union shall assume full responsibility for the disposition of all funds deducted.

15. The Union will indemnify and save the City harmless from any action growing out of deductions hereunder and commenced by an employee against the City (or the City and the Union jointly).

UNION REPRESENTATION

16. The City recognizes the right of the Union to select Chief Stewards, Stewards, and Alternate Stewards in accordance with past practice to represent the employees, upon request, on grievances arising under this Memorandum. An Alternate Steward shall act as a steward when the Steward is absent from work. Chief Stewards and Stewards shall remain in their departments and on their respective shifts during their term of office, but this Paragraph in no way restricts the right of the City to discharge, suspend, or demote such employees for proper cause.

17. Stewards shall process grievances with proper regard for the City's operational needs and work requirements, and shall cooperate in good faith with the City in keeping to a minimum the time lost from work due to grievance handling. If any steward fails or refuses to comply with this requirement, the City retains the right to impose disciplinary action.

18. The Union shall furnish the City with a written list of stew-

ards, indicating the department and shift to which each is assigned, and, further, shall promptly notify the City in writing of any changes therein.

UNION VISITATION—BULLETIN BOARDS

19. The accredited representatives of the Union shall be permitted to enter the City's premises during working hours, but at no time shall such visitation rights interfere with the work requirements of any employee or disrupt operations in any way unless expressly permitted by the City.

20. The City shall provide the Union with a bulletin board at a mutually selected location. Provided, that—

(a) no notice or other writing may contain anything political, controversial, or critical of the City or any City official or any other institution or any employee or other person;

(b) all notices or other materials posted on the bulletin board must be signed by the President or Chief Steward of the Union or an official representative of District Council #78;

(c) upon request from the appropriate Commissioner or his designee, the Union will immediately remove any notice or other writing that the City believes violates this Paragraph.

PROBATIONARY PERIOD

21. New employees shall be on probation in accordance with the rules and regulations of Civil Service, and probationary employees shall have no recourse to the Grievance Procedure under this Memorandum concerning any disciplinary action.

22. If an employee is discharged or quits and is later rehired, he shall be considered a new employee and subject to the provisions of Paragraph 21.

SENIORITY

23. Seniority shall be an employee's uninterrupted length of continuous service with the department, or job classification, or City, depending on the question involved and in accordance with the rules and regulations of Civil Service. An employee shall have no

seniority for the probationary period provided in Paragraph 21, but upon completion of the probationary period seniority shall be retroactive to the date of hire.

24. Seniority shall be broken (or terminated) when an employee:
(a) Quits;
(b) Is discharged for cause;
(c) Is laid off for a period of more than eighteen (18) consecutive months;
(d) Is absent without leave for three (3) or more work days, unless proper excuse for the absence (and if no notice was given, the failure to give notice) is shown;
(e) Fails to report for work when recalled from layoff within ten (10) working days from the date on which the City sends the employee notice by registered mail (to the employee's last known address as shown on the City's records).

LAYOFFS

25. Whenever it is necessary because of lack of work or funds, or whenever it is advisable in the interest of economy or efficiency, to reduce the working force of the City, employees shall be laid off in the following order:
(a) Temporary employees who have not completed their probationary period.
(b) Temporary employees who have completed their probationary period.
(c) Certified employees who have not completed their probationary period.
(d) Certified employees who have completed their probationary period.

26. Within the categories enumerated above, employees shall be laid off on the basis of classification seniority in accordance with the rules and regulations of Civil Service. When a classification seniority of two (2) employees is equal, they shall be laid off alphabetically from "Z" to "A."

27. Employees shall be recalled in the reverse order of layoff in accordance with the rules and regulations of Civil Service. An employee on layoff will be given ten (10) working days' notice of recall from the date on which the City sends the recall notice to the

employee by registered mail (to his last known address as shown on the City's records).

28. When reasonably possible, regular full-time employees shall be given a minimum of two (2) weeks' advance written notice of layoff indicating the circumstances which make the layoff necessary.

29. In the event an employee is laid off, he may, upon request, receive payment for earned but unused vacation as quickly as possible but not later than thirty (30) days after layoff.

LEAVES OF ABSENCE

30. An employee will be granted a leave of absence with pay, to be charged against his accumulated sick leave with pay, in the event of the death of his spouse, mother, father, child, brother, or sister, as follows:
(1) If the funeral is within the State of Ohio—3 days
(2) If the funeral is outside the State of Ohio—5 days
To be eligible for funeral leave, an employee must provide the City with a funeral form (to be supplied by the City) and must attend the funeral, and failure to do so, or a misrepresentation of facts related to a funeral leave, shall be proper cause for disciplinary action (including forfeiture of pay for the leave).

31. *Jury Duty Leave.* An employee serving on jury duty will be excused, with pay, for the time lost during his basic work week, provided he turns in to the City Treasurer any pay received for such jury service and presents a receipt from the City Treasurer to his supervisor.

32. *Military Leave.* An employee shall be granted an extended leave of absence without pay for military duty in accordance with law and after discharge shall be restored to employment with the City, upon request, in accordance with law.

33. Employees who are drafted or who enlist shall be granted a one (1) day leave of absence with pay, to be charged aaginst accumulated sick leave or paid vacation, for the purpose of taking a military physical.

34. A regular (non-probationary) employee of the City who is temporarily called to active duty (e.g., summer training) shall be granted a leave of absence for the duration of such active duty and shall be paid the difference between his regular pay and his service

pay (upon receipt of a service pay voucher) for a period not to exceed thirty-one (31) days in any calendar year and, further, shall accumulate vacation and sick leave with pay credit during the period of such leave.

35. Employees on military leave who thereafter return to employment with the City shall receive retirement credit for all time spent in active military service.

36. *Union Leave.* At the request of the Union, a leave of absence without pay may be granted to any employee selected for a Union office, employed by the Union, or required to attend a Union convention or perform any other function on behalf of the Union necessitating a suspension of active employment.

37. *Education Leave.* An employee may be granted a leave of absense without pay for educational purposes relating to the operations of the City.

38. *Maternity Leave.* An employee shall be granted upon request a leave of absence without pay on account of pregnancy, subject to the following conditions:

(a) She must have completed her probationary period at the time she applies for such leave;

(b) Application for such leave must be made at least four (4) months before the anticipated delivery date, as certified by the employee's physician;

(c) The duration of such leave will be flexible, depending upon the circumstances (*e.g.*, medical advice, departmental needs), but must commence at least one (1) month before the anticipated delivery date and will not extend more than six (6) months beyond childbirth;

(d) A certificate of the employee's physician as to her fitness to perform her required duties shall be a prerequisite to her return to work at the expiration of the leave. An employee who has been on maternity leave may be required at the City's expense to submit to and pass a physical examination before being permitted to return to work.

In the event of a difference of opinion as to the employee's physical status between the employee's physician and the City's physician, the issue shall be submitted to a mutually selected and paid for "third" physician.

39. *Sick Leave With Pay—Salaried Employees.* Employees on sal-

ary shall be credited with paid sick leave at the rate of ten (10) hours per month or fifteen (15) work days per year. Unused paid sick leave shall be cumulative and available for future use provided that the balance of the credit of the employee at the end of any month shall not exceed 960 hours or 120 days.

(a) No paid sick leave shall be granted unless the division authority is notified of the sickness within two (2) hours of the employee's scheduled starting time.

(b) A certificate from a physician may be required for any sickness, and a certificate from a physician must be provided for any sickness extending beyond three (3) days.

(c) Paid sick leave shall be granted only for actual sickness or injury, confinement by reason of a contagious disease, death or serious illness of a member of the employee's immediate family, or visit to a doctor or dentist for medical care.

40. *Sick Leave with Pay—Hourly Rated Employees.* Regular full-time employees on an hourly rate shall be credited with paid sick leave at the rate of ten (10) hours per month or fifteen (15) work days per year. Unused paid sick leave shall be cumulative and available for future use provided that the balance of the credit of the employee at the end of any month shall not exceed 960 hours or 120 days.

(a) No sick leave will be granted for the first four (4) hours of an employee's absence, unless during his absence the employee is hospitalized, in which case sick leave may be granted for the first day of absence.

(b) No paid sick leave shall be granted unless the division authority is notified of the sickness within two (2) hours of the employee's scheduled starting time on the first day of the absence on account of sickness.

(c) A certificate from a physician may be required for any sickness, and a certificate from a physician must be provided for any sickness extending beyond three (3) days.

(d) Paid sick leave shall be granted only for actual sickness, confinement by reason of a contagious disease, death or serious illness of a member of the employee's immediate family, or visit to a doctor or dentist for medical care.

41. *Sick Leave Without Pay.* After an employee has exhausted his sick leave with pay, he shall be granted a leave of absence without

pay for a period not to exceed six (6) months because of personal illness or injury upon request supported by medical evidence satisfactory to the City if the employee has reported such illness or injury to his department head or immediate supervisor by no later than the second day of absence. If the illness or injury continues beyond six (6) months, the City may grant additional sick leave under this Paragraph upon request. An employee on sick leave is expected to keep the City informed on the progress of his illness or injury as circumstances allow. Any employee who has been on sick leave for three (3) or more consecutive days may be required to submit to and pass a physical examination before being permitted to return to work.

42. *Personal Leave.* For those employees who have completed their probationary period, personal leaves of absence may be granted without pay for good cause shown for a period not to exceed ninety (90) days. The granting of such leaves will be based upon the operational needs of the employee's department.

43. *General.* All leaves of absence (and any extensions thereof) must be applied for and granted in writing on forms to be provided by the City. An employee may, upon request, return to work prior to the expiration of any leave of absence if such early return is agreed to by the City. When an employee returns to work after a leave of absence, he will be assigned to the position which he formerly occupied or to a similar position if his former position is not vacant or no longer exists.

44. If it is found that a leave of absence is not actually being used for the purpose for which it was granted, the City may cancel the leave, direct the employee to return to work, and impose disciplinary action.

45. An employee who fails to report to work at the expiration or cancellation of a leave of absence or fails to secure an extension of such leave shall be deemed to be absent without leave and shall be subject to loss of seniority under Paragraph 23.

ASSIGNMENT OF WORK—TEMPORARY TRANSFERS

46. All employees shall be required to perform any and all temporarily assigned duties, regardless of their usual or customary duties

or job assignment. A temporary transfer shall not exceed thirty (30) working days, except (1) to fill a vacancy caused by an employee being on sick or other approved leave of absence, (2) to provide vacation relief scheduling, (3) to fill an opening temporarily pending permanent filling of such opening, or (4) to meet an emergency situation. When an employee is temporarily transferred to another job classification——

(a) if the rate of pay for such other classification is lower than his regular rate, he shall receive his regular rate;

(b) if the rate of pay for such other classification is higher than his regular rate, he shall receive an adjustment in pay within his own classification commensurate with the work he is doing in the other classification if he works in the other classification for the time period established by law.

JOB EVALUATION AND CLASSIFICATION

47. The administration and operation of a job evaluation program, including job descriptions and job classifications, are the functions and responsibilities solely of the City.

48. Job evaluation, job descriptions, and/or job classifications shall not be subject to the provisions of the Grievance Procedure. Provided, however, that the City recognizes the right of a regular full-time employee who has completed his probationary period to appeal any disciplinary action based upon failure to meet the required standard of job performance either to the Civil Service Commission (more than 30 days) or the Grievance Procedure (less than 30 days).

49. If substantial changes in the method of operation, tools, or equipment of a job occur, or if a new job is established which has not been previously classified, the wage rate for such job shall be determined by the Office of Personnel Administration. Before putting such rate into effect, the Office of Personnel Administration will promptly notify the Union in writing, but once this is done the City may put the rate into effect without any further delay. Thereafter, the Union can file a grievance on the single issue of whether the rate established by the Office of Personnel Administration is reasonable or unreasonable.

PROMOTIONS AND TRANSFERS

50. When a vacancy occurs, or a new job is created, employees shall be promoted or transferred in accordance with the rules and regulations of Civil Service. (50-a) There shall be no discrimination in promotions on the basis of race, color, creed, religion, or Union membership.

GENERAL

51. It is the obligation of each employee to keep the City advised of his current address and, for purposes of this Memorandum, the City may rely on the last address supplied by an employee.

52. An employee may exercise his job classification seniority within his own department for the purpose of changing shifts or work weeks when an opening occurs within his classification on another shift or work week so long as he has the ability to perform the work involved and the department's operational needs permit such a change. An employee who desires a change of shift or work week may make an application in writing (on forms provided by the City) to his supervisor requesting a transfer to the shift or work week he prefers, and the employee shall retain a copy of the request.

53. No employee shall lose any benefits as a result of this Memorandum unless such benefits were specifically eliminated or modified during the negotiations which preceded this Memorandum.

HOURS OF WORK

54. The normal work week for all regular full-time employees covered by this Memorandum shall be forty (40) hours of work in five (5) eight (8) hour days, exclusive of time allotted for meals, during the period starting 12:01 A.M. Monday to midnight Sunday, except where different hours are necessary to meet operational requirements. Provided, that this Paragraph shall not constitute or be construed as a guarantee of hours of work per day or per week, and the City reserves the right, as operational needs and conditions require, to establish and/or change work hours and work schedules.

WAGES

55. Effective June 1, 1968, all hourly rated employees in the job classifications covered by this Memorandum shall receive an increase of twenty cents (20¢) per hour.

56. Effective June 1, 1968, all salaried employees in the job classifications covered by this Memorandum shall receive an annual increase of Four Hundred Twenty Dollars ($420.00) (prorated to June 1, 1968).

57. Effective June 1, 1968, all hourly rated and salaried employees covered by this Memorandum shall receive any additional increases (if any) which are awarded by the Fact Finder under the special fact finding agreement attached hereto as Exhibit B.

58. Effective July 1, 1969, all employees in the House of Correction Guard job classification shall receive a wage increase of five per cent (5%) plus ten cents (10¢) per hour.

59. Effective July 1, 1969, all employees in the job classifications covered by this Memorandum other than the one referred to in Paragraph 58 shall receive a wage increase of five per cent (5%).

VIRDEN SALARY SCHEDULE

60. Effective October 1, 1968, all employees in the Clerical, Administrative, and Professional job classifications covered by the Virden Salary Schedule shall be reclassified and thereafter progress in accordance with the following schedule:

Starting	Step 1	Step 2	Step 3	Step 4	Step 5
Rate	After	After	After	After	After
	1 year	2 years	3 years	4 years	5 years

	Step 6	Step 7	Step 8	Step 9
	After	After	After	After
	6 years	7 years	10 years	13 years

Thereafter, all employees will progress automatically from step to step unless held back because of poor work performance, and any hold-back on this basis can be appealed through the Grievance Procedure under this Memorandum.

OVERTIME

61. The City shall be the sole judge of the necessity for overtime.

62. The City shall retain the sole and exclusive right to determine work schedules and the number of shifts required. All overtime will be distributed in a fair and reasonable manner.

63. Effective October 1, 1968, all employees in the job classifications covered by this Memorandum shall receive time and one-half ($1\frac{1}{2}$) their regular rate of pay for all hours worked in excess of forty (40) in one (1) work week (excluding supervisory employees who do not qualify for overtime pay).

HOLIDAYS

64. All regular full-time employees shall be entitled to ten (10) paid holidays as follows:

New Year's Day	Labor Day
Lincoln's Birthday	General Election Day
Washington's Birthday	(November)
Memorial Day	Veteran's Day
Independence Day	Thanksgiving Day
	Christmas Day

65. To be entitled to holiday pay, an employee must be on the active payroll (i.e., actually receives pay) on his last regular workday before and his first regular workday after the holiday unless absent because of bona fide illness or injury or funeral leave, but in no case shall an employee receive holiday pay if he receives no pay during the holiday work week (regardless of the cause of the absence).

66. If any of the above holidays fall on a Sunday, the following Monday shall be observed as the holiday. If any of the above holidays fall on a Saturday, the preceding Friday shall be observed as the holiday for those employees for whom Saturday is not a regular working day.

VACATIONS

67. All regular full-time employees shall be granted the following vacation leave with full pay for each year based upon their length of City service as follows:

Years of Service	*Vacation*
After 1 year	2 weeks
After 8 years	3 weeks
After 12 years	4 weeks
After 22 years	5 weeks

The administration of vacations (including eligibility requirements) shall be in accordance with the rules and regulations established by the Office of Personnel Administration and the Union and attached to this Memorandum as Exhibit A.

68. If a recognized holiday falls within an employee's vacation leave, the employee shall receive an additional paid vacation day in lieu of the holiday (either at the beginning or at the end of his vacation).

69. Employees may take their vacation during the calendar year at the convenience of the City. During the first quarter of each calendar year, employees will be given an opportunity to indicate on a form provided by the City their vacation leave preferences, and promptly thereafter a written vacation schedule (by departments) will be prepared by the City with priority given to employees according to their departmental or job classification seniority to the extent consistent with operational requirements. Once the departmental vacation schedule is determined, it shall not be changed without the consent of the involved employee(s) except in response to an operational emergency. Any employee who fails to make his vacation application during the appropriate period will be given his vacation leave without regard to seniority based upon when his application was made.

CALL-IN PAY

70. An employee who is called in to work at a time when he is not regularly scheduled to report for work shall receive a minimum

of four (4) hours of work at his applicable rate of pay. If an employee is called in and works more than four (4) hours, he shall receive eight (8) hours of work at his applicable rate of pay.

HOSPITALIZATION

71. Effective June 1, 1968, all regular full-time employees in the job classifications covered by this Memorandum shall be entitled to an allowance for hospitalization protection equivalent to the cost of Blue Cross ward service hospitalization coverage upon such terms and conditions as the Board of Control shall establish and in accordance with the rules and regulations established by the Office of Personnel Administration as agreed to by the City and the Union.

72. Effective July 1, 1969, all regular full-time employees in the job classifications covered by this Memorandum shall be entitled to an allowance for hospitalization protection equivalent to the cost of Blue Cross ward service hospitalization coverage plus $1.50 per month upon such terms and conditions as the Board of Control shall establish and in accordance with the rules and regulations established by the Office of Personnel Administration as agreed to by the City and the Union.

LONGEVITY PAY

73. Effective January 1, 1969, all regular full-time employees shall receive longevity pay as follows:

Years of Service	Annual Benefit to Employee
5 years	$ 30.00
10 years	60.00
15 years	120.00
20 years	150.00
25 years	180.00

74. The administration of longevity pay (including eligibility requirements) shall be in accordance with the rules and regulations established by the Office of Personnel Administration as agreed to by the City and the Union.

UNIFORMS

75. All employees in the job classifications of House of Correction Guard, Meter Reader, Parking Attendant, and Auditorium Usher shall receive an annual uniform credit of one hundred twenty-five dollars (125.00) (prorated initially to June 1, 1968) from a mutually agreed upon uniform supplier.

DISCIPLINE

76. An employee who is suspended, demoted, or discharged shall be given a written notice, with a copy to his Steward, stating the reason for the disciplinary action within three (3) working days thereafter. In case of suspension or discharge, the employee shall be advised that he has a right to have his Steward present and, if he so requests, shall be promptly granted an interview with his Steward before he is required to leave the premises. Thereafter, all disciplinary action involving a discharge or suspension of thirty-one (31) days or more (and any other disciplinary action within the exclusive jurisdiction of Civil Service) can be appealed to the Civil Service Commission in accordance with Civil Service rules and regulations, and all disciplinary action involving suspensions of thirty (30) days or less (and any other disciplinary action not within the exclusive jurisdiction of Civil Service) can be appealed through the Grievance Procedure under this Memorandum.

GRIEVANCE PROCEDURE

77. A grievance is a dispute or difference between the City and the Union, or between the City and an employee, concerning the interpretation and/or application of any provision of this Memorandum, including disciplinary suspensions of thirty (30) days or less and other disciplinary action which is not appealable to Civl Service, and when any such grievance arises the following procedure shall be observed:

Step 1. An employee who has a grievance may take it up orally with his immediate supervisor, either alone or accompanied by his steward if the employee so wishes, within two (2) working days after the employee has knowledge (or should have had knowledge) of the event(s) upon which his grievance is based, and the supervisor shall give his answer to the employee within two (2) working days after the grievance was presented to him.

Step 2. If the employee's grievance is not satisfactorily settled at Step 1, the grievance, shall, within five (5) calendar days after receipt of the Step 1 answer, be reduced to writing and filed with the employee's Commissioner (or his designee) setting forth the complete details of the grievance (i.e., the facts upon which it is based, the approximate time of their occurrence, the relief or remedy requested) and dated and signed by the employee. The Commissioner (or his designees) shall meet with representatives of the Union within seven (7) calendar days after the written grievance has been filed, and a written answer shall be given within seven (7) calendar days after the Step 2 meeting.

Step 3. If the grievance is not satisfactorily settled at Step 2, the Union may within seven (7) calendar days after receipt of the Step 2 answer appeal in writing to the Director of the Department or Division. The Director (or his designees) shall meet with representatives of the Union within fourteen (14) calendar days after the grievance was submitted to the Director, and a written answer shall be given within fourteen (14) calendar days after the Step 3 meeting.

Step 4. If the grievance is not satisfactorily settled at Step 3, the Union may, within thirty (30) calendar days after receipt of the Step 3 answer, submit the matter to arbitration. Upon written notice of the Union's intent to arbitrate a grievance, the parties shall each designate a representative who will attempt to agree upon an impartial arbitrator. If the designated representatives are unable to reach agreement within seven (7) calendar days, the parties shall jointly request the American Arbitration Association to submit a panel of seven (7) arbitrators, and the arbitrator shall then be chosen in accordance with the Association's then applicable rules. The fees and expenses of the arbitrator shall be borne equally by the parties.

78. A policy grievance which affects a substantial number of employees may initially be presented by the Union at Step 2 of the Grievance Procedure.

79. In the event a grievance goes to arbitration, the arbitrator shall have jurisdiction only over disputes arising out of grievances as to the interpretation and/or application of the provisions of this

Memorandum and in reaching his decision the arbitrator shall have no authority (1) to add to or subtract from or modify in any way any of the provisions of this Memorandum; (2) to pass upon issues governed by law or applicable governmental administrative rules and regulations thereunder which have the effect of law; or (3) to make an award in conflict with such laws, rules, and regulations.

80. All decisions of arbitrators consistent with Paragraph 79 and all prearbitration grievance settlements reached by the Union and the City shall be final, conclusive, and binding on the City, the Union, and the employees. Provided, that a grievance may be withdrawn by the Union at any time and the withdrawal of any grievance shall not be prejudicial to the positions taken by the parties as they relate to that grievance or any future grievances.

81. The time limits set forth in the Grievance Procedure shall, unless extended by mutual written agreement of the City and the Union, be binding and any grievance not timely presented, or timely processed thereafter, shall not be considered a grievance under this Memorandum and shall not be arbitrable.

LEGALITY

82. It is the intent of the parties that this Memorandum comply, in every respect, with applicable legal statutes, charter requirements, governmental regulations which have the effect of law, and judicial opinions, and if it is determined by the Law Director or other proper authority that it is, in whole or in part, in conflict with law, that provision shall be null and void.

SPECIAL AGREEMENTS

1. The Water Servicemen wage progression schedules will be reduced by six (6) months from forty-eight (48) months to forty-two (42) months.

2. The Recreation Department and Parking Meter Servicemen shall be brought under the Virden Salary Schedule or a comparable wage progression system.

3. Those employees classified as Water Servicemen who regularly work on meter repair shall, in addition to the regular wage increases set forth in the Memorandum of Understanding, receive two (2)

special equal increases effective June 1, 1968 and July 1, 1969 to bring them to the top of their pay band. Thereafter, the City may at its convenience create a new job classification of Meter Repair Serviceman which will have a starting rate the same as Water Serviceman and a top rate of approximately Four Hundred Dollars ($400.00) less.

4. To the extent practicable, when a regular payday falls on a weekend or a holiday, the pay will be distributed on the last regular working day before payday rather than the first regular working day after.

DURATION

83. This Memorandum represents a complete and final understanding on all bargainable issues between the City and the Union, and it shall be effective as of June 1, 1968, and remain in full force and effect until July 1, 1970, and thereafter from year to year unless at least ninety (90) days prior to said expiration date, or any anniversary thereof, either party gives timely written notice to the other of an intent to negotiate on any or all of its provisions. If such notice is given, negotiations shall be promptly commenced, and this Memorandum shall remain in full force and effect until an amended Memorandum is agreed to or, on or after July 1, 1970, either party gives fourteen (14) days' notice of an intention to terminate this entire Memorandum.

EXHIBIT A

Any employee who has completed one year of continuous employment by December 31, of the previous year shall receive two (2) weeks vacation.

Any employee who has completed less than one year of continuous employment by December 31, of the previous year shall receive one work day off for each month worked prior to December 31, of the previous year, but not to exceed two weeks. New employees whose starting date is prior to the 16th of the month shall be credited with one day of vacation for that month.

Any employee who has completed eight (8) years of continuous employment by December 31, of the previous year shall receive three (3) weeks vacation during every year thereafter.

Any employee who has completed twelve (12) years of continuous employment by December 31, of the previous year shall receive four (4) weeks vacation.

Any employee who has completed twenty-two (22) years of continuous employment by December 31 of the previous year shall receive five (5) weeks vacation.

For vacation purposes, an employee's continuous employment is defined as the period of time during which he is continuously listed as an employee on the rolls of the City, including authorized paid leaves of absence.

If an employee is discharged for cause or quits, and is reemployed at a later date, his length of continuous employment will be computed from the date of his re-employment.

An employee who is laid off and later re-employed shall be given credit for his service before the lay-off but no credit will be given for that period of time during which the employee did not work.

Time in authorized leave of absence shall be deducted for purposes of computing the amount of continuous employment.

An employee transferred from one department to another shall be given credit for his service elsewhere with the City, providing such employment has been continuous.

An employee who is on leave of absence without pay for a period totalling more than thirty (30) calendar days in any calendar year, shall earn vacation leave at the rate for which he is eligible based on length of service, as follows: less than eight (8) years service—1 day per month, not to exceed two weeks; eight years but less than twelve (12) years service 1½ days per month, not to exceed three weeks; twelve years but less than twenty-two (22) years service—2 days per month not to exceed four weeks; twenty-two years service—2½ days per month, not to exceed five weeks.

An employee may use any vacation leave earned prior to December 31, of the preceding year. Vacation leave being earned currently in any calendar year may not be used until after December 31, of that year.

APPENDIX J

Selected Documents (Cleveland)

Cleveland, Ohio, August 19, 1969

To: All Water Service Foremen
From: T. E. Stanton, Commissioner
   Division of Water and Heat
Subject: Supervisory Personnel

Dear Sir:

This letter is formal notification that all water service foremen are considered to be first-line management personnel, and shall be part of supervision.

Very truly yours,
T. E. STANTON
Division of Water and Heat

cc:

Director Stefanski
Mr. John Minder

Cleveland, Ohio, August 25, 1969

To All Employees of the City of Cleveland:

As you know, Local 100 of the American Federation of State, County and Municipal Employees is engaged in illegal strike activities in direct violation of the no-strike, no-work stoppage provisions of the agreement between that union and the city. The same provisions are contained in the agreements between the city and all other unions representing city employees.

Since Local 100 appears to be bent upon spreading its illegal walkout, you may be confronted by illegal picket lines or other illegal appeals to you to leave your job.

This is to advise you of the proper response in such cases:

1. Do not join in any interference with any fellow employee's lawful entry to or exit from any city office or facility.
2. Do not intimidate, threaten or harass any fellow city employee or member of the general public.
3. Do not argue, harass or converse with any illegal picket or pickets.
4. If you yourself are physically abused in any way, you should notify your supervisor immediately and ask him for further instructions.

The city is exerting every effort to bring about a peaceful, prompt solution of the present dispute.

Sincerely,

WALTER A. BURKS

Director of Personnel

AGREEMENT

The American Federation of State, County and Municipal Employees, AFL-CIO, agrees that the Memorandum of Understanding between the City of Cleveland and Local 100 and District Council #78, American Federation of State, County and Municipal Employees, AFL-CIO, will be honored and observed by the union and, particularly, that Paragraphs 5 through 9 and 77 through 81, dealing with strike prohibitions and dispute settlement procedures, will be observed. The City also affirms its obligations under the terms of the Memorandum of Understanding.

IN WITNESS WHEREOF, the parties have hereunto set their hands this 29th day of August, 1969.

AMERICAN FEDERATION OF STATE,
COUNTY AND MUNICIPAL EMPLOYEES,
AFL-CIO   CITY OF CLEVELAND

JERRY WURF	CARL B. STOKES
International President	*Mayor*

BIOGRAPHICAL NOTES

W. Ellison Chalmers is director of the Racial Negotiations Project of the Institute of Labor and Industrial Relations at The University of Michigan-Wayne State University. He holds degrees in labor economics from Brown University and the University of Wisconsin. His experience in government includes serving with the Federal Mediation and Conciliation Service. For many years, Chalmers was a professor of Industrial Relations and Economics at the Institute of Labor and Industrial Relations at the University of Illinois and served that Institute both as chairman of its graduate study program and as director. He has participated in and written about numerous empirical studies of collective bargaining, particularly in the United States, but also in Finland, India, and Singapore.

Gerald W. Cormick is assistant director of the Racial Negotiations Project. He has degrees from the University of British Columbia and The University of Michigan in business administration and has taught at the University of New Brunswick, Canada, for several years. He has written of the collective bargaining experience of Canadian nurses and will be presenting a dissertation on the establishment of power resources in racial disputes.

Preston Wilcox's academic background includes Morehouse College, New York University, City College of New York, and Columbia University School of Social Work. He has taught at Columbia University and Atlanta University. His recent activities have been concerned with community involvement in the area of public education. He is the president of Afram Associates, a consulting firm in Harlem and served as a consultant to the I.S. 201 experimental school district there.

F. Ray Marshall is professor of economics at the University of Texas at Austin. He received his doctor's degree from the University of California at Berkeley and taught at the University of Mississippi, Louisiana State University, and the University of Kentucky before assuming his present post. Some of his major works have included

The Negro and Organized Labor (1965); *The Negro and Apprenticeship* (1967), co-authored with Vernon M. Briggs, Jr.; and *Labor in the South* (1967).

Arvil Van Adams received his doctor's degree in May, 1970, from the University of Kentucky, where he is now a research associate. Prior to entering the University of Kentucky, he attended William Jewell College and Memphis State University. He is presently co-directing a study of Negro employment in firms involved in conciliation procedures under Title VII of the 1964 Civil Rights Act. This study is funded by the United States Equal Employment Opportunity Commission.

James E. Blackwell is professor and chairman of the Department of Sociology and Anthropology at the University of Massachusetts at Boston. His academic background includes two degrees from Case Western Reserve University and a doctorate from Washington State University. At the time of the study, he was an associate professor of sociology at Case Western Reserve University. He has also worked and lived in various parts of Africa and Southeast Asia.

Marie R. Haug is an assistant professor of sociology at Case Western Reserve University and is research director of the Institute on the Family and the Bureaucratic Society. Her academic background includes a degree from Vassar College, graduate work at Yale University and the New York School of Social Work, and the M.A. and Ph.D. degrees in sociology from Western Reserve University. She has co-authored numerous books and monographs in the field of sociology.